LOST PROMISE

How CIA Analysis Misserves the Nation

AN INTELLIGENCE ASSESSMENT

John A. Gentry

UNIVERSITY PRESS OF AMERICA

Lanham • New York • London

University Press of America,® Inc.
4720 Boston Way
Lanham, Maryland 20706

3 Henrietta Street
London WC2E 8LU England

Printed in the United States of America
British Cataloging in Publication Information Available

Library of Congress Cataloging-in-Publication Data

Gentry, John A., 1949–
Lost promise : how CIA analysis misserves the nation : an intelligence assessment / John A. Gentry.
p. cm.
Includes index.
1. United States. Central Intelligence Agency. Directorate of Intelligence. 2. Intelligence service—United States. I. Title.
JK468.I6G46 1993 327.1'273—dc20 92–36974 CIP

ISBN 0–8191–8951–0 (cloth : alk. paper)

The paper used in this publication meets the minimum requirements of American National Standard for Information Sciences—Permanence of Paper for Printed Library Materials, ANSI Z39.48–1984.

To my father, Dr. John T. Gentry, who by example
taught me the meaning and importance of integrity,
and to my daughter Allison.

Table of Contents

PREFACE

This book reflects the frustrations and concerns of a former analyst of CIA's Directorate of Intelligence (DI). It contains parts of nearly 12 years of personal experiences, as well as thoughts and concerns of colleagues who are also friends. It reflects sadness—for I once intended to make CIA my career—and the anger of a citizen who sees his tax dollars frittered away and his nation's security potentially compromised. It also springs from the unhappiness of knowing that good people continue to labor in the miserable working conditions of parts of the DI. I hope that this work will help stimulate the cleansing of the Directorate.

The observations in this book pertain primarily to the DI's five offices that follow regions of the world and to the Office of Resources, Trade, and Technology. Some comments reflect DI practices generally. These six offices have exclusive or major responsibilities for the Directorate's main analytical duties, meaning that my comments refer to the offices that produce a large percentage of the DI's judgments. The Office of Leadership Analysis, the Office of Scientific and Weapons Research, and the Office of Imagery Analysis operate somewhat differently, while the DI's other offices have support missions that generally lie beyond the scope of this analysis. The judgments of this book generally do not pertain to scientific and weapons intelligence analysis.

I concentrate on the negative aspects of the Directorate of Intelligence, but in every office many good analysts and managers strive to do the best they can. They often do fine work. I mean no blanket condemnation of any part of the DI or any part of its work force. The strengths and weaknesses of individual offices vary considerably. My concerns are as great as they are because I view the Directorate as a national resource that has self-inflicted wounds. It needs restoration and improvement. As a citizen I hold the DI, as a potentially key contributor to the nation's defense and its foreign policy, to a higher standard of performance and integrity than it has achieved since the early 1980s—the standards of objectivity, selflessness, and service it claims for itself and which it largely attained during its first 30 years.

Over the course of several years, I repeatedly have talked about the problems of the DI to many analysts, other Agency employees, and observers of CIA. Some of the ideas expressed herein came to me from them. Through these discussions, several colleagues have helped me focus my thoughts. They remain nameless here to protect them from the enemies of CIA and their own managers' wrath. I have gathered other insights from former Agency employees, journalists, and current and former Congressional intelligence oversight committee personnel. Three capable people helped with the final editorial work.

The examples cited in this work come from several sources. Some come from my own personal experience. Many others represent anecdotes or physical evidence shared with me by responsible people. I have omitted from this work a number of anecdotes uncomplimentary to DI management; I felt less than fully confident of the veracity of some, and discarded others for stylistic reasons. Each of the examples cited refers to specific people in specific circumstances. I have made many of these names available to CIA's Inspector General without, as of this writing, any apparent effect.

The Agency's Publications Review Board, part of the Office of Public and Agency Information, has scrutinized this book to determine that it does not contain classified information. It recommends the following disclaimer: "This material has been reviewed by the CIA to assist the author in eliminating classified information, if any; however, that review neither constitutes CIA authentication of material nor implies CIA's endorsement of the author's views."

John A. Gentry
July 1992

CHAPTER ONE

BACKGROUND AND PURPOSE

The intelligence community of the United States generally, and the Central Intelligence Agency in particular, long has been a target of critics on many grounds. While these generally center on such issues as covert action and the role of intelligence in a democratic nation, senior US government users of American intelligence products, Congress, and lay observers of the US foreign intelligence community also have criticized aspects of intelligence analysis—the process by which information is processed into evaluations and judgments useful to policymakers. These complaints have centered on issues such as quality, objectivity, policy-relevance, and timeliness even as the critics praise some analytical work.

Some academic and government critics have attacked "analysts" as actors central to the problems of US intelligence analysis. In some of these views, analysts are inadequately prepared through lack of area familiarity or language skills, and are too likely to view the world through an American culture perspective; they are likely to be too academic in approach for busy government officials and to work too independently of the needs of the policymakers they ostensibly serve. Some observers attribute this isolation—at CIA especially—to the belief that analysts should track foreign events independently—that is, divorced from the immediate concerns of policymakers—to ensure that intelligence analysis is not corrupted.[1] In the view of some, this alleged isolation reduces the accountability of analysis, promotes intellectual complacency, and encourages analysts to reject legitimate criticism as unwarranted politicization.

Other complaints charge that analysts are too conservative to offer valuable warnings until information becomes so voluminous as to be either obvious or too late to give the government time to act. Still other comments have centered on the bureaucratization of intelligence and parochial fights between intelligence agencies.

Some Congressional and academic critics, in particular, have attacked intelligence analysis on intellectual grounds, charging that errors of fact, judgment, or methods have led to serious misunderstanding of foreign actions and capabilities that, in turn, have led to dangerous and/or expensive US policies and programs. These types of comments in recent years have concerned, for example, judgments about Soviet defense spending and gross national product estimates. They have been especially loud when the intelligence community agencies, particularly CIA, have revised estimates sharply. They also recur, of course, when the administration and Congress are surprised and officials want to know why they did not receive warning.

More generally, critics of American intelligence have accused the member agencies of the intelligence community of institutional biases reflecting ideological bents or the parochial interests of the departments they serve—as the propensity of the Defense Intelligence Agency (DIA) for finding military threats to justify defense spending, for example. Others have argued that alleged liberals at the Department of State's Bureau of Intelligence and Research (INR) and CIA see the world through rose- (or pink-) colored glasses.

More virulent critics have charged that intelligence agencies purposefully "cook the books" by skewing reported information and judgments to support specific policies. The late Director of Central Intelligence William J. Casey received pointed public criticism from a number of quarters for allegedly altering a National Intelligence Estimate on Mexico in 1984. Director William H. Webster was a target of Congressional criticism that he used intelligence to support Administration policies in the Persian Gulf in 1990.[2]

The central thesis of part I of this book is that the problems of CIA's analytical arm—the Directorate of Intelligence—are far deeper than those alleged by most critics of the Agency. The regular critiques are symptoms of deeper institutional and cultural problems that reflect the organization of the DI, personnel management, and the management of the intelligence production and review processes. More importantly, they concern senior DI managers' de facto policies about the Directorate's mission, the organization's bureaucratic priorities, and the intellectual integrity of the institution. These policy decisions and ethical standards together lead the Directorate to produce intelligence analysis that is sometimes "cooked" to serve policy agendas, but just as often is purposefully shallow, self-serving, and sometimes just cheap.

These failings are tragedies in several senses. Intelligence analysis done properly offers a hope, if not a promise, of better warnings of threats and a more secure nation. CIA long has promised that its analysis is the most objective possible, but in recent years it has thrown that virtue away in a scramble by senior Agency officers to satisfy personal and bureaucratic agendas. And, not least, the enormous intellectual promise of so many fine, bright CIA people, was damaged in the 1980s and early 1990s by the parochial interests of senior CIA executives.

Part II addresses some of the many public misunderstandings and simple ignorance of CIA analytic practice as demonstrated in the literature on CIA intelligence analysis. It clarifies some DI practices and proposes ways for the policy making and academic communities to help keep CIA accountable.

Notes to Chapter 1

1 This view is widely attributed to Sherman Kent, especially as espoused in his Strategic Intelligence for American World Policy *(Princeton, N.J.: Princeton University Press, 1949).*

2 Senator Ernest Hollings on January 12, 1991, during Senate debate over whether to authorize President George Bush as Commander-in-Chief to attack Iraq, charged that Director Webster's public comments on intelligence judgments about the prospective effectiveness of sanctions against Iraq had supported the Bush Administration's views, while CIA briefings to Congress had painted another picture. Hollings, a member of the Senate Select Committee on Intelligence, said that Webster "should be ashamed of himself."

CHAPTER TWO

PART I

CIA'S DIRECTORATE OF INTELLIGENCE

"And ye shall know the truth and the truth shall make you free."

— John 8-23

(Inscription in entry of CIA headquarters)

"Certainly intelligence must not be an apologist for policy, but this does not mean that intelligence has no role in policy formation. Intelligence's role is definite and simple. Its job might be described in two stages: (1) the exhaustive examination of the situation for which a policy is required, and (2) the objective and impartial exploration of all the alternative solutions which the policy problem offers."[1]

"Like many a producer of consumers' goods, intelligence will have its greatest marketing success when its product bears the unmistakable signs of superior research, cautious development, sound design, and careful production."[2]

— Sherman Kent, 1949

The Directorate of Intelligence (DI) is the analytical arm of the Central Intelligence Agency and is one of its four major components, or directorates (see figure 1). As the last processor of intelligence information within CIA, the DI—alone among US intelligence analysis organizations—directly feeds intelligence judgments to the president and other policymakers in all executive branch departments, to the Congress, and to US allies on a selective basis. A healthy DI thus is essential.

The Directorate's stated mission is to "analyze and interpret foreign intelligence information" for the United States government; put differently, the DI's responsibility "is to provide timely, accurate, and comprehensive intelligence information of vital importance to the U.S. policymaker and the security of our nation."[3] The DI produces "finished intelligence," which requires the analysis, evaluation, and integration of information from all sources—publicly available data, and the fruits of clandestine or technical collection of information, for example—into a variety of products ranging from short oral briefings to lengthy assessments.

CIA analysis is heavily oriented toward the future. Data collection and analysis of historical and current events serve primarily to improve the Agency's ability to forecast future events, assess their implications, and assist policymakers in making decisions. Thus, for example, evaluations of the Soviet Union's past investments in defense industrial activities have helped DI analysts, and the entire government, understand future Soviet military order of battle as weapons flow from factories, as well as possible arms control negotiating positions. This focus on the future is a key difference between DI analytical work and the largely historical emphasis of many academics and other analysts.

The Directorate of Intelligence has existed in varying forms since the inception of CIA. It has received new names, organizations, and duties as its perceived mission has evolved and its budgets permitted.[4] For most of its existence, it has had its current name. In 1978-82, it was the National Foreign Assessment Center—a modest attempt by the Carter Administration to distinguish still more the difference between the largely white collar, office-bound, nature of analysis and the field work of CIA's Directorate of Operations (DO).

Despite its re-designation in 1982 as a directorate, the DI retains significant differences in mission, outlook, and culture

Figure 1

Organization of the Central Intelligence Agency

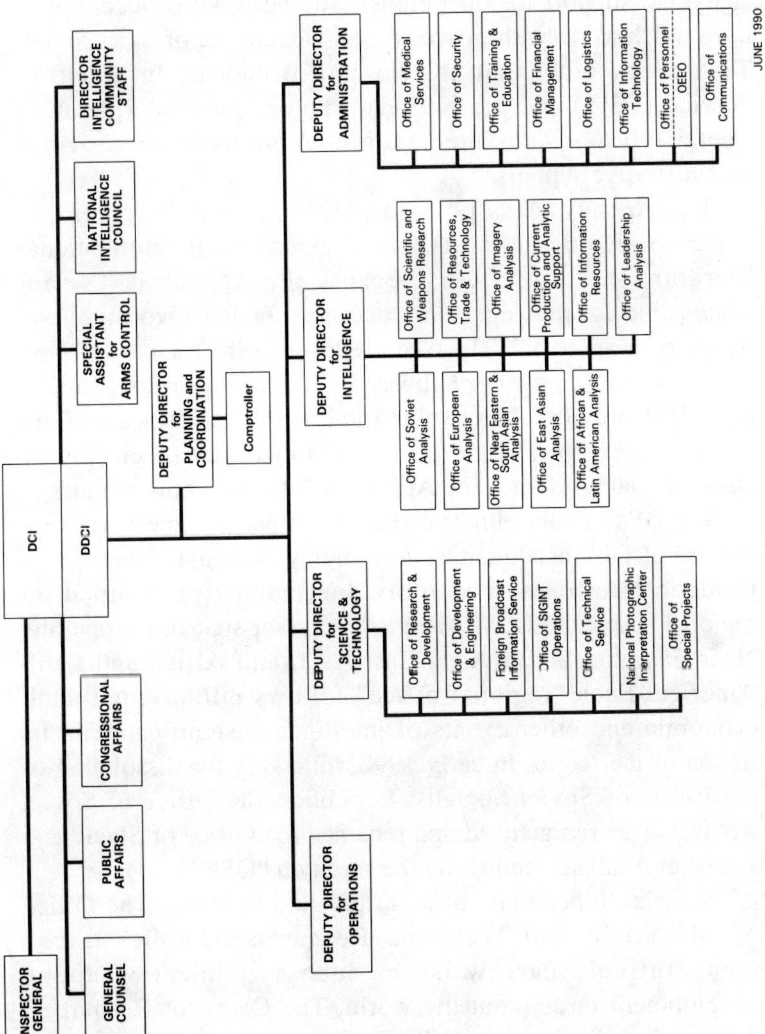

Source: CIA brochure, " Factbook on Intelligence."

from the other directorates. The differences between the DI and the DO—where the "spies" and covert operators reside—have been especially strong, despite analysts' reliance on the informational fruits of case officers' work and the potential for analytical support for operations.[5] Similarly, DI officers rarely have much to do with offices in the Directorate of Science and Technology other than the Foreign Broadcast Information Service (FBIS) and the National Photographic Interpretation Center (NPIC). The Directorate of Administration provides administrative support.

The Agency takes pointed public pride in its claims of objective reporting and analysis. It asserts in its informational literature that this occurs because the Agency is "... not responsible for making policy decisions or for advocating one policy over another."[6] The CIA credo—a Bill Casey innovation that hangs in a first floor hallway at CIA headquarters—says in part, "We provide objective and unbiased evaluations and are always open to new perceptions and ready to challenge conventional wisdom." See Appendix A for the entire credo.

The DI's 11 subordinate offices and most of its personnel are located at CIA headquarters in Langley, Virginia. Five offices produce intelligence on individual countries grouped on regional bases: the USSR (and its successor states); Europe; the Near East and South Asia; East Asia; and Africa and Latin America. Each "regional office" follows military, political, economic and other events of intelligence significance in its region of the world. In early 1992, following the dissolution of the Union of Soviet Socialist Republics, the Office of Soviet Analysis was reorganized and renamed the Office of Slavic and Eurasian Analysis, known by the acronym "OSE."

The six "functional" offices operate differently. The Office of Scientific and Weapons Research (OSWR) tracks comparatively narrow issues such as nuclear weapons development throughout the world. The Office of Resources, Trade, and Technology (RTT) follows a diverse mix of economic and technological issues on a global basis, as well as topics like terrorism, narcotics, and weapons transfers that are

Photograph 1. The Directorate of Intelligence occupies space in the Agency's headquarters complex in Langley, Virginia. The main entrance to the Original Headquarters Building, completed in 1963, is at left. The large green New Headquarters Building at right was begun in 1984 and essentially completed in 1989. The white "bubble" at lower left, as it is known, is the Agency's auditorium.
Source: Central Intelligence Agency.

world-wide phenomena; it was reorganized from the Office of Global Issues (OGI) in June 1990, when it dropped several responsibilities and increased its emphasis on others. The Office of Imagery Analysis (OIA) uses photography and other images as its primary sources of intelligence information for evaluating events throughout the world. The Office of Leadership Analysis (LDA) follows world political leaders and other important people and organizations. The Office of Information Resources (OIR) provides information support services. Finally, the Office of Current Production and Analytic Support (CPAS) publishes the Directorate's papers and performs a variety of other functions, including briefing White House personnel and staffing the Agency's Operations Center. In addition, the DI has staffs that provide intelligence support on such issues as arms control, and DI personnel serve on interagency intelligence committees and in posts abroad.

DI offices are subdivided for functional and administrative reasons. Each office has several divisions, which are themselves divided into branches—just like much of the rest of government—where analysts reside. Some offices have clusters of divisions called "groups." There also are hybrid organizations called "centers" which tackle specific, knotty, and sometimes multi-directorate problems; these allow considerable organizational flexibility and cover issues such as international terrorism.

The creation of five "regional" and six "functional" offices creates overlapping jurisdictions and interests that generate considerable opportunity for "cross fertilization" as well as turf fights. The directorate-wide reorganization of October 1981 was designed to place specialists from different academic backgrounds—political, military, and economic, for example—into the same branches so that they could interact more productively and produce better intelligence. Previously, these analysts had been in separate offices organized along functional lines. The regional reorganization was only partial, however—as the continuing existence of the functional offices attests—often creating the need for extensive intra- and inter-office coordination.

While the organizational structure requires significant coordination of views and judgments between offices having overlapping responsibilities, there are usually clear lines of ultimate responsibility for every product—either from the beginning or after a turf fight by competing offices or even divisions within an office. A single analyst, a branch chief, a division chief, and an office director typically determine the shape of lengthy projects that sometimes take a year or more to complete. Coordination comments can be ignored for perceived cause and more senior officials in the review chain make judgmental or editing changes in drafts, taking or leaving the prose and recommendations of their subordinates as they see fit.

With the office of the Deputy Director for Intelligence (DDI)—the head of the Directorate—in the late 1980s and early 1990s usually having relatively modest review comments, the office director is the key determinant of the shape of papers originating in his office.[7] He can heavily control the analytic position the Central Intelligence Agency takes to the president and the intelligence community generally on all issues over which his office has primary responsibility. This responsibility regularly involves designating an officer—and a position—to represent CIA during the coordination of National Intelligence Estimates.

The significant responsibility granted managers for approving, killing, reshaping, refocusing, or otherwise modifying analysis is a key, purposeful aspect of the "review process"—the mechanism by which an analyst's draft is converted into a CIA paper. The process works by passage of drafts to reviewers who incrementally mandate changes. A branch chief, for example, makes changes until he is satisfied. Then he passes the paper to his division chief. If the division chief's required changes are more than minor, the analyst must pass the paper back through the branch chief for review again before it goes back to the division chief. And so on. This transit of a paper through the review chain continues until the most senior reviewer is satisfied (see figure 2).

Figure 2

Passage of a Paper Through the Review Process

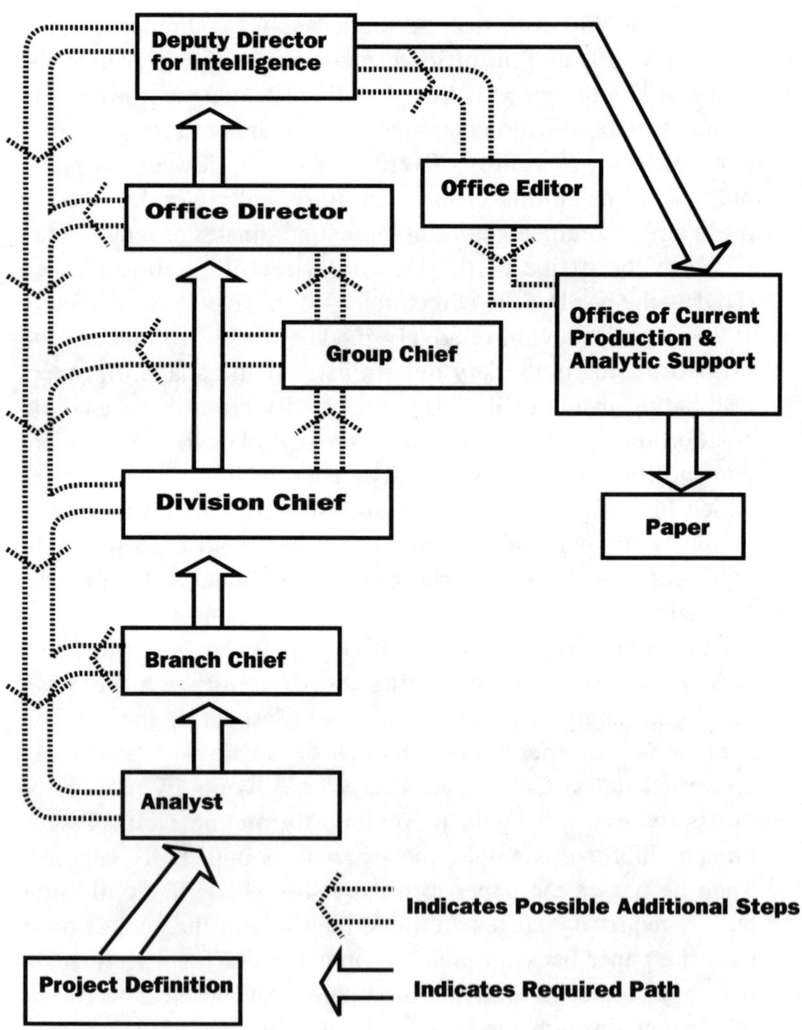

The review process theoretically exists to ensure that DI products meet DI standards for quality of analysis, format, and style. As such, it is essential. It also is a process despised in practice by virtually all analysts and many managers as the least appealing part of a career in the DI. Analysts widely regard it as slow, wasteful, frustrating, and far from certain of attaining the objective of better analysis. Extensive complaints by analysts and lengthy discussions within the Directorate over the years have failed to yield a better way to assure publication of sound papers that meet Agency standards, whatever they may be.[8]

The DI decides to work on intelligence topics for several reasons. Often, a topic simply is obviously important, either because it poses a tangible threat to US interests or because it already appears on the pages of newspapers; this is particularly true for "current intelligence" items. Sometimes the president or other senior policymaking or intelligence officials ask that an issue be addressed. Senior Agency officers often mandate longer term projects as part of research program packages. These help manage DI analytical resources and show the president and Congress that CIA is responding to their concerns; they also serve as marketing tools to justify CIA funding requests. Analysts and lower ranking managers often make proposals that receive blessings, particularly on current intelligence issues.

The DI has a large number of "art forms" in which to present its analyses. Sometimes intelligence "consumers" specify a form, but usually DI management and the responsible analyst have considerable flexibility in chosing a medium. These range from phone calls to oral briefings and videos. A host of written forms—with varying style, format, and timeliness characteristics—gives the analyst many options if he can complete his work and get it through the review process. At the same time, these varying characteristics sometimes limit analysts considerably; the particularly stringent format rules for current intelligence journals, for example, may force an analyst to give more cursory treatment to a complex but fast evolving issue than he may think desirable. The pace of change may, however, force him to use such a publication despite its limitations. The inventory of DI products does not, however, include National Intelligence Estimates.[9]

As his career progresses, the recruiting brochures promise, the DI analyst will have unique opportunities to "make vital contributions to the nation."[10] He will "work for the President of the United States and national leaders" and "form part of the foundation on which they make national policy decisions."[11] His work will be "exceptionally important."[12] By implication, he will be a satisfied employee and citizen.

* * *

The recruiters' brochures and public relations claims reflect a view of the mission of intelligence that guided the Agency in its early years and is probably best stated by Sherman Kent in *Strategic Intelligence for American World Policy*, first published in 1949. Kent was a history professor at Yale University who became a senior analyst in the Office of Strategic Services (OSS) during World War II. He later was director of CIA's Office of National Estimates—a predecessor of the Directorate of Intelligence.

Strategic Intelligence provided a philosophical grounding for American intelligence analysis and discussed many of the issues that remain unresolved to this day. These include: the proper role and distance between intelligence producers and consumers; methodological problems; organization; and, the importance of analytical objectivity.

Kent viewed intelligence as composed of three basic, but overlapping elements: descriptive, reportorial, and speculative-evaluative. Descriptive intelligence, in Kent's scheme, is essential to the others. It is the basic groundwork—the accumulation of facts and figures—that allows analysts to spot change and "speculate" about, or assess or evaluate, the meaning of the changes. Kent's concern about basic information developed from his experience during World War II, when ignorance of even apparent trivia like the widths of streets in small towns, for example, sometimes played crucial roles in the outcomes of military operations.

The Agency in its early days shared Kent's concerns and for years devoted considerable resources to the development of basic information, especially about potential enemies with closed societies like the Soviet Union. CIA generated massive amounts of data and compiled them periodically in volumes called the *National Intelligence Survey* (NIS) series—standard format documents that provided a wealth of information on the political, demographic, military, geographical, and other aspects of foreign countries.

Kent's reportorial intelligence refers to the need to report and, to some extent, assess change. This is the journalistic, or "current," side of intelligence. Reporting may be oral, but more often it is formalized into publications that have evolved over time and consist now of such publications as the *National Intelligence Daily* (NID) and the *President's Daily Brief* (PDB). Articles typically are quite short and may be relatively light on analysis because of that brevity.

Kent described "speculative-evaluative" intelligence as the "most important and most complicated element of strategic intelligence"—an opinion I suspect most analysts share. It also is the challenging part of the job—one that attracts most of them to the DI and provides the largest amount of satisfaction. It builds on the other two elements of intelligence. It is the difficult job of making sense of a complex mixture of often inadequate, conflicting information to make judgments that policymakers want, need, and will use. Kent wrote:

> "Speculative knowledge is not common and it is not to be had for the gathering. It is the rarest ingredient in the output of intelligence and is produced only by the most competent students this country possesses. It requires of its producers that they be masters of the subject matter, impartial in the presence of new evidence, ingenious in the development of research techniques, imaginative in their hypotheses, sharp in the analysis of their predilections or prejudices, and skillful in the presentation of their conclusions. It requires of its

producers the best in professional training, the highest intellectual integrity, and a very large amount of worldly wisdom."[13]

Kent devoted specific attention to the issue of objectivity and the methodological means to guard against bias of any sort—including those of culture and language—and to ensure objectivity:

> "Now an intelligence staff which must strive for reasoned and impartial analysis, if it is to strive for anything, has its own difficulties with view, position, slant, and line. After all, it is made up of men whose patterns of thought are likely to color their hypotheses and whose colored hypotheses are likely to make one conclusion more attractive than the evidence warrants. The main difference between professional scholars and intelligence officers on the one hand, and all other people on the other hand, is that the former are supposed to have had more training in the techniques of guarding against their own intellectual frailties. Policing their inescapable irrationalities is a twenty-four-hours-per-day task. Even so, it is not always successful."[14]

For Kent, these psychological and methodological concerns had implications for the proper relationship between intelligence producers and consumers:

> "If intelligence under the best of conditions finds itself guilty of hasty and unsound conclusion, is it likely to find itself doing more of this sort of thing when it is under the administrative control of its consumers in plans or operations? My answer is yes. I do not see how, in terms of human nature, it can be otherwise. I do not see how intelligence can escape, every once in so often, from swinging into line between the policy of the employing unit and prostituting itself in the production of what the

Nazis used to call *kaempfende Wissenschaft* (roughly "knowledge to further aims of state policy"). Nor do I see how, if the unexpected occurred, and intelligence invariably came up with findings at variance with the policy of the employing unit, intelligence could expect to draw its pay over an indefinite period. I cannot escape the belief that under the circumstances outlined, intelligence will find itself right in the middle of policy, and that on occasions it will be the unabashed apologist for a given policy rather than its impartial and objective analyst. As Walter Lippman sagely remarks, 'The only institutional safeguard (for impartial and objective analysis) is to separate as absolutely as it is possible to do so the staff that executes from the staff that investigates. The two should be parallel but quite distinct bodies of men, recruited differently, paid if possible from separate funds, responsible to different heads, intrinsically uninterested in each other's personal success.' "[15]

"For these reasons, what is gained in guidance, may well be lost in the integrity and objectivity of the operation."[16]

"The only way out of the dilemma seems to me to lie in the very compromise that usually is attempted: guarantee intelligence its administrative and substantive integrity by keeping it separate from its consumers; keep trying every known device to make the users familiar with the producers' organization, and the producers with the users' organization."[17]

"Proper relationship between intelligence producers and consumers is one of utmost delicacy. Intelligence must be close enough to policy, plans, and operations to have the greatest amount of guidance, and must not be so close that it loses its objectivity and integrity of judgment."[18]

For Kent, organization and tolerance for diversity also were important to production of the best intelligence. While organization charts could vary, Kent observed that:

> " ... intelligence organizations must be not a little like a large university faculty. They must have the people to whom research and rigorous thought are the breath of life, and they must accordingly have tolerance for the queer bird and the eccentric with a unique talent. They must guarantee a sort of academic freedom of inquiry and must fight off those who derogate such freedom by pointing to its occasional crackpot finding. They must be built around a deference to the enormous difficulties which the search for truth often involves."[19]

Kent's views, and those of similar minded people, provided a firm intellectual and even ethical base for CIA analysis for over 30 years. In recent years, however, the organization has begun to act much differently.

Notes to Chapter 2

1 Kent, Strategic Intelligence, *p. 201.*

2 Ibid., p. 76.

3 CIA recruiting brochure, Directorate of Intelligence, Central Intelligence Agency, Careers that can make a difference, *p. 2.*

4 For a brief history of the organization of the Agency, see Charles D. Ameringer, U.S. Foreign Intelligence *(Lexington MA: Lexington, 1990) pp. 201-224.*

5 While cooperation between individuals in the two directorates sometimes is very good, many analysts view DO officers as action-loving cowboys who are not interested in or capable of collecting the information they need to do good analysis. At the same time, many operations officers see analysts as egg-heads with little savvy who perversely enjoy a weirdly competitive life in a headquarters environment they prefer to avoid. As a measure of their affection, they commonly call analysts "geeks."

6 CIA brochure Directorate of Intelligence, Central Intelligence Agency, Careers that can make a difference, *p. 2.*

7 For stylistic reasons, third person singular pronouns in this paper are masculine. In fact, the DI employs many women analysts and female managers up through the position of office director.

8 The review process is a regular topic of discussion by individuals and the "Friends of Analysis," an informal group within CIA, and particularly the DI, that exchanges views and communicates outsiders' critiques of intelligence analysis.

9 The National Intelligence Estimate (NIE) is a product of the intelligence community as a whole, and reflects the coordinated comments of the members of the community. It is approved by the DCI as Director of Central Intelligence, not as the head of CIA. A National Intelligence Officer (NIO) has staff responsibility for production of each estimate. Normally, the responsible NIO chooses as "principal drafter" a knowledgeable senior analyst from one of the larger agencies of the community, who prepares the initial draft either on his own or in collaboration with others. Rarely, an NIO drafts an estimate himself. CIA in recent years has supplied a large number of principal drafters.

10 CIA recruiting brochure, Directorate of Intelligence, Central Intelligence Agency, Careers that can make a difference, *p. 2.*

11 Ibid., p. 6.

12 Ibid.

13 Kent, Strategic Intelligence, *pp. 64-65.*

14 Ibid., p. 199.

15 Ibid., pp. 199-200.

16 Ibid., p. 200.

17 Ibid., pp. 200-201.

18 Ibid., p. 180.

19 Ibid., p. 74.

CHAPTER THREE

THE DI IN PRACTICE

The Directorate of Intelligence in practice operates much differently than its credo mandates and its brochures claim. While some offices' managers and analysts are capable, competent, and dedicated to sound service, other offices with significant responsibilities fall far short of what many seasoned observers consider satisfactory performance. In virtually every arena in these poorly managed offices, the Agency's stated performance promises are not met and institutional objectives are at least partially different. The trend, in the view of many DI analysts and some managers, in the 1980s and early 1990s was toward still worse performance.

A "typical" week in the life of an analyst illustrates some of the kinds of activities, pressures, frustrations, and pleasures of life as a DI analyst. This hypothetical week applies to a "country analyst"— one who follows current and longer-term events in a specific country. This example is a composite of many common analysts' experiences and is, I believe, representative of the working lives of many "country" analysts. Other analysts have more generic or "functional" responsibilities for similar activities in many countries, produce different mixes of products, and have different experiences.

My reason for devoting so much attention in this fictional story— and later in the book— to the institutional and cultural pressures on analysts, as well as their goals and frustrations, is that these constitute major influences on the quality of DI analysis. One cannot understand the strengths and weaknesses of the

DI without an appreciation of the effects of these influences on the key producers of CIA judgments— the analysts and first-line managers. My references to incentives, procedures, and poor morale are designed not to complain that life should be easier for analysts, but rather to point to the ways that CIA managers mold and sometimes politicize analysis, while too often managing valuable resources poorly.

On Monday morning, Bill, the political analyst who covers Bugland, comes in early to read his "traffic"— reports that have come in overnight. Bugland is a small developing country in a strategic and troubled part of the world. Bill's traffic is always heaviest after a weekend and he is anticipating word on the results of a meeting the previous day of a faction of the ruling party. Prime Minister Smith, a friend of Washington, is in trouble and could be dumped by party elders. Bill plans to read his electronic mail first, then check the newspapers and "hard copy" traffic when they arrive later.

Bill quickly notices that two sources have reported that Jones, a stridently anti-American populist who has vowed to end US military basing rights in Bugland, has outmaneuvered Smith and has the votes to topple him at a full party conference on Thursday. The better report comes from one of the Agency's best human sources in Bugland. Bill feels a little thrill; he thought this might happen and had been pressing the clandestine service to watch for tensions in the party. His work has paid off.

The worst is about to happen for US interests, and Bill decides a current intelligence article is warranted. He quickly tells his branch chief, Tom, of the news and asks that the office list a "brief"— a full page of analysis— for tonight's *National Intelligence Daily* (NID), the Agency's main current intelligence publication and "publication of record." He smiles a little "I-told-you-so" smile. Tom concurs and sends the supporting reports to Mary, their division chief. Mary in the past has thought Bill too worried about the extent of Jones' alleged anti-Americanism but, after a quick read of the cables, agrees to list a "note"— a two-paragraph article— on the NID "menu." She reminds Bill that the DDI last week said there had been a lot of articles on base issues lately, and that it would be best to emphasize the bilateral political side of things. Besides, her counterpart Mark of the Security Issues Division has been moving his division's analysis more into political matters and she does not want to have to list the note as a joint piece. Bill agrees but senses trouble. He knows that Bugland military analyst Fred, with whom he must "coordinate" his article, thinks that US access to the airfield and port complex at Pica, and some prepositioned military stocks there, are essential to our ability to deter aggression in the region. Fred is particularly concerned about on-going negotiations to build a large dry dock in the harbor at Pica.

Bill begins to draft. He knows his subject well and only looks in his files for a little detail before taking the draft to Fred for comments; he wants to head off trouble early. Fred is working on his own NID article on a big arms purchase by a neighboring country, so Bill drops off a copy and asks him to call back as soon as possible. Twenty minutes later Fred walks to Bill's desk with concerns; he thinks the potential military significance of this development is far greater than Bill suggested, and Bill's draft uses specific language about the base at Pica different than Fred has used in earlier papers. The office should be consistent. Fred backs off a little and offers a sentence on the importance of the dry dock facilities. Bill reluctantly agrees. He has to juggle the rest of the draft because it is now too long for the note format and the dry dock reference does not fit his heavily political story very well; Bill works to cram the dry dock into one four-sentence paragraph of "facts" and a similar paragraph of "comments." He gets the draft to Tom at 11:15 AM and calls off his planned lunch with an old friend in the cafeteria as he waits for Tom's comments.

Tom has changed the draft significantly and cut out the dry dock reference. He asks Bill with some irritation if he had heard Mary's instructions this morning. Remembering Mary's comments, he has softened Bill's assessment about Jones' alleged anti-Americanism by adding that Jones had gone to a "university in the US," knowing that reference in DI publications to most specific names of American persons and institutions is forbidden. Bill responds that Jones had quit school and left the country hastily after being beaten up by factory workers and arrested for burning an American flag. Tom says "oh," and deletes the change. Tom finally agrees that a short dry dock reference is needed to keep Mark at bay. Tom and Bill work over more changes and get the draft to Mary. It is 1:30 PM.

Mary has some concerns. She is worried about the dry dock and is trying to decide whether the piece should discuss prospects for a Jones government's ties to the West generally and NATO. Should that be added? Where in the draft? She finally decides not to add NATO, especially given its state of flux, and approves the text with several word changes. Bill thinks some of the changes are marginal but harmless, and is pleased that some of the language Tom changed is back as he wanted it. It is 2:30.

Bill gets the draft to his office editor, who quickly makes a few editorial changes and gets it back to Bill while he waits. It is a little better; some of Mary's phrases had been a little obtuse, and the editor clarified a phrase of his own that had been bothering Bill all morning. He then puts it in the NID box, where the office director, Joe, will pick it up for review. Bill goes back to his desk in a cubicle in the large "bull pen" office he shares with the other analysts in his branch and waits anxiously. The word could come at any time and he can not get his mind re-focused on another project. At 3:45, he gets good news. The deputy office director did the office-level review and did not change a thing. That is no surprise to Bill; the deputy director is just an economist and does not understand political matters. Bill runs upstairs to the NID staff, plops his draft in the in-box, and returns to his phone to wait.

At 5:15, NID editor Stan calls to say Bill's draft is ready. It has been edited. He can come to see it. Bill is a little apprehensive. He, like many analysts, believes that NID editors have little purpose in life except changing language and cannot justify their existence by simply approving good drafts; and, Stan is worse than most. Sure enough, Stan has chosen to call Jones a leftist and not a populist. Bill tells Stan the difference and gets nowhere; the Secretary of Agriculture has told the DDI that he considers himself a populist and does not appreciate that honorable label being applied to foreign left-wingers. They compromise on other language. To make matters worse, Stan tells Bill that the piece is marginal and may not run. The NID has only so much space and it has been a busy day in the world. The DDI and the senior editors will decide.

Bill goes back to his office to tell Tom of developments. Tom is tending to his career— socializing with Mary, Mark, and Joe and slurping a beer— but manages to break away for a few minutes to listen to Bill. It is 6:15, and there is nothing more for Bill to do. He goes home to his own beer.

On Tuesday morning, Bill immediately checks the NID. His note has turned into a "snowflake"— a four-line Kiplinger Letter-style piece of several phrases but no complete sentences. Jones is still a leftist and there is no dry dock mentioned. Tom shrugs and allows as how at least Bill got most of his message to policymakers. Fred calls to ask what happened to the dry dock; he is not happy and hints ominously that he might talk with Mark about the deletion. Bill makes copies of the snowflake for the branch and his personal production files, and enters the production in the office's none-too-user-friendly computer production file. Every little bit will help come career board time.

After reading his traffic and seeing nothing worth a follow-up NID, Bill turns to his article on the internal dynamics of the ruling party that is scheduled to run in the next edition of his office's serial publication. After changing his characterization of Jones from "populist" to "leftist" throughout the draft, he works steadily until Rachel from the Office of Leadership Analysis (LDA) walks in with a draft for coordination. She is doing a paper on foreign policy decisionmakers in Bugland and asks that he return coordination comments by close of business Thursday. Bill takes a quick look and discovers that the paper heavily discusses Smith and Jones— and how they operate within the party to line up support— as well as officials of the

Ministry of Foreign Affairs. It comes perilously close to infringing on his turf. Besides, she has some things wrong. Bill shows the draft to Tom, who promptly reports to Mary that LDA is at it again. Mary declares that she will get Joe to complain to the director of LDA. Bill puts the draft aside and decides to look at it late Thursday afternoon.

On Tuesday afternoon, Mary calls Tom to her office and tells him to close the door. Joe has finished reviewing Bill's Intelligence Assessment (IA) on growing regional tensions and prospects for instability in Bugland, and the word is not good. They had reviewed the draft and made a number of changes in it, but an analyst's paper is always his ultimate responsibility. They talk about what Joe did not like and how Bill might have gone wrong. A meeting in Joe's office is scheduled for 3:00 Wednesday afternoon— plenty of time for criticism before the end of the work day. Tom goes to tell Bill of the meeting's time and little more. Bill knows the news is bad.

Word that Joe has finished review of Bill's paper after three weeks— with negative implications— spreads quickly in the branch. In the bull pen, conversations are easily overheard. His colleagues smile wryly and offer condolences. Some have been there before, can empathize, and are glad it is him and not them. Others sympathize and want to learn as much as possible of Joe's objections so they can avoid similar trouble. They like Bill and wish him well, but those at Bill's grade cannot help think that his misfortune to cross Joe on an Intelligence Assessment— a major project that analysts must do well to succeed in the DI— will give them an edge for promotion at the next career board meeting.

Bill's economist counterpart Rose is supportive but is excited about news of her own. Her last typescript memorandum on Bugland's land reform program prompted complimentary comments from our ambassador in Bugland City and kudos from the DDI, who said he liked it; Joe just gave her a small cash award. She is elated by the rare tangible evidence that someone appreciates her work. Bill congratulates her but feels a twinge of jealousy and remembers that he gave her good ideas about how the government of Bugland convinced land owners to go along.

On Wednesday afternoon, Bill is nervous. He works a little on his party dynamics article and reads his paper traffic from the stack in his in-box, discarding most of it until he fills up his last "burn bag" for classified trash. Then he talks with his counterparts in the Directorate of Operations and at State while waiting for the meeting with Joe.

Bill, Tom, and Mary are at Joe's open door at 2:55. They talk little. Joe gets off the phone at 3:05, signing off with a jovial laugh, and calls them in. He tells them that the paper is not what he wants. Bill screws up his courage and says that the paper is consistent with the outline and terms of reference they all had agreed to, and that Tom and he had made sure of it during branch review. Tom doodles silently as Joe tersely says that he wants something else and does not care what the outline says. Joe tells them what he wants in general terms and they begin to take copious notes. Mary and Tom ask a few clarifying questions as Joe explains the reorganization, changes in emphasis, additional topics, and "tightening" of language he wants. Given the success of Rose's paper, he wants more on agrarian/urban tensions and less discussion of ethnic and regional strife. He directs a series of specific substantive and editorial "fixes." He asks if all understand his desires. Bill picks up the draft on the way out of Joe's office.

Mary, Tom, and Bill go to Mary's office to assess the damage. They discuss what they heard Joe say he wanted and which of his contradictory comments should be disregarded. Bill thumbs through Joe's remarks, made with the fountain pen he always uses to review papers, and shakes his head occasionally. They agree that Joe's concerns are editorial, not substantive from the analytic standpoint, but that they nevertheless are major. It is a black mark for all of them, but especially for Bill. Mary and Tom resolve that they will ensure that Bill's next draft meets all of Joe's requirements; they do not want to go through this again. They agree that Bill will evaluate Joe's comments and that they will meet again Friday morning to discuss Bill's conclusions about how to fix the draft.

On Thursday, Bill is alternately angry and sad. He thinks Joe has demonstrated inconsistency, ignorance, impatience, and caprice in his comments. Some, like stray question marks, make no obvious sense but will require some wording changes to demonstrate that Bill is responsive. Joe has butchered whole sections that were important and reduced other thoughts to trivia. Bill remembers that both Mary and Tom declined to defend Bill or language they had insisted on adding to the text. He struggles for a reorganization formula that will satisfy Joe, and cover the subject completely and well. He tries to include all the points Tom and Mary made about what Joe indicated he really wants.

On Friday morning Bill briefs Tom and Mary on his review of Joe's written comments. He decides not to point out that Joe has made some factual and judgmental errors in his somewhat contradictory comments that reflect true ignorance of Bugland. He knows they are team players and are uninterested in discussions about Joe's mistakes. If there were misunderstandings, they are Bill's fault because DI analysts are in the communication business.

Bill knows that the only route to take is to figure out how best to satisfy Joe. They discuss new approaches, leaning heavily on the notes they took on Wednesday to divine Joe's real wants. They agree on a scheme and a schedule; three weeks of hard work probably are needed to fix the draft. The reorganization will require a whole new set of important transition paragraphs. The paper Bill enjoyed creating is gone and work on modified draft will not be very much fun for him. Mary tells Tom to review the paper especially carefully to ensure that it is consistent with Joe's written and oral instructions. She then will do the same. Branch and division review will be even tighter this time.

Bill glumly starts to work. Analyst colleagues float by to ask for lessons of the review sessions; they file them in their mental books on Joe's preferences and the reactions of Mary and Tom to them. Late Friday afternoon, Bill remembers that he owes coordination comments to Rachel. He looks over her draft quickly and calls with a few, apologizing for being late. Bill is exhausted, but resolves to be in the office early Saturday morning. He will ignore the article on party dynamics and maybe, just maybe, he yet can satisfy Joe and get the paper published before his career board meets next.

The story of Bill, while entirely imaginary, reflects some of the practices and attitudes common in many parts of the Directorate of Intelligence. It provides some lessons about the DI as well.

Analysts, and low- and middle-managers, often craft analysis heavily to serve senior Agency officials, not the president or the US government. This occurs because the review process and the personnel management system place both substantive review of analysis and near total control over promotions in the hands of a single individual; the office director has complete control of low- and middle-ranking analysts and much influence on higher paid individuals. Because the review chain has such absolute power, and because promotional decisions are often made on the basis of the "ease" or "difficulty" of the review process, analysts at minimum must keep in mind the concerns of management about even such trivial matters as personal quirks about word choices; some analysts keep informal "dictionaries" of the English language according to a key reviewer. At worst, the bureaucratically ambitious analyst ignores the needs of the administration and the nation, and devotes his analytic attention to satisfying the review chain. It has become axiomatic among analysts that analysts do not write for the president, they "write for the seventh floor"— where Agency executive suites are located.[1]

This attitude (and trend) is amplified by the demands and the language of management, particularly the office directors. For longer analytic projects like IAs, which consume most of analysts' time and usually are the primary basis of performance appraisals, these managers specify what they "want" before the analyst sets to work.[2] It is common for an office director to review a three- to five-page project proposal, then specify explicitly length, style, and even judgmental guidance before an analyst has completed his research. Indeed, some managers regularly counsel analysts to tailor their research efforts to support pre-determined conclusions; research thus becomes a search for facts to buttress a judgment.

The analyst and intermediate reviewers will, throughout the rest of their work on that project, keep prominently in mind what the office director said he wanted. Because analysts often view these comments as unclear or half-baked— the office director often will have made his decisions quickly on the basis of limited personal knowledge of the subject at hand— the sound analyst will repeatedly ask himself how he can satisfy the office director while preparing a useful paper that is judgmentally sound and factually accurate.[3] He faces a considerable ethical dilemma if these objectives cannot be reconciled. To make matters worse, office directors' wants are often transient and may be considerably different during the review process than they were during discussions about a project's scope.[4]

Office directors' (or other managers') "wants" for their offices' analysis vary, of course. The good ones share the values of CIA's credo, its heritage, and the recruiters' promises. The objects of their wants are methodologically sound, objective analysis, with conclusions and implications for specific policies being chips to fall where the analysis leads. Other motives concern the results of analysis.

Some managers, and thus analysts, seeing heavy interest in a subject by administration officials, devote more resources to specific issues of concern. Managers interpret policymakers' interests and broad guidance according to their own political views and those of their allies and potential mentors. They also act to serve the bureaucratic purpose of making the Agency appear responsive and thus deserving of at least its current budget. Changes in resource allocations may help make intelligence at least appear more "policy-relevant," assisting the Agency in making budget requests, for example. (If handled poorly, they may also increase the chance that the Agency will receive criticism for getting involved in a policy issue; antagonists on an issue also may use or leak Agency data or judgments that support their positions.)

Other Agency and DI resource re-allocations serve to keep Congress and the administration off management's collective back by making the Agency appear responsive to their concerns. Reorganizations like the evolution of the Office of Global Issues into the Office of Resources, Trade, and Technology in 1990 also occur for this reason. Finally, some managers simply have personal interests they wish to satisfy through expenditure of analytical resources. These may reflect good or poor decisions.

Analysis too often is not objective; it is deliberately slanted to serve personal, political or bureaucratic purposes. This occurs for several reasons, is far more extensive than the public criticisms Casey received, and has insidiously become ingrained in the review process.

Some managers, and thus ambitious junior managers and analysts, actively promote specific political policy positions through slanted intelligence analysis. These individuals may have links to Republican or Democratic officials or candidates, or serve more senior Agency officials they think have such ties. In 1988, for example, rumors swept parts of the DI and the Department of State that a senior DI official had close ties to the presidential campaign of George Bush— a violation of Agency policy at minimum and potentially a criminal violation of the Hatch Act. While unconfirmed, the rumor was plausible to many who heard it, given the manager's past stated attitudes. Much more commonly, the worst managers make clear that they expect their units' products to reflect their own judgments, whatever facts indicate or analysts' judgments may be.

Critics of CIA analysis repeatedly have attacked intentional slanting, but pointedly directed alteration of language by very senior officials like Casey over the objections of DI analytical offices is fairly rare for at least four reasons. First, some senior officers— like Deputy Directors for Intelligence (DDIs) Richard Kerr and John Helgerson, and Director Webster— appear to have few interests or opinions strong enough to lead them into explicit conflict with their subordinates over substantive issues.

Director Casey and DDI Robert Gates, however, had strong views and expressed them.

Second, the overt injection of personal opinion into analysis over the objections of analytic organizations makes bad press. Widely publicized charges that Casey politicized analysis mainly involved National Intelligence Estimates (NIEs)—national-level documents that require extensive coordination with the intelligence organs of executive branch departments.[5] These have their own bureaucratic and political agendas and have many avenues to leak complaints about a heavy-handed DCI.

Third, there generally is no need. A senior officer can "politicize" analysis subtly during the review process or even before it begins. Presumably unintentionally, DCI Webster conveyed a strong message when he told officers following the Middle East in August 1990 that he would very much like to give President Bush intelligence analysis that he believed Bush wanted to hear— that international economic sanctions would force Iraq to withdraw from Kuwait without US and allied resort to military force. One can only speculate about the influence Webster had on NESA analysts and managers, and the consequences for subsequent analysis and briefings that eventually led to Senator Ernest Hollings' assertion on the floor of the Senate that Webster himself had politicized CIA judgments on the Iraq-Kuwait crisis in 1990— by providing briefings unjustifiably supportive of Bush Administration policy.

Finally, a senior official can pick a drafter who, by inclination or prior agreement, will provide a draft that satisfies the commissioning officer. These "analysts" are known as "hired pens" in the same sense that "hired guns" in Western movies serve a master. These people normally know their role and sometimes candidly admit the function.[6]

Much more common is politicization by alteration of drafts during the production and review process. This occurs either directly from managers' actions, or indirectly by analysts or junior managers trying to win favor by adopting the perceived or explicitly stated political positions of their superiors. This slanting, or politicization, of analysis occurs by both commission and omission (or suppression). In the 1980s and early 1990s, DI analysis on the Soviet Union, Eastern Europe, China, and Central America was particularly subject to bias; the bias itself took several forms, ranging from mild cases of "clientitis"— the development of an affinity for a country as a result of growing familiarity— to virulent anti-communism. Analysts and managers following other areas more successfully resisted pressures from above, if they existed.

DI treatment of Eastern Europe is an extreme but telling example of politicization of analysis. Managers in the division following Eastern Europe made clear in the mid- to late 1980s (prior to the beginning of the collapse of communist regimes) to the division's analysts that the regimes were to be treated harshly. These were enemy countries in conflict with the United States. CIA, these managers made clear to some analysts, would demonstrate this hostility.

These managers directed conclusions to analysts prior to the evaluation of facts— not the legitimate managerial role of specifying subjects for investigation. This difference is major. It indicates an ideological intent and cannot be dismissed as either aggressive investigation or incompetence. These managers dispatched analysts to find data supporting their beliefs and to draft papers of specified length and format supporting those opinions.

In one case in mid-1987, for example, a division chief directed me to show a linkage in a current intelligence piece between an East European government and an international terrorist group despite much information to the contrary, my objections, and those of two other DI components concerned with the issue— the Office of Near East and South Asian Analysis (NESA) and the Counter-terrorism Center. He ordered the article after reading of similar accusations in a partial translation of an article in a West German magazine with a long-standing reputation for sensational, and sometimes incorrect, reporting. The LaBelle disco bombing in West Berlin only a little over a year earlier (in April 1986) had cost American lives and been publicly attributed to terrorists operating from East Berlin. He knew that there was continuing interest— within CIA and in the Reagan Administration— in any East European government connection with terrorists, because they might (or would, in the view of some) indicate a Soviet connection to international terrorism.[7] Any evidence, or reporting, of such a connection would be welcomed in some parts of government.

The responsible branch chief took his instructions from his rater literally and insisted that the division chief's message be printed. During the course of discussions about the merits of the case and the views of other offices, the branch chief accused me of lacking loyalty to the Office of European Analysis. He did not mention the DI, the Agency, the president, the nation, or sound analysis. These managers purposely relegated me to the role of research assistant and propagandist and chastised me for objecting to their inappropriate directives. After three days of work designed to both satisfy my managers and avoid providing erroneous or misleading intelligence, a uselessly bland two-paragraph article appeared in the NID. Only the taxpayers' collective wallet, readers' respect for DI analysis, and my relationship with my bosses had been hurt.

In another case at about the same time, this same branch chief directed me, as I was preparing a lengthy paper known as a Research Paper (RP), to alter judgments to show significant anti-American consequences stemming from alleged Soviet mischief in the Third World. The topic of the paper was the training of people from Third World countries in a Warsaw Pact country. The paper documented numbers and nationalities of trainees in a broad spectrum of activities at specific locations. The branch chief wanted to show that these trainees had acquired senior positions in their governments and organizations— some of which had committed terrorist acts or otherwise acted in ways opposed to US interests. This would allow him to spin the analytical line that the training connection assured continuing control by the country that did the training, and hence the Soviets because this country was a Warsaw Pact member and therefore a Soviet surrogate. The final thread of argument was that this alleged Soviet control meant Soviet proxy war against the United States and Western interests generally.

I countered that this overstated the case considerably. Facts did not support some judgments. When discussions failed, I complained to the division chief, who abdicated his basic managerial responsibilities by declining to become involved at all. The paper when printed contained factual errors and a series of biographies of alleged trainees who by implication, but not by demonstration, were nefarious agents of international communism. (Ironically, there was no need for this dishonesty. The East European government in question demonstrably did many things not in American interests and had virtually no claim on the sympathies of readers of the paper.)

The branch and division chiefs responsible received no apparent bureaucratic damage from the incidents. Both later moved to more senior positions in another office. Pointed analysts' complaints to EURA's deputy director in 1987— by me and others— had no effect except to damage the complaining analysts by branding us malcontents. Other examples, although usually less blatant, are numerous.

Politicization by omission is more difficult to identify, but is probably more prevalent and is just as damaging to the Agency's avowed mission. In these cases, analysts or managers avoid issues or omit even unevaluated data that they expect will offend the political or bureaucratic sensitivities of either senior Agency officials or a consumer agency.

The Office of Resources, Trade, and Technology (RTT), for example, regularly slanted its economic reporting and analysis to avoid offending senior officials of the Treasury Department in the late 1980s and early 1990s. It avoided language that might cast doubts on the effectiveness of the so-called Brady Plan— the Bush Administration's scheme to reduce the burden of indebtedness of Third World countries. It also avoided publication of data, independent of analytical commentary, indicating that Treasury's desired result had not occurred.

RTT managers were responding as bureaucrats to unfavorable reactions to intelligence reports by Treasury officials— particularly those of outspoken Undersecretary for International

Affairs David C. Mulford, the plan's principal architect. Many Agency employees believed that then-DCI Webster had one primary objective: the avoidance of the controversy and criticism that marked the Casey years, the maintenance of the Agency's organizational interests, and conduct of "no-risk" Agency activities, to use Nathan Miller's term.[8] Aware that senior Agency officials wanted smooth relations with executive branch departments, aware that potentially controversial material would be excised during the review process in support of these objectives, and aware that their performance evaluations were dependent on the smoothness of the review process and their ability to satisfy their seniors, branch chiefs and analysts simply stopped writing the judgments they really held. In this way they practiced self-review or, more accurately, self-censorship. According to one RTT analyst who participated in this politicization, these lower level individuals responded to Treasury's reactions, particularly those of Mulford, even as reported in the newspapers.

Managers of the Office of African and Latin American Analysis directed that ALA's analysis not contradict the underpinnings of initiatives by Assistant Secretary of State Chester Crocker in the mid-1980s to broker a solution to the Angolan civil war. According to a former ALA analyst, office managers stipulated that ALA adopt the position that government forces (the MPLA) were strong enough to survive against opposition UNITA forces if Cuban troops withdrew; this meant that Cuban armed might was less essential to the survival of the MPLA. It supported Crocker's hope that Cuba could be enticed to leave—an easier chore if leaving would not condemn the regime in Luanda to defeat. Crocker's perseverance and the interests of the parties eventually led to a solution, but DI managers' efforts to please State Department policymakers hindered their potential ability to help improve American foreign policy.

Analysis of events in Central America for years during the 1980s suffered from politicization of several general sorts— and one peculiar to Central America. The intense domestic political struggle over US policy in the region ensured that the Agency would receive kudos from the White House for demonstrating, for example, that the Sandinista government of Nicaragua was aiding Salvadoran guerrillas. At the same time, reporting of other developments in the region could be used by Congressional opponents of American policy.

Uniquely, much of ALA's information on the area came from the same Directorate of Operations element— the Central American Task Force— that was conducting a very public "covert action" in the region— support of the Nicaraguan "Contra" rebels. This organization faced a problem: it wanted to accomplish its "covert" mission, but might find that more difficult if it fully satisfied another usual mission of reporting accurately on developments in its area of operations to the DI and to the rest of the government. The operators had good reason to believe that DI "geeks"— as some operations officers call analysts— would use even unfavorable information in their analyses, prospectively upsetting their operations by giving their critics in Congress further reason to oppose their efforts.

Over time, ALA analysts came to believe that the DO was censoring the information it released to ALA, and that senior ALA managers knew of the policy. This generated a feeling that a significant part of ALA reporting on Central America during the mid-1980s was flawed, and caused sometimes severe bitterness. In 1984, four analysts, known in the DI as the "Gang of Four," complained directly to DDI Robert Gates of this politicization. All soon thereafter received new assignments. Later, one resigned and at least two went on rotations from ALA. One became an Assistant National Intelligence Officer for Latin America and remained, in my judgment, bitter about the entire experience years later. The episode became widely known.

Politicization of analysis on Nicaragua, combined with widely disliked and disrespected office directors, contributed to chronic, very poor morale. Analysts voted with their feet and ALA had very high attrition. This episode represented, in my view, a clear failure of the general policy that separation of the operations and analytical components of CIA helps ensure both appropriate security and the objectivity of analysis. It also points to yet another practical reason not to conduct "covert" actions in public.

In another case in the late 1980s, an Office of Global Issues (OGI) analyst following technological developments throughout the world received information that a government friendly to the United States was about to encourage one of its private commercial firms to act in a way detrimental to US economic and technological interests. The information held that the foreign government was taking its actions for political as well as economic reasons. The OGI analyst believed the development sufficiently important and time-sensitive that a *National Intelligence Daily* article was warranted. The analyst then contacted an analyst in the Office of East Asian Analysis (OEA) who followed the country on a daily basis, and who was the appropriate coordination point. After initial concerns about the veracity of the report, the OEA analyst agreed that a current intelligence piece was justified.

In the meantime, however, discussion about the information and the NID proposal had grown to include branch and division chiefs in both OGI and OEA. The debate about accuracy of the raw intelligence continued, but quickly was overshadowed by OEA managers' political concerns. OEA branch and division chiefs made clear that they were worried about the bureaucratic ramifications of such an article. The OEA managers said they believed that the US policy community was happy with the bilateral relationship with this major trade partner as it then stood, and would be unhappy with unpleasant news about the foreign government's actions and political motives. They said they expected bilateral relations to suffer as a result of publication of the news in the NID. They further indicated that they feared that CIA would be blamed for bearing such bad news and that CIA would suffer bureaucratically for it. The OEA managers thus refused to coordinate on the proposed NID article, effectively killing it. OGI managers considered bucking the issue to the office director level, but had wearied of the struggle and gave in.

The information contained in the raw intelligence report was not published, and policymakers did not have an opportunity to intercede with the foreign government before its company took action. Thus, OEA officials served parochial CIA bureaucratic concerns at the explicit, conscious cost of denying the US government information it needed to defend the nation's economic interests. OGI managers, not wanting to offend colleagues they would have to deal with again, failed to insist that the debate about the merits of running such a piece be kept to issues of fact and intelligence judgment; they thus abdicated their responsibilities as well. The two relevant analysts, at the end in general agreement, played effectively no role in the final decision to kill the article.

The staff that directly serves the intelligence needs of the president— known as the "PDB staff" because it produces the *President's Daily Brief*— long has disdained regular coordination activities with other DI components and provided its own intelligence to presidents. For example, while it has a number of methods of procuring articles and other media for its senior consumers, a common one is use of the drafts of articles also submitted to the staff that publishes the *National Intelligence Daily*. The PDB staff selects articles, and rewrites and edits them as it sees fit. While normally it coordinates with the drafts' authors, it often has ignored their concerns.

Once, during the Reagan years, I objected to a PDB staff editor's substantial rewrite of one of my articles. I was concerned that both factual error and poor judgment had been injected, and that the PDB version had become quite inconsistent with the NID's edited draft. This was important because the NID also goes to the very senior officials who receive the PDB, and their staffs use the NID in their work; significant inconsistencies could hinder the work of policymakers and make CIA look foolish as well. In response to my concerns, the PDB editor observed that my views were irrelevant. The PDB staff "knew what the president wanted." She went ahead and prepared a substantially different article than the one I gave her. Because the PDB staff is part of the Office of Current Production and Analytic Support (CPAS), it is beyond all but the most vocal objections of analytic office directors; moreover, its head had held his position for years and was a dangerous man to cross. For these reasons it was not unheard of during the Reagan years for an analyst to purposefully skip submitting a draft to the PDB staff— and thus prospectively to President Reagan— over concerns about the PDB's objectivity in handling analysis.

The long-time head of the PDB staff gave a good indication of his own commitment to objective analysis and service to the president in early 1991. During the series of major events in the Soviet Union affecting issues like the prospects for then-President Mikhail Gorbachev's political survival, the man said that it did not matter what happened in the USSR; the Agency had forecast each of the possibilities and thus was "covered" against criticism that it had missed a call in any event. My source said that the man made his comments in a "gleeful" manner.

More generally, analysts and even middle managers argue that they cannot change the review process during which much politicization occurs, and fighting for objective analysis (or other issues involving judgment or integrity) would simply be ineffective but career damaging behavior. "Not worth falling on my sword," is a fairly common expression in some offices. Some express modest regret. Others say they simply are doing as they are told. Because this practice is so widespread, the good soldier Schweik— a literary character who always took orders— is a fairly common reference, and object of comparison, in some DI offices.[9]

After a short time, analysts and junior managers understand the wants of senior managers with political or bureaucratic agendas. They need little additional communication to assure that only politically correct judgments and data enter drafts. The politicization thus becomes implicit, with few regular oral admonitions or paper trails to "prove" that the DI has strayed from its mission of providing objective analysis.

In many cases, the slanting of analysis thus reflects a decision to satisfy someone and subservience of the desire most DI employees have to serve the more general national interest by providing sound objective analysis. Analysis is personalized. By satisfying a rater or a more senior official, who in turn wants to satisfy or avoid offending someone else, one enhances his own career prospects and makes his days more pleasant. Because of its predominance in current DI culture, many in the DI also have come to believe that satisfying perceived *wants* of specific individuals constitutes service, whatever national intelligence *needs* may be, with sometimes little regard for the consequences of this attitude.[10] This philosophy reflects a major evolution of the de facto mission of the Agency from its early days, when objective analysis was the clear first priority.

This is not a claim that CIA determines or should decide what is important to the government. CIA clearly has a duty to examine issues raised by policymaking officials— including those who intend to use intelligence data and judgments in partisan policy battles. However, CIA has a duty to alert policy officials of unpleasant foreign events and the consequences of US policies gone awry. It also has a duty to scan the international scene for events of importance to the United States that go beyond the scope and time horizon of a politician worried about his next poll approval ratings. Agency managers increasingly in the late 1980s and early 1990s ignored these latter duties.

Even as it caters to some policymakers, the DI peremptorily rejects requests for intelligence assistance from officials it deems unimportant— that is, who can neither help nor hurt the Agency. While intelligence resources are limited and priorities must be set, it is CIA officials, not any executive branch or Congressional body, who decide the merits of specific requests. Budgets and research plans are sufficiently general to provide this leeway for senior DI executives, whose rejections of requests are often terse and even rude. Thus, for example, the DI summarily ceased providing support to the government's telecommunications policy community— a relatively weak constituency— in 1986. The DI since has refused at least one request for assistance from a part of this community.

The DI review process implicitly views readers of its large distribution publications not as national leaders but as dumb, lazy, governmental amateurs who want to be entertained.

Sometimes even explicitly stated, these are the characteristics management imputes to the policymaking community when guiding analysts on style, sophistication, and depth of analysis. More tactfully, a well-respected DI manager advising other managers on how to train analysts wrote:

> "Intelligence is written for generalists who are grappling with real problems… New people are also slow to realize and often doubt another truth— that after a few months on the job they are among the most knowledgeable people in government on a particular issue, and, for the first time in their lives, they are writing for an audience that knows less than they do."[11]

This generalization also applies, although to a lesser extent, to projects done at the request of a specific policymaker or government agency.[12] Most analysts were well aware that the average tenure of officials of the rank of deputy assistant secretary and above during the early Reagan years was short; this meant and still means, so the thinking goes, that such officials cannot be experts in foreign affairs and that they need to be spoon-fed intelligence judgments.[13] Analysts knew that Reagan liked video news and generally presume that photos and graphics serve entertainment as well as informational purposes; senior management periodically has reminded analysts of the need for such "texture" in DI products.

Management's frequent presumption that "the reader" is stupid or lazy translates into dicta that papers be short and easy to understand, regardless of the scope or complexity of issues. Office directors often specify length (in exact numbers of double spaced typed pages per section) during sessions to discuss the concept of a paper— despite their sometimes minimal understanding of its subject. Analysts also receive regular admonitions to keep drafts clear.

However, this admirable interest in clear-headed analysis and good writing too often deteriorates into a search for simpleness and sometimes into mandated simple-mindedness.[14] A division chief in the Office of Global Issues (OGI) in 1990 declared that there should be only one thought contained in each paragraph of even a Research Paper— which by definition is one of the longest, most detailed papers in the DI product inventory. Any extenuating, mitigating, or clarifying data or judgments therefore, in his view, are "extraneous." One of my early supervisors declared his policy of cutting the length of all drafts he received for review, however "tight" they might be; this simply encouraged analysts to purposefully place some "fluff" in drafts in the hope that this man of modest intellect would choose it, not important parts, for his editorial ax.

Managers often tailor drafts for the mythical "reader" far more than analysts, who better appreciate that their readers vary in interests, expertise, and policy responsibilities. Indeed, analysts draw up the paper distribution lists that managers rarely deign to examine. The proverbial reader, as an abstraction who may or may not bear any resemblance to any of the perhaps several hundred addressees of a major paper (and many more who have access to it), thus is a creation of the personality and experiences of each reviewer. The target reader thus changes regularly— and sometimes considerably— as a paper moves through the drafting and review process.

Because the presumed "reader" cares for big picture judgments and little for "extraneous" detail, drafts usually are short of detail to support judgments, often lack methodological statements, and often do not provide means for careful readers to replicate analyses. In the view of a manager providing advice to other managers on analysis, "... the value of a paper is proportional to its clarity, brevity, and focus on issues."[15] Detail deemed uninteresting to a busy reader but still of value can be crammed into an appendix. Management insists on this despite the standard inclusion of short "summary" or "key judgments" sections at the beginning of big papers (Research Papers and Intelligence Assessments) that are designed to give overviews to busy readers. The process of coordinating drafts with perhaps several other DI units, often through compromises in language, tends to further reduce judgments to their "lowest common denominator"— a term commonly and derisively used in the DI in this context.

While there are many exceptions to this generalization, the DI thus regularly publishes shallow papers that purposely, condescendingly fail to serve the knowledgeable senior government official who is a career civil servant or capable political appointee— the competent officials who arguably are the government's most important users of intelligence. These are institutional embarrassments to the Central Intelligence Agency; they also are often personal ones to the analysts whose names appear on title pages.[16] For these reasons and the general pain of the review process, it is not uncommon for an analyst to feel a greater sense of relief than accomplishment upon publication of major papers.

A former Congressional oversight committee staff officer recounted his experience in discovering the shallowness of much of intelligence analysis. After describing the lack of usefulness of much that he read, he said that he and his colleagues once compared notes after listening to a briefing on the situation in the world as a whole.[17] Each of them thought initially that the briefer did not provide much of use about his own area of responsibility, but certainly was knowledgeable about other subjects. Each thus realized that the briefing was generally shallow. This same former staffer noted, however, that his impression of DI analysts' knowledge and judgment as displayed in one-on-one discussions was very favorable. Thus, the review process and its targeting of mythical "readers"— for both written and oral briefings— is a key reason that DI analysis has such a poor reputation among some consumers despite the often considerable abilities of DI personnel.

Undaunted, senior Agency management in the 1980s moved the DI away from the research-oriented think-tank environment of years past toward that of a newspaper producing quick, short articles. The reorganization of 1981 largely eliminated the word "research" from offices' titles. Over the years, management's increasing focus on "production"— the number of papers printed— has de-emphasized research on a daily basis as an analyst's job; a division chief in the Office of European Analysis put it succinctly when in 1987 he declared to his division that research was to be dispensed with first if a paper appeared to be in danger of missing a deadline.[18] Explicitly, no effort would be made to speed the review process.

Research, in some offices, became an expensive luxury that interfered with the race for production quantities. While managers recognized that it was necessary to some extent, they cautioned analysts against a propensity to study rather than produce. Some managers conveyed clear messages that they regarded research as an effete academic pursuit that real intelligence analysts eschew; to make the point clearer, they negatively cited some analysts' propensity for research in giving poor performance appraisal reports or "PARs"— official Agency personnel records.

In March 1990 the director of the Office of Training and Education (OTE) went still further, declaring to a class that analysts in fact do not do analysis. Instead, he argued, they are in the "investigative journalism" business. The director's comments are not the random observations of an irrelevant official. OTE is the Agency's training arm— the organization that instructs analysts and managers on Agency expectations of them, and teaches courses on analysis and writing. Its director was a former senior officer in the DI's Office of Soviet Analysis. These attitudes contrast sharply with Sherman Kent's observation that: "Research is the only process which we of the liberal tradition are willing to admit is capable of giving us the truth, or a closer approximation to truth, than we now enjoy."[19] The DI, however, long ago stopped producing NIS papers and other products that Sherman Kent called "descriptive"— those dedicated to the development of a base of knowledge from which judgments can be made.

With research and even analysis increasingly denigrated by Agency management, it is not surprising that expertise is also less respected that it was a few years ago. It is not much needed, especially when the task at hand is to summarize incoming State Department cables (or other reporting) for a current intelligence article. The development of expertise, including investments in foreign language skills, also requires time and work that get in the way of management's goal of boosting "production." Management generally rejects, explicitly or implicitly, the argument that the DI must invest in human capital— by committing time for research and study— before analysts can make quick but accurate judgments.[20] Instead, management generally confers "expertise" to analysts on the basis of position description; thus, an assignment to follow political developments in Sri Lanka, for example, confers de jure bureaucratic authority within the DI over those matters.

Recognizing the diminished importance of expertise, many analysts and managers move regularly from account to account as they "punch tickets," develop the personal contacts that will help advance their careers, or (too commonly) move on because they want less oppressive supervisors.[21] The decision to move regularly thus may or may not reflect a conscious decision to take a "generalist" versus a "specialist" career track.

Despite the rigors of the review process, the DI has few institutional checks on the quality of analysis and seems to care little about the wisdom of judgments or the accuracy of forecasts after papers are printed. There is no regular review by any DI organization of how well its papers' forecasts stand the test of time. Reflective assessments occur with few exceptions for the purpose of finding a reference in some DI publication to deflect the periodic charges of intelligence failure; even if contradicted by other CIA products, that scrap is useful for arguing that CIA did its job but the policy community did not listen or act.

No analyst or manager is punished for producing flawed or useless work. Neither does he usually receive credit for prescience except by his colleagues. Good writing skills, the ability to engineer a smooth review, and a kudo at the time of delivery of a paper are far more important attributes for bureaucratic success.[22]

Some wags in SOVA once examined the career tracks of senior DI managers, comparing bureaucratic success with the accuracy of their major forecasting judgments. They claim to have found a fairly strong inverse relationship between accurate forecasts on major issues (like whether the Soviets would invade Poland in 1981 to crush the Solidarity movement, for example) and promotions.

Satisfactory work during the process of paper production and receipt of "kudos" from readers continue to be many DI analysts' and managers' primary goals. I recall a branch chief in EURA who, reacting to the legitimate concern of a new analyst that he was not quite ready to write a current intelligence article, said something close to, "who cares if its right, you're getting a publication, aren't you?"

The review process often is extremely slow, wasting time and money, generating frustration, and failing to satisfy the Agency's ostensible objective of timely intelligence support. The review of a paper often takes as long as the research and drafting phases and may take considerably longer; this is especially true for larger, less time sensitive projects. Each reviewer normally works in isolation from other reviewers. Each is likely to have a number of priorities at any one time or be undecided about how to alter a paper to satisfy the perceived wants of someone up the review chain. Thus, a paper may languish unattended for substantial periods that can be, in a bad case, many months; my office director in 1984 took 105 days to return a draft with minimal changes, for example. In rare cases, years may elapse between submission of a paper for review and its final publication.[23] Still other papers intended to provide forecasts are *overtaken by events*— "OBEed" in analyst vernacular. Managers kill some of these papers because slow review of drafts about fast moving events— not infrequently by themselves— renders them superfluous.

Substantial review delays are most likely for long, low priority papers, but occur on almost all product types. Very high visibility or priority papers may be delayed if numerous offices want a piece of the action in hopes of receiving kudos, or because reviewers want to be especially confident of the result. Sometimes sheer personal insecurity or incompetence prevail, especially when a manager was appointed for his loyalty characteristics rather than his knowledge or managerial skills.

Perhaps in part for all of these reasons, SOVA delivered to the White House only three of 30 papers it requested prior to the December 1989 Bush/Gorbachev summit off Malta; the other 27 sat on SOVA middle managers' desks until after President Bush left Washington.[24] In this case, even the existence of a clear deadline for a very high priority consumer was insufficient to assure timely review and publication. Despite failures like this, many analysts prefer tight deadlines caused by specific events like summits; they place at least a little pressure on reviewers to do their jobs promptly and help insure that papers do not drag on interminably.

Reviewers are also slow because they claim they want to send forward papers that are as perfect as possible. While excellence is a worthy ambition, the object is not so often sound judgment or accurate communication as it is a style that is polished and consistent with personal preferences, or the real or perceived wishes of senior reviewers. These "reviewers" thus spend often enormous amounts of time editing, or "wordsmithing" as analysts often call it. For some, this editing and re-editing borders on the compulsive.[25] Often, this work is nearly wholly wasted as more senior reviewers do the same thing, but with a different set of stylistic preferences. It is common, for example, for a word like "which" to be changed to "that" and back again several times during the review process.[26]

In addition to the editorial work erroneously labeled "review," each long paper passes through at least one distinct editorial office in CPAS and perhaps one in its author's home office. These editors, in addition to preparing a paper for publication, do genuine editorial work like knowing the proper usage of "which" and "that." They do not have the bureaucratic agendas of reviewers. They also serve the valuable function of allowing the analyst one last opportunity to circumvent what he may consider bone-headed review changes; if challenged by reviewers after paper publication about alterations of specific language, the adroit analyst can attribute the changes to the

CPAS editors— who safely lie beyond the range of bureaucratic vindictiveness of all but very senior reviewers.

While waiting for review comments, many analysts have virtually nothing to do. Management sometimes rationalizes that it makes little sense to assign another topic to an analyst when perhaps substantial changes may be mandated at any moment. Conscientious analysts and junior managers move to other papers or commence research on other projects independently, but many person-years of the Directorate's analytical talent are wasted annually as reviewers slowly complete their work.[27]

Reviewers wearing their managers' hats seemingly care little for this waste. It is normal and to be expected. If blame is to be assessed, it goes to the analyst because reviewers by definition would not have to spend time on a draft if it was good in the first place.

An analyst is less and less likely to interact personally with the policymakers he ostensibly is serving. Management purposefully is segregating analysts from policymakers despite the recurrent consumer and academic charges that analysts do not know policymakers' needs. Instead, management acts as go-between, passing the sifted messages of the policy community to analysts through as many as five layers of filters, not counting the liaison staffs that may be the actual messengers: the DCI, the DDI, office directors, division chiefs, and branch chiefs. In some offices, managements formally forbid analysts to deal with the rest of government except at the low, "worker bee" level.[28] The result is that the average analyst has no good idea of the wants or needs of the policy community and thus may not know exactly how to respond to a consumer's request for intelligence support. As in the children's game, messages change as they are repeated.

Analysts also get only periodic feedback on consumers' reactions to their papers. Most of the work of an analyst thus seems to him to disappear into a "black hole," contributing to nagging questions about whether his efforts make any difference at all. Consumers' regular lack of reactions to DI products indicate that the concern is indeed legitimate. This phenomenon accounts for Rose's pleasure at her recognition in the Bugland story.

Similarly, the average analyst, who is a presumed expert, is unlikely to brief a senior policymaker. The trend since the mid-1980s has been for senior management to do more briefings. Senior managers, in turn, relying on briefings from more junior managers, perhaps analysts, and briefing books for their own preparation. The result is a reverse filtering process.[29] This is particularly unfortunate when senior managers are very ignorant on important questions. Judge Webster's lack of an intelligence or foreign affairs background thus was an ongoing concern to many Agency employees, even though many Agency officers who dealt with him regularly noted that he learned a lot on the job— a way to put a positive spin on the Judge's initial lack of knowledge and experience in foreign intelligence matters without commenting on how much more learning might be desirable.

This pattern has changed over the years as the Agency has aged and become more bureaucratic, and is markedly different in individual DI offices. Internal DI statistics show a sharp variation in numbers of analyst briefings by regional office. As a general rule, the office directors who send analysts to brief in their stead or take analysts along with them have far happier employees and enjoy smaller attrition rates in their offices. They also probably do a better job of briefing.

An anecdote by a retired division chief illustrates the change. As a junior analyst, this man followed events in Hungary. When the Soviets invaded in late 1956, he daily went to the White House and alone briefed President Eisenhower. This is beyond the realm of imagination today; bureaucratic procedure, managerial ambition, and managerial fear that analysts would somehow annoy the president or pass unwelcome news make such a practice unthinkable.

More generally, managerial attitudes in some offices reflect a low level of respect for analysts as intellects and as human beings. This reality is in sharp contrast with DCIs' regular claims that the Agency's most important assets are its people. It is, however, consistent with the view that analysts are the servants of senior managers who can be used or verbally abused at will. It also translates in some cases into nasty, demeaning comments on drafts during the review process, as well as simple rudeness. This tendency varies sharply by office and by smaller unit. The Office of Near East and South Asian Analysis for years in the 1980s had a reputation for treating its analysts better than other offices; DI statistics show sharply differing rates for key figures like attrition, analyst briefings of senior government officials, and others that indicate tangibly the difference between NESA's regard for its analysts and the practices of more poorly managed offices.

Some DI personnel attribute the treatment they receive as people to an extension of the values of the Directorate of Operations— an organization that is in the business of recruiting, co-opting, and using people. Individuals are useful or they are not. Value is often fleeting. Loyalty is sometimes transient. Whatever its origin, many managers convey clearly the belief that analysts are assets or tools to be used. If these tools are "broken," or made unpopular by changes in intellectual fashion or personal preference, they can be discarded, ignored, or treated miserably with ease and impunity. This attitude has the predictable consequences on analyst morale, eroding gradually what often is an extremely high level of dedication in new employees.

This managerial attitude was stated explicitly by the man who became Associate Deputy Director for Intelligence in late 1991. In October 1986, the then-director of the Office of Global Issues addressed a conference of the OGI division that followed international security issues. In recounting his own career at CIA, according to a conference participant, the director, referring to Agency employees, said something close to: "I've splattered a lot of people all over the walls." The audience, according to my source, was stunned to hear such words from a man who had the power to "splatter" them as well.

Management's lack of respect for its people as human beings, combined with a willingness to compromise on the objectivity of analysis, reflects an institutional lack of integrity that extends throughout daily DI life. A compromise of integrity on a paper usually indicates a willingness to violate other tenets of the Boy Scout oath as well. With satisfaction of bureaucratic superiors the prime objective, personal honesty, loyalty to colleagues and subordinates, and simple truthfulness become dispensable. Analysts' anecdotes of back-stabbing and simple lies by managers are voluminous. In the view of some DI analysts, dishonesty is rampant and is a management tool. Petulance and personal vindictiveness are as common, leading most analysts to be very careful about what they say, with whom they talk, and with whom they are seen talking. Managers in EURA in the mid-1980s employed secretaries to report on the comments of analysts, for example.[30] This kind of behavior, in combination with the vagaries of the review process and personnel management actions, is hardly conducive to the production of quality analysis. It makes for an unpleasant working environment— independent of the less than ideal physical working conditions of most offices that are a regular source of low-level gripes.

The Agency implicitly encourages this management-by-expediency by failing to provide ethical standards for its managers. As late as 1989, the Agency's introductory course for new managers— a week-long affair filled with personnel manipulation techniques— devoted not a single minute to the Agency's expectations about employees' integrity. By strong implication, the lack of discussion suggests a lack of Agency concern about integrity— intellectual or personal. It is another indication that Casey's credo is irrelevant. It is noteworthy as an indicator of actual Agency practice during the tenure of Director William Webster— whose strong suit by virtually all accounts is his own personal integrity. It also indicates yet another weakness of the polygraph as a tool to identify character flaws.

At the same time, the Agency expects little in the way of leadership from its managers. Use of the word itself is rare. Some managers possess fine leadership skills, strong senses of integrity, and loyalty to their analysts, but they are incidental to the training and expectations of the Agency. Incongruously, the

DI operates an Office of Leadership Analysis but has little use for leadership itself.

Far from receiving support and encouragement to do objective analysis, the analyst is likely to face serious ethical dilemmas in balancing desires for a successful career, satisfying service, and honest analysis. Most new analysts, I believe, find the recruiters' promises attractive and want to serve CIA and the nation well. They quickly learn, however, that they have behavioral options that will determine heavily the course of their careers.

The analyst who gets a lot of papers through the review process with minimal review changes, or has otherwise impressed senior management, can hope to be promoted rapidly. As his career progresses, he begins to ponder a major choice: does he want to remain an analyst or enter management? He knows that promotional (and hence financial) opportunities are far superior on the management track, and he knows that the review process will not change, no matter how senior or well respected he is as an analyst. He is likely to believe it is better to be a reviewer than an object of review. Most ambitious analysts thus opt for management, whatever their aptitude for dealing with people.

A few analysts decide early that satisfying a bureaucratic superior is lucrative and determine to satisfy superiors as a first priority, with goals of sound analysis, service to the country, and intellectual integrity secondary objectives. These men and women thrive on bureaucratic intrigue. They know that their success must come at someone else's expense and actively work to do well in comparison to other analysts. They sometimes operate against their ostensible colleagues and co-workers, furthering what is often an intensely competitive DI environment.[31] Some of these people are now in senior positions in the Directorate. Because this tactic has been so successful for some, and reflects what many DI people perceive to be a key element of Director Robert Gates' own bureaucratic success, practitioners of this behavior are widely known as "Gates clones." In this way, the DI operates like many large organizations in this country.

Most other analysts put the development of expertise at the

fore, reasoning that they must know what they are doing before they should advise the president and the rest of government. They expect rewards to come to those who work hard and perform well. They have courage of conviction and will defend their judgments. Most soon learn, however, that intellectual debate in the review process is not desired and modify their own behavior at least somewhat. Many learn to bend intellectually when they know they cannot prevail, rationalizing that it is better to run and live to fight another day than commit useless bureaucratic suicide. They often are self-critical of their intellectual subservience to the financial expediency of keeping a job. They loathe the review process for the intellectual prostitution it sometimes forces on them, but remain intrigued by the basic work that brought them to the DI in the first place. These people are the backbone of the Directorate.

Some analysts become simply content to do as the bosses say. For these people, the review process is a series of instructions. They ply their data developing and drafting skills in the service of others. They stay intellectually aloof and will not strongly argue a position because they have learned that holding a view is bureaucratically dangerous. They do not venture speculative ideas. These analysts often dislike and usually fear management. They are not particularly happy at work, but have children to feed and mortgages to service. They are likely to leave promptly at quitting time each day and expect to retire as soon as they are eligible. They usually are good people who have become discouraged bureaucrats.

A key analysts' dilemma concerns a decision whether to seek or accept a branch chief's job. Aside from legitimate questions about his temperament and suitability, the analyst must decide if he is willing to conduct himself in the ways many senior managers expect their branch chiefs to act. For some the answer is no. For a few, ethical beliefs prohibit acceptance of an appointment to a management position.

Others simply wear out and finally leave, the recruiters' promises long since discarded. Agency statistics indicate that attrition in the DI was higher in 1989 than in the other directorates. Management long has professed unconcern while scrambling to recruit; it rationalizes that there will always be malcontents, people who can not adjust to office reorganizations, and offers of mythical six digit salaries in the private sector. In fact, the Agency's Director of Personnel told me in 1989, CIA's exit interviews were so perfunctory that no one knew why employees left. Agency management seemingly continues to ignore the sharp differences in attrition by office— good hints about varying levels of employee satisfaction that also should be tips about the quality of management.[32] It seems not to notice the stream of DI employees moving to other directorates, with but a trickle of people entering the DI from elsewhere in the Agency. Likewise, management seems generally unconcerned about the significant attrition of expert, mid-career analysts— arguably the DI's best assets— and has for years been unable to attract and retain enough economists as analysts.[33]

The Directorate does poorly in selecting its managers. Some senior managers admit as much— generally citing cases in other offices or in the past— even as they punish analyst "complainers" and do nothing to correct the situation. The Directorate has no clear criteria for managerial selection except existence for a time in certain pay grades. Appointments to management are largely driven by the personal preferences of senior managers. Selections may reflect personal likes, loyalty, and perceived good performance as an analyst. Senior management regularly assumes that "good" analysts— largely defined by the ability to get papers quickly through the review process— make good managers despite voluminous evidence to the contrary, common sense, and regular complaints within the DI about manager selection criteria.

The vagaries of the relatively capricious selection process are compounded by the fact that new managers normally receive training only after they have assumed their positions, and then generally only as the press of business permits. Thus, an organization that so carefully chooses its analysts— months usually elapse before an applicant becomes an employee— cavalierly appoints managers and in essence assumes that they will do fine. It is a truly heroic assumption.

Aside from the potential for, and reality of, politically-motivated appointments, the selection reflects a fundamental value judgement: that promotion to management is a reward for good service as an analyst. This is a strong implicit statement of the modest value the organization puts on its analysts. In important respects, one's years as an analyst are spent demonstrating mettle— prominently including one's willingness to be a "team player"— that warrants elevation to management. This is so clear to most analysts that even those with little inclination to, or ability for, management seek managerial positions because a management appointment represents the natural progression of a successful career.

Senior managers often become personally linked with their selections for subordinate managers. They may wait until it is more than obvious that a manager is a problem before transferring him or returning him to the ranks of analysts. Such a failure reflects poorly on a senior manager's own judgment in selecting his subordinate managers. For that reason, some senior managers fight criticisms of their appointees with the vigor of a defense against a personal attack.

Often, failed managers receive "senior analyst" positions— higher paid positions ostensibly reserved for capable people who want to stay analysts. Many of these positions in fact house managerial deadwood who need assignments consistent with their elevated pay grades— to the detriment of analysis and general morale. With fewer senior analysts positions available for analysts who want to stay analysts, and their status cheapened by association with failed managers, the DI communicates in yet another way that it values analysts much less than it claims.

Other managers who perform "poorly" by the often inconsistent standards of the DI get rotations to non-line assignments. Ostensibly broadening experiences, these rotations serve to get trouble out of the immediate concern of office directors; besides, they might be off to another assignment before the person on rotation returns, shunting the problem of what to do with a well-paid problem to one's successor. Because the rotation has become such a common personnel management tool, significant numbers of relatively senior people unwanted by their offices constantly float through sometimes key parts of the Agency and the rest of government. For example, a EURA branch chief relieved for cause in 1986, his deputy office director confirmed to me, received consecutive rotations to: the Office of the Secretary of Defense in the Pentagon; a "plum" intelligence liaison position in a southern hemisphere capital; and, a position on the PDB staff. Another EURA manager relieved for a second time as a division chief— after, among other things, threatening in his office to kill an analyst— received a second "plum" liaison assignment in a European capital. (Note, however, that some rotations are indeed broadening experiences and some are much sought.)

Another commonly used tack is blaming others for recognized problems. For example, one office director in 1990 admitted before a large group that politicization had indeed occurred in his office previously, but said that he had stamped it out since his arrival in March 1989; this claim elicited wry smiles from observers who regarded him as more politically motivated than his predecessor. The alleged offender, meanwhile, continued to hold another senior Agency position, suggesting that very senior Agency management either did not believe the charge or did not care if it was true.

Large numbers of analysts simply do not trust management. Many anecdotal examples exist. For example, management several years ago broached the possibility of redoing the DI's personnel management system to, among other things, establish pay bands with merit the deciding decision criterion. This potentially also could have reduced the decisive pay advantages managers have over analysts by allowing some senior analysts pay grades higher than junior managers— an Agency variant of a proposal receiving wide government assessment at the time. The Agency seated a committee of analyst volunteers to provide inputs. The analysts objected to key portions of the management proposals, in particular citing the opportunity for still more arbitrary and capricious management rewards and punishments of analysts due to the very vague definition of "merit." When the committee refused to drop its opposition, management summarily dismissed it and created another, more pliant committee. The personnel system reform proposal ultimately died, but the experience left unpleasant memories.

At least some Agency management courses encourage the development of adversarial relations between managers and analysts. The introductory course for managers, for example, encourages the development of manager networks to help protect themselves from "employees"— a category of humanity that does not include them as managers. This adaptation of a factory management technique is particularly unfortunate in an environment where genuine teamwork among professionals could improve collective performance considerably. The mistrust and animosity is often greater than what I experienced between officers and enlisted personnel in the Army in the bad years of the 1970s. The DI, however, has many fewer of the disciplinary and command requirements that make rank a military necessity. Moreover, any sound military leader would act swiftly to correct similar levels of mistrust in his command.

DI management does not like intellectual competition and maintains no mechanism, other than the review chain, for processing alternative views or suggestions. The Team A versus Team B approach to disagreements over analysis of Soviet defense activities in the mid-1970s has few adherents among DI bureaucrats who dislike intellectual competition internally, let alone one with potential external critics. The DI's lone experiment in alternative analysis in recent years— a journal called *Contra* ostensibly devoted to contrary views— folded in the early 1980s after it degenerated mainly into a forum for bureaucratically naive analysts to reveal themselves as "problem employees" by criticizing management. Criticisms of the DI in the Agency's classified quarterly *Studies in Intelligence* come mainly from non-DI officers and have no apparent influence on management.[34] Some offices' serial journals offer ostensible opportunities for uncoordinated views that in practice are (bureaucratically) politically acceptable and may be as innocuous as trip reports.

Management as a whole refuses to recognize a systemic, institutional problem. Problem managers are isolated, unfortunate cases, not something to be much worried about. They are to be identified by managers alone. Indeed, the director of the Office of European Analysis in the late 1980s and early 1990s repeatedly made clear that he regarded analyst criticism of management as evidence of poor analyst performance.

DDI John L. Helgerson told me pointedly in July 1989 that he was happy with his management team and saw no reason for changes. In our discussion, he also used what I believe is a common CIA senior managers' device to ignore criticism. After listening to my concerns, he noted that I indeed felt strongly about the situation in the DI. He indicated that the depth of my concerns— I indeed had come to talk with him specifically about the issue and was not selling Girl Scout cookies— constituted an "emotional" attitude that, he hinted broadly, meant that he could and should dismiss my comments. He thus created for himself a useful dichotomy: if employees' concerns are genuine, they can be dismissed as emotionalism; if they are meekly stated, they are ignorable as minor complaints.[35] Later, he employed similar logic to claim that the large number of fired managers occupying senior analyst positions was a virtue; these people, he argued, had valuable management experience.[36]

True to his word to me, Helgerson made no significant personnel changes for cause in the succeeding three years. Indeed, he has bent over backwards to ignore obvious problems. In mid-1991, for example, the DI Management Advisory Group (or MAG, pronounced as a word)— which traditionally has concerned itself with relatively innocuous issues like quantities of floor space per employee— roused itself and conducted a survey of employees' feelings about the management of the Office of Soviet Analysis. The survey ranked division managers and placed at the bottom of the list a man whose performance and ethics I had discussed with Helgerson in 1989. Angered, the man requested another survey of his division. The second round was even more critical, with 18 of 22 respondents saying they would move to another division if they could. The MAG reported its findings to Helgerson, who took the unusual step of meeting with the division. Analysts again were very critical. Helgerson again apparently did nothing. The miscreant remained in his job.

Helgerson, however, did respond to my widely circulated resignation letter of November 16, 1990, which accused management of politicizing analysis, among other things (see Appendix B). In a June 14, 1991, message to DI personnel, he dismissed my comments but admitted "general concerns about this issue among analysts." See Appendix B. Helgerson stated DI policy, and said he "recommended" inclusion of the topic of analytical integrity into training courses.[37] Left unstated was an admission that the importance of integrity had not been there before.

Whatever their managerial flaws, senior Agency executives also have personal pecuniary reasons not to notice problems. These officials rotate the sharing of cash awards that typically are in the $10,000 to $20,000 range. They ostensibly are awarded for good, ongoing, general performance. By contrast, specific merit awards for lower ranking officers— such as Rose in the Bugland example— may be $500 before taxes. Serious remedial action against subordinate managers would indicate poor earlier judgment in appointing them that could endanger future potential for receiving awards. Such action also would violate the unwritten rule that while animosities, troubles, and bureaucratic conflict among managers might be intense, management problems should not be made known to "employees."

The Agency's Public Affairs Office (renamed the Office of Public and Agency Information after Robert Gates became DCI) has been equally oblivious to management problems. When asked about charges of politicization in my letter of resignation from the Agency, spokesman Mark Mansfield said, "the rigorous and searching internal review of the agency's analytic product helps ensure that policymakers receive the best, most objective information possible. ... This process has maintained the credibility of CIA analysis over the years."[38] This reasoning is akin to claiming that the foxes are doing a wonderful job of guarding the chicken coop.

Notes to Chapter 3

1 Other intelligence organizations work very differently. For example, a former DIA analyst told me, "We never wrote for our 'seventh floor' because we knew they [senior managers] would never read more than the executive summary."

2 Analysts' actual assignments vary considerably, of course. Crises typically increase considerably the amount of current intelligence that analysts with country (as opposed to functional) responsibilities perform. Other analysts do long-term work almost exclusively.

3 While some office directors long have worked in the area they supervise, some have no substantive experience in the areas their offices follow. For example, the director of the Office of Slavic and Eurasian Analysis named in early 1992 was a West European political analyst and had West European responsibilities as a manager; he never worked on the USSR. The director of the Office of Near East and South Asian Analysis named in 1990 was a long-time OGI manager with no recent Middle East or Asian or even country-specific responsibilities.

4 Office directors often change their instructions, leaving even their immediate subordinates unsure what they want. A division chief in RTT told me he rarely knew what the office director wanted and was constantly surprised by the office director's capricious reactions to papers.

This same office director in May 1990 told an analyst that he did not like a draft of a major paper. He indicated that he did not care what the paper's revised terms of reference stated, recognized that his written and oral comments were not helpful, and said he would recognize a good paper when he saw it. He offered no apology for his poor management, leaving the analyst with the task of divining yet again what the office director "really" wanted. This is an extreme case but is not unique.

5 Casey received pointed public criticism for allegedly interfering with the production of an NIE on Mexico in 1984. National Intelligence Officer for Latin America John Horton left the Agency in part over unhappiness with the handling of the estimate. Whether Casey politicized that estimate remained a topic of debate within the Agency years later.

6 United States Senate, Transcript of Proceedings before the Select Committee on Intelligence, Nomination of Robert M. Gates to be Director of Central Intelligence, Evening Session, September 25, 1991, pp. 24 and 40, (sanitized).

7 See Bob Woodward, Veil: The Secret Wars of the CIA 1981-87 *(New York: Simon & Schuster, 1987) pp. 127-129.*

8 Nathan Miller, Spying for America, The Hidden History of U.S.

Intelligence *(New York: Paragon House, 1989) p. 441. Miller's observation refers to Judge Webster's controls on the activities of the Directorate of Operations, but his characterization of Webster's conservatism applies equally to analysis.*

9 The reference is to the protagonist of The Good Soldier: Schweik, *by Jaroslav Hasek, a story about a soldier's life in World War I.*

10 In a minor example of this desire to please, or to avoid offense, the DI in the late 1980s altered its normal editorial style policy of translating foreign words into English when discussing a small, radical foreign political party whose name in English is "Republican." Instead, it used the foreign language original. It did not want to offend the Reagan/Bush Administrations by using their party's name in association with this group.

Former Office of Soviet Analysis analyst Jennifer Glaudemans recalled another example in her "Written Statement of Jennifer Lynn Glaudemans for the Senate Select Committee on Intelligence," September 25, 1991, p. 12. Referring to politicization in SOVA by its director, "Mr. Kolt," in 1989, she wrote, "I would like to tell you that at this time, SOVA went through a linguistic nightmare. The political terms "reformers and conservatives" in the Soviet context referred to reformers and hard-line communists who were opposed to reform. The Soviets use the term "conservative" to refer to these hardliners. Because the Soviets use the term, Sovietologists use the term. But because in the American political context the term "conservative" is affiliated with the current administration, concern was raised that the use of the word conservative might somehow offend the sensitivities of the President. Thus, we were all forced to call Soviet conservatives, orthodox (which made them sound religious) or traditionalists (which made them sound like pro-tsarists). It was silly and bizarre, but I tell you it is a demonstration of the degree to which SOVA is willing to be politically sensitive."

11 An article on the "Art of Intelligence Analysis" entitled "Managing/Teaching New Analysts," written by "One DI Manager for Other DI Managers"— a sanitized version of an article that appeared in CIA's quarterly Studies in Intelligence, *Fall 1986, p. 4.*

12 A significant publication medium is the typescript memorandum, known simply as the "typescript," which typically answers relatively narrow questions within a fairly short period of time for specific readers. This allows greater definition of, and tailoring for, the consuming reader. However, DI offices, in their desire to boost readership and kudos, typically add dozens of sometimes only peripherally related individuals and agencies to distribution lists— again tending to encourage analysts and reviewers to aim at the lowest level reader. They also send typescripts to Agency senior managers, meaning that senior managers' quirks must be taken into account as well.

13 Robert Gates quoted the conventional wisdom that the average tenure of deputy assistant secretaries at one time was 21 months in his article "The CIA and Foreign Policy," Foreign Affairs, *Vol. 66, No. 2, Winter 1987/88, p. 226.*

14 This is particularly common when reviewers have little educational background in the subject area of the paper they are examining— a branch chief with a political science background reviewing an economic paper, for example. The reviewer is prone to impute his own ignorance to the "reader." Such reviews can help avoid jargon and improve the communication of key points, but they also can lead to what one analyst wryly calls "cross-sterilization."

15 "Managing/Teaching New Analysts," p. 4.

16 This practice repeatedly has prompted me to muse that intelligence analysis too often is to analysis what classic comic books are to classics.

17 This particular briefer was an INR analyst, but the lesson to be learned applies to the DI as well, in both my view and that of my source.

18 The DI continues to have a publication type known as the "research paper" or RP. However, this art form receives generally lower levels of review and printing priority than shorter papers.

19 Kent, Strategic Intelligence, *p. 155.*

20 The Agency at times has been generous in some respects about allowing time off for full-time training. It also maintains a host of internally run courses. However, managers often frown on the idea of analysts sitting at their desks reading, ruminating, or sharing thoughts with colleagues, judging such behavior to be "goofing off." Yet it is precisely this kind mental freshening that is most helpful to improving analysis, generating ideas, and doing the job better.

21 I once asked an experienced analyst why he had transferred from the Office of East Asian Analysis to a notoriously poorly managed division in the Office of European Analysis. He said that he did indeed know that his new division was a "hell-hole," but he wanted to work in a different "hell-hole." He later resigned from the Agency.

22 In the mid- and late-1980s, the Senate intelligence committee also gave short shrift to post-mortems on CIA assessments; in 1990, however, the staff director created a staff position known as the "Chief of Hindsight," who was tasked to look at CIA's analytic performance. Its first incumbent was a former DI analyst who, in the words of a former Congressional colleague, "left the Agency in disgust." The House intelligence committee more regularly evaluated some DI papers in the mid- to late-1980s. According to House committee spokesman Mike Sheehy, chairmen sometimes express their "pleasure or concern" over selected papers—undoubtedly contributing to the tendency of senior DI officials to tailor assessments to please key audiences.

23 The anecdote of a former analyst and friend is an extreme, but not unique, case. This individual completed an assessment of prospects for the economy of a European country and submitted it for review. While waiting for its return, his frustration with the DI reached the point that he finally decided to transfer to the Directorate of Operations as a case officer. Considerably later, after he was posted abroad, I met him in his duty station and asked him, among other things, how the paper had come out. He laughed and said that it had just been printed; he felt that while it had been good analysis at the time he submitted the draft, it appeared as only a mediocre history.

24 My source for this information was a SOVA employee with direct knowledge of the preparation of the papers.

25 For many reviewers, this process goes well beyond a desire to assure quality or clarity. Some readily admit that they like to re-edit their own editorial changes. One RTT branch chief graphically compared what a reviewer does to a draft to what a male dog does to a fire hydrant. He did not exclude himself from this characterization and offered no apology; he was describing common practice.

26 In some offices, managers commonly use the word "fix"— as both a noun and a verb— to describe this stylistic reworking. This usage has the effect of conveying to analysts the message that there is but one acceptable formulation, and that any other combination of words reflects a broken paper that needs repair. This has the none-too-subtle effect of encouraging analysts to pursue stylistic orthodoxy, at minimum.

27 This procrastination or incompetence is most wasteful when management requires completion of a project under review before it releases an analyst to move to another office. The individual can only begin to "read in" on his new assignment. The director of RTT, for example, in 1990 delayed the rotation of one of his analysts to another office for about six months as he insisted on incremental word and minor substantive changes that included a petty objection to the phase "capital flight"— a standard economic term used to refer to the tendency of wealthy people in unstable countries to move their money to safe havens abroad. The analyst wastefully remained in RTT until his paper was printed, well after it received final review blessing. This same office director earlier refused to allow publication of the term "high-definition television"— a standard industrial term for a new type of television technology then under development.

28 In an extreme case, an analyst in the Office of African and Latin American Analysis told me that his branch chief forbade any contact by his analysts with any other government employee on intelligence business except by specific permission.

29 Some of these briefing books for senior Agency officers are purposefully short on data and contain rudimentary judgments. The books often simply do not allow a briefer who is relying heavily on the book alone to elaborate much, or answer even fairly simple questions. The rationale is that senior briefers themselves are busy people who do not want to become immersed in most issues.

30 Secretaries who declined requests to inform explained to me how the recruitment process worked. First, a manager noted that the secretary works for him, not for analysts despite the regular interaction of analysts and secretaries during the paper production process. The branch chief, he reminded the secretary, writes performance appraisals on him or her, and implied that cooperation would help improve the appraisal. The secretary could help him identify "problem" analysts. Alert to the success of this recruitment tactic, analysts in one division of EURA had fun by feeding disinformation to management by making outrageous but innocuous comments within earshot of co-opted secretaries. Sure enough, the comments came home during conversations with managers. Management appears to have kept its end of the bargain; co-opted secretaries enjoyed receipt of a num-

ber of Agency awards involving cash payments.

31 Competition between analysts takes many forms. Common ones include crossing turf bounds to grab part of the action on a high-visibility issue, exaggerating contributions on joint papers, and personal attacks on writing or analytical abilities. Managers often implicitly encourage this kind of behavior through their own demands and expectations, while displaying similar meanness in their dealings with other office managers. In offices with poor management, this analyst competition can be intense, leading to the fairly common use of the term "dog-eat-dog" to describe it. This kind of environment is not conducive to the conduct of sound, objective, collegial analysis.

32 The Agency agreed to release attrition figures in response to my Freedom of Information Act request, but had not provided the figures by press time.

33 There are at least three reasons that cut to the heart of DI management philosophy. First, many economists believe that non-economist reviewers often insist, in the name of clarity, on reducing methodologically sound economic analysis to pabulum. Second, economists tend to be more interested in research than quick current events articles most suitable to political "stories." Third, some senior managers in offices like SOVA have made clear that they believe economics is a profession of politically naive bean counters who at best serve the needs of political analysis.

34 The winter 1990 issue contains a brief but harsh critique of DI managers in a review of the analytic portion of Intelligence Requirements for the 1990s *(Lexington, MA, Lexington, 1989), edited by Roy Godson. The author was an instructor in OTE who specialized in analysis.*

35 I remembered this conversation as I drafted my letter of resignation from the Agency. I opted to be blunt rather than meek and obscure in making my points and to "err," if at all, by being too harsh. Clearly the letter struck a responsive chord at CIA; it was widely distributed within the Agency and reached news organizations in the United States, Canada, and Europe, at least.

36 The DDI apparently clings to the view that management is sound. He declined to respond in any way to a letter I delivered to his secretary on May 25, 1990 offering suggestions for ways to improve the Directorate.

37 John L. Helgerson, "DDI Message to the Directorate on the Subject of Politicization," June 14, 1991.

38 Bill Gertz, "CIA officials 'cooked books,' ex-analyst says," Washington Times, *March 27, 1991, p. A3.*

CHAPTER FOUR

HOW IT GOT THAT WAY

"Policy relevance pays the bills around here."[1]

"Intelligence can never be neutral."[2]

— Robert M. Gates

There is no simple explanation for the malaise that grips much of the DI. The changes have come incrementally. Many CIA people rationalize the changes simply as the natural evolution of an organization from the dynamic young outfit of the immediate post-World War II period into a big bureaucracy.[3]

Perhaps so, but a clear change in direction occurred during the tenure of Robert M. Gates as the DDI and later as Casey's deputy director. In January 1982, new DDI Gates shocked the Directorate by declaring in a dramatic address to DI employees that the DI's performance was substandard and that significant improvements needed to be made.[4] He complained that the Directorate was producing products "irrelevant or untimely or unfocused or ... all three"; for "failure by analysts to foresee important developments or events"; for "close-minded, smug, arrogant responses to legitimate questions and constructive criticism"; for "flabby, complacent thinking and questionable assumptions combined with an intolerance for others' views, both in and out of CIA"; for "poor, verbose writing"; and for "a pronounced tendency to confuse objectivity and independence with avoidance of issues germane to the US government and policymakers."[5]

Photograph 2. Robert Michael Gates—Deputy Director of Intelligence (1982-86), Chairman of the National Intelligence Council (1983-86), sixteenth Deputy Director of Central Intelligence (1986-89), and fifteenth Director of Central Intelligence (1991-?).
Source: Central Intelligence Agency

Photograph 3. Official CIA portrait of William Joseph Casey, thirteenth Director of Central Intelligence (1981-87). It hangs on a wall in a first floor corridor of the Original Headquarters Building. Portrait by Everett Raymond Kinstler, 1984.
Source: Central Intelligence Agency

Photograph 4. William Hedgcock Webster, fourteenth Director of Central Intelligence (1987-91).
Source: Central Intelligence Agency

Photograph 5. Richard J. Kerr, Director of the office of East Asian Analysis, Associate Deputy Director for Intelligence, Deputy Director for Intelligence (1986-89), and seventeenth Deputy Director of Central Intelligence (1989-92).
Source: Central Intelligence Agency

With those last words especially, Gates challenged the legacy of Sherman Kent and—while not stating the point explicitly—began to establish a tone (or culture or environment or atmosphere) which led many subordinate managers and analysts to believe that the message of analysis was as (or more) important than its objectivity. Gates also criticized analysts "pretending to be experts ... who had spent little if any time" in the country they followed—a humorous and hypocritical comment to many in the DI given the fact that Soviet "expert" Gates had not then visited the USSR and did not go until after he left CIA in 1989.[6]

Gates ordered more and better quality analysis. He directed new review procedures and a number of administrative changes. He reminded his subordinate managers that they were responsible for the output of their units—a fairly obvious point that nevertheless generated much nervousness in DI managers' offices. Gates' dicta reflected his experiences on rotation from the Agency in 1974-79 to policy positions, his stint as National Intelligence Officer for the USSR, conversations with consumers, the legacy of criticisms of analysis during the Carter years, scathing critiques of analysis by President-elect Reagan's intelligence transition team in 1980-81, and DCI Casey's concerns about analysis, among others. He had heard complaints and decided to redress them.

Gates, with Director Casey's help and prodding, had a vision for intelligence analysis and made concrete changes in DI practices and procedures to help actualize that vision. He decided to review personally many types of Directorate production and instituted a set of forms for intermediate reviewers to signify their speedy review and approval of attached drafts. He stated his position clearly in a 1984 *Washington Post* article:

> "I am the final approving official for all of CIA's daily production of current intelligence that goes to the president and other senior government officials. The director (sic) of Central Intelligence (DCI) sees it at the

same time as the policy-maker. I also approve all longer-range assessments."[7]

By so directing, he intended clearly to encourage tighter quality control. Gates worked long hours, completed his reviews quickly, and returned numerous drafts with sometimes extensive comments and queries. This emphasized clearly to managers that they needed to work hard to satisfy Gates. It also increased their apprehension and insecurity considerably. Managers and analysts alike generally viewed extensive splashes of ink as evidence of dissatisfaction—whatever their nature—and determined to avoid them next time.

Gates' micro-management reflected supreme self-confidence in his own capabilities and made clear to most DI personnel the importance of packaging to suit his tastes and limited time. While handling a host of other duties, Gates claims that he reviewed and approved some 700 research studies in the first nine months of 1984 alone.[8] That amounts to over two and a half papers per calendar day. These papers probably averaged 30-40 pages each, excluding key judgments, appendices, text boxes, and tables—an enormous work load.

DI employees' interest in satisfying Gates was reinforced by their study of Gates' career path. Analysts and managers—most of whom were and are former analysts—employed their skills to study Gates. They gleaned that Gates' meteoric rise was due at least partially to his adroit shifts in positions to exploit career opportunities and his ability to find patrons, including Bill Casey. Perhaps such a strategy would work for them, too.[9]

DI personnel noted the apparently close personal as well as professional ties between Gates and Casey. Some thought a near father/son relationship developed.[10] Whatever the personal ties, Casey expressed his confidence in Gates tangibly. He made Gates chairman of the National Intelligence Council (NIC), which prepares NIEs among other things, as well as DDI; he thus placed those responsibilities on one person for the first time. Some believed that Gates ghost-wrote some of Casey's speeches and published articles. Gates thus enjoyed the reputation of a strong DDI with backing of an activist DCI who was a cabinet officer and a confidant of the president—not a man to cross carelessly.

Gates' demonstrably keen interest in the individual words of papers—rather than general guidance or broad questions to ensure high quality—and a desire to please him soon led to a major ongoing study of the concerns, interests, and desires of Gates himself. The DDI's "wants" became key concerns to virtually all, and a dominant topic of staff meetings. DI managers, in particular, scrutinized hints about changes in them as carefully as Kremlinologists once studied photos of the Soviet Communist Party hierarchy for hints about internal power struggles. Analysts had even tougher jobs; in preparing papers, they had to divine not only what Gates "really" wanted, but also how each intermediate reviewer would interpret both Gates' comments and their superiors' evaluations of Gates. For some, this became the key intelligence question, with analysis of the topic of a paper a secondary concern.

Gates' obviously close association with Casey, a man with strong views, solidified the belief that he had a political/ideological agenda as well. The Soviet Union was a major personal interest of Ronald Reagan and Casey, according to numerous accounts, and the subject of Gates' graduate education.[11] Simultaneously, in the early Casey years, Gates' vice chairman of the NIC was Casey appointee Herb Meyer, an ascerbic man who former DDI, Deputy Director for Operations, and Deputy DCI John McMahon recalled, "was disliked, especially for injecting politics into the analytic process."[12] National Intelligence Officer for Latin America Constantine Menges appeared to some similarly prone to look for politically favorable data.[13]

DDI and NIC Chairman Gates acquiesced to subservience of DI analysis on nuclear proliferation issue to NIO David Low, a Casey protege on the NIC. Low regularly, according to DI analysts who experienced the subordination of DI analysis to the NIC, watered down DI analyses of the nuclear activities of politically sensitive countries like China, Pakistan, and

Argentina; his aversion to reporting on Chinese activities was particularly strong just prior to President Reagan's trip to China to sign what turned out to be a rather meaningless nuclear cooperation agreement. DI managers did not object to Low's activism or apparent political bent; Gates made no apparent effort to reign Low in.

Casey himself was so sure of some things that, while some Agency personnel admired his curiosity and willingness to learn, others agreed with former National Intelligence Officer John Horton who called Casey an "intellectual bully."[14] Moreover, many in the DI already sensed what Senate intelligence committee staff director Bernie McMahon later concluded of Gates:

> "Bob wasn't going to talk to the boss the way [John McMahon] did. He's not the kind of guy who's going to say to Casey, 'That's a stupid idea, and if you go through with it, I'm walking out the door.'"[15]

Gates both actively monitored and shaped Soviet analysis during his years in senior CIA positions. Gates also contributed to the establishment of a "party line" that limited the parameters of "successful" analysis. Long-time SOVA manager John Hibbits explained the influence:

> "Over time managers and eventually analysts in SOVA understood what would and would not get through the front office and there developed within the office, divisions, branches, and minds of the analysts a self-censoring atmosphere. Some reaction was subtle and some more obvious. In planning our research program, for example, a paper on Soviet use of chemical agents in the Third World was rejected at the middle management level because it would have no payoff; it would not show clear Soviet use and therefore would likely only upset Gates. So I had to tell the analyst who had proposed the subject in hopes of clarifying the record to work on something else."[16]

"How well agency managers could craft intelligence that would keep criticism from the DDI to a minimum became a measure of one's value and there arose a danger of being out of the loop if you were not responsive. Many professionals adjusted without seriously compromising the essential integrity of the product in their own mind, but it became difficult to remain completely objective. As professionals, many began to anticipate criticism and write papers that Gates would like or at least find convincing. Even with these constraints, many of us were able to write and manage a number of what I believe were solid intelligence analysis (sic), but the process was very difficult. Others simply sought jobs outside SOVA or the Agency."[17]

A DI officer who served as an Assistant National Intelligence Officer during the Casey years saw the pressure on the NIC as well. Casey and Gates, in this man's view, reduced much of intelligence analysis to the US-Soviet struggle and pushed analysis to address issues in those terms. NIOs quickly learned what was expected of them and "hunkered down" out of a "sense of survival." Those who dared to dissent received often "nasty" memos from Gates, although the former A/NIO noted that Gates could sometimes be convinced of another view. But the nastiness was strong enough that most, himself included, "got to a point where you were sort of beat down. You wouldn't put your head on the block when senior people wouldn't."

Even the senior, office-level managers who made life difficult for the Hibbitses of the DI sometimes were uncomfortable. A former office director repeatedly said to associates that he felt pressure from Gates and Casey to provide specific messages, not just ensure high quality analysis.[18] This office director nevertheless clearly made accommodations with Gates. He also had an excellent opportunity to tell the Senate Select Committee on Intelligence (SSCI) of his experiences during Gates' second confirmation hearings for Director in October 1991 and chose not to do so. Why not? I do not know, but two obvious candidates are a lack of personal integrity and legitimate fear of retribution. He still worked at the Agency in October 1991.

Gates made clear his intent to control dissent early in his tenure as DDI. After telling analysts and managers in his introductory speech that "it is essential that voices crying in the wilderness ... be heard," and inviting employees who believed their offices were not doing a good job in covering issues to "send me a memorandum setting forth these concerns and alternate views," he assured analysts "that no analyst will be penalized or suffer for taking advantage of this opportunity."[19] Fair enough. But he also told DI employees that any such concerns had to be forwarded through office directors, the very source of such problems in most cases, ensuring major potential for retribution if individuals actually did complain. Then he added ominously:

> "I do not expect this opportunity to be abused with frivolous subjects or trivial disputes within organizations... Let me just add that, in my view, this opportunity and other available channels provide ample opportunity for those who believe their views are not being taken into account. There is, accordingly, no excuse for breaching discipline and carrying complaints to outside audiences while ignoring these internally available opportunities for redress."[20]

Because such "opportunities" did not appear genuine, the implicit message was to keep quiet about concerns.

Gates made clear his wants in several ways. Sometimes, he simply demanded changes, or made them himself. For example, according to several DI people who watched him in action, Gates alone—without consultations or discussions with analyst authors or their managers—repeatedly altered the substance of articles in the *President's Daily Brief*. At other times he was more indirect. After a time, his revealed preferences became de facto instructions in the absence of specific comments.

Especially later in his tenure as DDI and as DDCI, he let trusted subordinates—particularly office directors—convey instructions and review products according to his definition of "quality."

After a while, Gates managed to suppress positions, and even entire subjects with relatively little effort—a reflection of his propensity to vindictiveness and the keen powers of observation of most DI personnel to discern such vindictiveness and apparent preferences. Former analyst Jennifer Glaudemans recounted to the SSCI during Gates' 1991 confirmation hearings the implications of an episode in which Gates killed a paper on Soviet-Israeli relations without explanation:

> "The implications of this event, however, went far beyond anything Mr. Gates probably intended and demonstrates the kind of atmosphere he was capable of creating and did nothing to fix. Mid- and lower level managers interpreted his killing of the paper to mean that he disagreed with the judgment and it became a tortuous effort to write anything on the subject of Soviet-Israeli relations again."[21]

Glaudemans also said that Gates ordered a study in 1986 based on the proposition that Soviet aid to selected countries in the Third World might be increasing, but discarded the paper when evidence indicated that such assistance actually was declining. After Gates' rebuttal testimony, Wayne P. Limberg, the chief of the SOVA branch that produced the study, submitted additional testimony to the SSCI. According to the *Washington Post*, Limberg indicated that Gates ordered the study because Casey had a hunch that Soviet aid to Marxist regimes—like those in Angola, Nicaragua, and Afghanistan, especially—was on the rise.[22] SOVA's details of Soviet aid activities over a five-year period showed the opposite, however. Gates made clear his displeasure with the result; he "threw it aside, literally," according to an analyst who worked on the study, "It never saw the light of day."[23] Gates chose not to include this episode in his 20-point rebuttal of charges of politicization at the conclusion of his confirmation hearings—suggesting that he had no defense.

In a direct suppression of intelligence, Gates moved to support Reagan Administration policy on Afghanistan by ordering for a time in the late 1980s that the DI publish nothing in the *National Intelligence Daily* concerning Pakistan's nuclear development program, according to an analyst who worked on weapons proliferation issues. In the spring of 1986, this policy so bothered analysts and junior managers in both the Office of Scientific and Weapons Research and the Office of Global Issues that several of them took the issue personally to then-DDI Richard Kerr, who responded by meeting with several DI people. My source participated in the meeting with Kerr and knows of no tangible remedial action Kerr may have taken.

The connection between Pakistani nuclear weapons and the Afghan rebels, or *mujahedin*, was only slightly indirect. Pakistan was a major US ally in supporting the rebels. However, Pakistan also was conducting nuclear weapons research and development. US law as provided by Section 620-E(e) of the Foreign Assistance Act of 1961 (as amended in 1981 and 1985) required administrations regularly to provide a so-called "Pressler Certification"—after Senator Larry Pressler—stating that: Pakistan had no nuclear explosive device; and, that provision of aid would significantly reduce the risk that Pakistan would develop the bomb. Otherwise, US aid would be eliminated. Moreover, Representative Stephen Solarz authored an amendment that aid be cut to nations even attempting to acquire certain nuclear equipment and technology outside of the procedures of international control regimes.[24]

Should US sanctions have been imposed on Pakistan, it seemed likely that the Pakistanis would be less cooperative on an issue of considerable interest to the United States—aid to and sanctuary for the Afghan rebels. Thus, evidently to ensure that CIA not contribute to a finding that might endanger a key Reagan Administration goal, Gates placed the Pakistani nuclear program temporarily off-limits to the NID—a publication that went to Congress and thus Congressional opponents of both the Pakistani nuclear effort and aid to the Afghan rebels.

Gates, however, denied any such suppression of intelligence in sworn testimony to the Senate intelligence committee. In a written statement dated October 10, 1991, Gates wrote: "I was not aware, nor did I direct, any steps to block the most accurate available information on the Pakistani nuclear program from reaching policymakers."[25]

Allegations of suppression of the subject in the NID flatly contradict Gates' sworn statement. Numerous current and former DI and National Intelligence Council personnel apparently had direct knowledge of Gates' role in politicizing intelligence on Pakistan. While the SSCI found no evidence to substantiate claims of politicization—my source did not talk to the Committee—it refused to grant Gates exoneration and said its investigation:

> "... did develop other of the allegations brought to its attention. Therefore, the Committee is continuing its investigation of these issues. The Committee also notes that certain of these allegations are the subject of on-going investigations within the CIA, and Departments of State and Defense."[26]

In another incident, Glaudemans recalled Gates' reaction to a paper addressing the likely effects of economic sanctions against Libya. While there is some confusion in the SSCI record about all of the facts of the matter and why Gates rejected the analysis, she recounted to the SSCI Gates' conduct with some DI personnel:

> "There was an unambiguous signal sent when Mr. Gates stormed into an analyst's office, criticizing a paper he had written that said economic sanctions against Libya were unlikely to be effective. The analyst's justification being that the value of Libyan crude is so highly valued on the open market and therefore economic sanctions were not likely to inhibit Qadhafi's actions. In front of not only an analyst, but in front of a branch chief of a

> division, yelled, *how can you say this when this is inconsistent with Administration policy* (emphasis added).[27]

In his role as chairman of the National Intelligence Council, Gates broke rules designed to ensure that the intelligence community as a whole agreed upon positions. In testimony to the SSCI during hearings on his 1991 nomination to be DCI, Gates admitted that he broke long-standing rules to push through in May 1985 a Special National Intelligence Estimate (SNIE), drafted by National Intelligence Officer for the Near East and South Asia Graham E. Fuller, warning of mounting instability in Iran and indicating that the Soviet Union had made significant gains in its relations with Iran at the expense of the West. This estimate, at odds with previous assessments and reversed in May 1986, was the intelligence basis for the Reagan Administration's decision to sell arms to Iran—and thus the Iran-contra scandal as well.[28]

In this episode, Gates suppressed CIA analyses that the Soviets had no such influence and relied on selected favorable evidence to support Director Casey's views. He mandated that the estimate contain no "footnotes," or statements of dissenting opinion. In his role as DDI, he could squelch CIA opposition, but he also faced major disagreement from the State Department's Bureau of Intelligence and Research (INR). To remedy this, he called Assistant Secretary of State Morton I. Abramowitz, the head of INR, and persuaded him to remove an INR footnote. In response to Senator Bill Bradley's question during his 1991 confirmation hearings, Gates admitted that there was no footnote in the estimate and claimed that he acted, "because I felt that the view that they had, as they had written their footnote, really didn't represent an alternative view."[29] This is poor reasoning and is irrelevant; intelligence community members long have had rights to footnote, whatever the competence of the argument, the views of anyone in CIA, or the opinion of the chairman of the NIC. Gates' actions represented a gross violation of his responsibilities as a representative of the intelligence community as whole, as opposed to those of a subordinate of Bill Casey.

According to the *New York Times*, INR analysts drafted three footnotes to the estimate, one of which concerned the Soviets.[30] The analysts were so unhappy with the basic argument of the NIE draft that they used the occasion of another Graham Fuller paper on the same subject, dated May 17, 1985, to write a critique of the argument to then-Secretary George Shultz. They complained, according to the *Times*, about "the politicization of the process."[31]

Former SOVA branch chief Wayne Limberg recounted in a sworn affidavit to the SSCI that Gates "wanted no footnotes" in NIE 11/10: "Soviet Policy in the Third World."[32] Named DI representative for coordination of the estimate in August 1984, Limberg had problems with several sections of the draft, expressed them to the NIO supervising the preparation of the estimate, and threatened to add CIA footnotes. This NIO complained to chairman of the NIC Gates who, as DDI as well, directed Limberg to "get the best deal I could but no footnotes." According to Limberg, the NIO knew of Gates' directive, making Limberg's task still more difficult.

Limberg told the SSCI of a similar experience in March 1985, during coordination of a SNIE on Libyan, Syrian, and Iranian support for international terrorism. Limberg's statement says:

> "We in SOVA were uncomfortable with it because we felt it overrated Soviet influence. Once again we were told we could take no footnotes. We had to depend on State/INR to make our case. In a sense, this estimate set the stage for the new (sic) infamous 1985 estimate on Iran."[33]

Gates responded that he recalled "no SOVA desire to take a footnote being brought to my attention."[34] According to a memo of the vice chairman of the NIC dated March 28, 1985, DCI Casey amended the draft estimate's key judgments after the estimate had been coordinated, stressing that "the three radical states shared certain common purposes; they were willing to consult regularly and to pursue numerous goals in tandem."[35]

To help sort out the controversy, the National Intelligence Council provided the SSCI with 16 NIEs and Special NIEs in which CIA (and thus the DI) took a footnote during the period 1983-86. Of the 16, twelve concerned Soviet military or technical matters. The only footnotes on political issues concerned countries other than the USSR; they argued that threats to US interests were greater than the text judged. There were no footnotes in any of the areas cited by any of the witnesses who expressed concern to the Committee about prohibitions on footnotes.[36] This effectively confirms the assertions of Limberg and Glaudemans, given the Agency's major efforts on Gates' behalf during the confirmation process.

Gates helped steer an April 1985 CIA assessment toward a conclusion that the Soviet KGB masterminded the assassination attempt on Pope John Paul II in 1981. A May, 1983 DI study entitled "The Papal Assassination Attempt: A Review of the Record" had judged that the Soviets were not behind the attack, arguing in part that it was inconsistent with known KGB methods of operation.[37] In 1984, the Directorate of Operations began to acquire information that the Soviet military, not the KGB, was behind the attack, and in 1985 author Clair Sterling claimed in *The Time of Assassins* that Papal assailant Agca worked with Bulgarian intelligence.[38] Casey, meanwhile, was convinced the Soviets were behind the attack.[39]

In 1985, the DI at Gates' direction began a new assessment uncharacteristically designed to present only one possibility—the case for Soviet involvement.[40] A joint OGI/SOVA work, it drew significant opposition from within SOVA at the time of its preparation; SOVA Director Douglas J. MacEachin was unhappy with it and forwarded a four and one-half page memo to Gates by SOVA manager John Hibbits outlining the case against Soviet involvement. Gates, however, already had disseminated the assessment with a cover memo indicating that the paper was the first "comprehensive examination" of the assassination attempt.[41]

Before the SSCI at his 1991 confirmation hearings, Gates claimed that he asked the DI's Product Evaluation Staff to review the assessment and asked a CIA officer to critique it. According to the *New York Times*, former analysts say Gates misrepresented the report's conclusions within the Agency.[42] The report, the so-called and now declassified "Cowey Report," says that many of the people the CIA Papal Task Force interviewed thought that:

> "... calling the paper 'The Case for Soviet Involvement' and marshalling evidence only for that side 'stacked the deck' in favor of this argument and ran the risk of appearing biased. This impression was further reinforced, they thought, by the 'unbalanced' treatment of counter-arguments in the text."[43]

Gates acknowledged under questioning by the SSCI on October 3, 1991 that he probably should not have sent a memorandum to then-Vice President Bush calling it the "first comprehensive examination of who was behind the attempted assassination ..."[44]

During Gates' tenure as both Chairman of the NIC and DDI—the period 1983-86—he had unique opportunities to debase the normal National Intelligence Estimate (NIE) or "estimative" process; he could direct both the NIOs responsible for supervising the preparation of estimates, and the CIA drafters and coordinators of them. Casey's decision to give Gates these two important hats thus reflected very poor judgment. The error has not been repeated and should never again occur.

At other times, Gates expressed his views—and implicitly his expectations for the content of DI future analysis—through comments and his own published analyses. Managers and analysts scrutinized them the way a good old Soviet communist party apparatchik would examine a party leader's speech for clues about changes in party doctrine. Gates' views generally reflected a hard line toward the USSR—consistent with Casey's views, Ronald Reagan's well publicized "evil empire" characterization, and the attitudes of prominent administration hawks. These articles would have provided guidance for acceptable SOVA analysis on the Soviet Union, independent of any overt politicization.[45] In his 1986 article and speech "War by Another Name," for example, Gates portrayed Soviet policy in the Third World with such words as:

> "Our continuing difficulty in formulating a coherent and sustainable bipartisan strategy for the Third World over two generations contrasts sharply with the Soviet Union's relentless effort there to eliminate western influence, to establish strategically located client Communist states, and to gain access to strategic resources."[46]

Gates added:

> "Let there be no mistake or ambiguity about it: the Soviet Union supports terrorism. It has directly and indirectly trained, funded, armed, and even operationally assisted terrorist organizations such as Fatah, Abu Nidal, and others. Nearly every terrorist group in the Middle East has links to the U.S.S.R. or one of its clients."[47]

Note that this article predated the mandated Eastern Europe/terrorist article cited in chapter 3 by only about six months.

Gates rewarded those who pleased him, selecting for promotion analysts and junior managers who saw satisfaction of Agency superiors—notably Gates and his mentor Casey—as critical performance goals. His selections validated the belief of many DI employees that who you know is more important than what you know or how you perform. They confirmed the value of a career strategy of sycophancy. Gates showed no recognition of, or dislike for, such behavior.

Because many of the managers Gates tapped for promotion

also had changed jobs often, DI people came to believe that regular movements within the Directorate and outside were "career enhancing." This further reduced the value placed on expertise—both by the organization and in analysts' and managers' minds. Surveys conducted by the Agency's Office of Medical Services, which monitors employees' attitudes and concerns to some extent, showed that a large share of the analyst corps continued in the late 1980s to believe that frequent position changes enhanced career prospects, and were more important than the development of expertise.

Gates and his favored subordinates also punished those who disagreed with their judgments, fostering and reinforcing an atmosphere of intimidation among analysts and many low- and mid-level managers. Former analyst and SOVA manager Melvin A. Goodman was "fired," in his own words, for failure to support Gates' line on Soviet activities in the Third World. Goodman, chief of the division that followed Soviet activities in the Third World, disagreed with Gates' harsh assessment of Soviet motives and activites—of the sort that he presented in his "War By Another Name" speech.[48] Gates reportedly wanted Goodman "out of the building," and Goodman received a senior analyst position until he could arrange a rotation to the National War College. Two other SOVA managers lost jobs for being "too bleak" about the Soviet economy and "too soft" on Soviet arms control policy, respectively, according to former analyst Jennifer Glaudemans in her testimony to the SSCI.[49] In a semantic exercise, Gates denied that he ordered Goodman removed, but made clear to SOVA Director Douglas MacEachen his preferences. MacEachen told the SSCI:

> " ... Mr. Gates did believe that it would be best for SOVA if he [Goodman] were not going to be heading that division, that he ought to be out of the office altogether. My view was that he was an asset to SOVA and should stay there, where we had him in the front office."[50]

Firings for failure to toe the Casey/Gates political line were common enough to intimidate other managers and analysts, particularly in politicized offices like SOVA. Glaudemans recalled to the SSCI the ramifications of such episodes. Referring to the dismissal of Goodman as chief of the Third World Division of SOVA, she said:

> "At an off-site conference shortly after his removal, a SOVA Group Chief did not deny this, when asked why he was 'fired.' In fact, it was said that the division's analysis was going to have to change. I remember at the time, the chilling effect this had."[51]

Referring to the actions of a branch chief who, reacting to Gates' review comments on a paper his branch produced, protested the changes, Glaudemans testified:

> "The Branch Chief, convinced of the inaccuracy of the judgment, went to Mr. Gates' office to argue on behalf of the original analysis. That the branch chief was successful this time speaks to the weight of the evidence, but he was also removed from SOVA shortly thereafter. That this branch chief's analytical track record was outstanding was irrelevant, unfortunately. It was clear that this branch chief was removed because he had challenged Mr. Gates too often. This was confirmed to me, when a senior manager said in the context of the Branch Chief's removal that 'this talking back to Gates has got to stop.'"[52]

Incessant battle with Gates and the awareness of politicization spawned weariness in SOVA. Glaudemans wrote:

> "People had been beaten and intimidated to the point where they stopped fighting losing battles, particularly when there was the belief that the Division Chief had been removed for fighting such battles. This is the nature of the politicization beast and the degree to

which analysis was corrupted; analysts and mid-level managers anticipated Mr. Gates' reaction and began censoring themselves."[53]

This experience was not unique to SOVA. An economist in RTT in 1990, long after Gates and his proteges had institutionalized the intimidation, characterized to me the analyst corps in the DI as "scared rabbits." He included himself in that category. According to the *Washington Post*, a 20-year DI veteran who left because of Gates called the DI an "unhealthy situation;" he added that Gates "destroyed the old DI and the integrity of analysis."[54] A source of the *New York Times* said, "Casey and Gates changed procedures and rewrote key judgments. Analysts who didn't pursue the policy agenda were basically ordered to get on board. It was a corruption of the process."[55] Long-time CIA officer Harold P. Ford declared to the SSCI at Gates' second confirmation hearings in 1991 that it was exactly such comments that led him to reverse his initial assessment that Gates was qualified to be DCI:

> " ... it is my view, based chiefly on the confidences of CIA officers whose abilities and character I respect, that other of Bob Gates' pressures have clearly gone beyond professional bounds and do constitute a skewing of intelligence ..."[56]

Regular reorganizations in SOVA provided convenient occasions to orchestrate large-scale musical chairs in which loyal subordinates found seats even as "problem" managers like Goodman lost their jobs. SOVA's case, while extreme, is illustrative of a management tactic that Gates criticized in 1982 but did not stop.[57] Jennifer Glaudemans told the SSCI:

> "From April 1986 until August 1987, I had four different branch chiefs and from April 1985 until August 1987 I had four division chiefs and I never changed jobs. With few exceptions, each successive reorganization

brought in less experienced managers. When I worked on Soviet policy toward the United States from January 1988 until I left in November 1989, I also had four different branch chiefs, two division chiefs and two group chiefs."[58]

"SOVA was created in the 1981 DI reorganization. It was then reorganized in March 1984, and in varying degrees in 1985, 1986, 1987, and 1989, and I believe there has been some more since. Some of this personnel turmoil was, I believe, the result of satisfying Mr. Gates' personal preferences. Some may justifiably reflect the needs of an institution to adapt to the changing situation in the USSR. I believe most of this turmoil, however, reflected an institutional inability to come to terms with conflicting demands: one, which required substantively qualified managers who could successfully lead a bunch of analysts, and the other, which required managers to be sufficiently pliant as to not 'rock the boat' with too many unwanted papers that cited too much unwanted evidence. One of the major impacts of this personnel turmoil was to put a break on the flow of papers getting out of the SOVA Third World Division. I think this, too, is credible evidence of politicization. If Mr. Gates was having a difficult time getting the analysis he wanted, then slowing down the process was a second best solution."[59]

Former division chief Mel Goodman addressed the role of personnel policy in facilitating politicization in his testimony before the SSCI in 1991:

"Personnel management is the most effective way to ensure consistent production of a desired intelligence line, and Gates' personnel policies produced a steady erosion of CIA's analytical mission. Replacing intelligence experts with people willing to cooperate became a vital element in Gates' approach to intelligence management, and the effects of this policy continue to hinder the production of quality intelligence. Junior analysts became responsible for analysis on Soviet domestic and foreign policy as senior analysts sought other positions inside the intelligence community and elsewhere. Nearly every senior analyst on Soviet foreign policy eventually left the Office of Soviet Analysis, and management positions that were once held by professionals with more than fifty years of collective experience currently are occupied with officers with virtually none. The picture for Soviet domestic affairs policy is similar, with the departure of most senior analysts and the introduction of managers with virtually no experience in Soviet domestic politics. The same pattern dominated the assignments of intelligence officers who covered the Caribbean and Central America. Bill Casey gave cash awards to officers linked to Irancontra (sic) such as Dewey Clarridge, Alan Fiers, and Clair George in 1986. In similar fashion, Gates' intelligence directorate used incentives to honor and promote managers and analysts who adhered to the company line."[60]

At least two experienced DI hands wrote memoranda to then-DDI Richard Kerr complaining about perversions of the analysis/review process without effect. Thomas M. Barksdale, a senior analyst working on Iran, wrote a 10-page memo dated December 2, 1986 charging that the intelligence used in 1986 to justify covert arms sales to Iran as part of what became the Iran-contra scandal represented "... a perversion of the intelligence process staggering in its proportions. It violates the professional standards of conduct that have governed me and most of my colleagues during my 18 years as an intelligence officer."[61] See Appendix B, page 276. Barksdale wrote:

"My concern is not only the exclusion of DDI analysts from playing an intelligence role in recent event.

> I do not believe this is an isolated case that is already past history. I believe the Iranian affair has revealed serious problems about the intelligence process..."[62]

He wrote:

> "Iranian analysts in the DDI (sic) were never consulted or asked to provide an intelligence input to the covert actions and secret contacts that have occurred. In my judgment, this exclusion of expert opinion contributed significantly to the current foreign policy disaster."[63]

Barksdale added a warning about the general implications of the procedural failings of the Iranian fiasco:

> "I believe that the system as it has worked in regard to Iran over about the past 18 months has resulted in distorted, uninformed, and in some instances inaccurate information being presented to officials of this government who presumably believed they were receiving the collective judgment of this Agency. I am appalled that in the midst of a grave foreign policy crisis this helter-skelter, ad hoc, uncoordinated way of doing business has continued. I worry that we risk repeating or perpetuating the mistakes that contributed to the onset of the crisis."[64]

In a January 1987 memo to Kerr, then-SOVA Director Douglas MacEachin complained about the May 1985 Special National Intelligence Estimate on Iran, saying that skeptical views of his analysts (about Iranian/Soviet relations) were suppressed, and other statements added to a section they had drafted, without their knowledge or coordination. MacEachen wrote that "significant changes" had been made in NIO/Near East Graham Fuller's draft "without informing SOVA."[65]

Barksdale and MacEachen were not just complaining that their bureaucratic turf had been trampled. Coordination rules were established to ensure quality by eliminating most chances for injection of unchallenged personal judgment, or bias. Gates had broken, or permitted to be broken, a fundamental rule. The recurrent violation of such a basic precept meant that others, particularly officer directors, could disregard it as well. Episodes like those that led to the two memos helped change the institutional framework of DI analysis in fundamental, and negative, ways.

Gates' emphasis on more (and better) analysis predictably led to increasing managerial concern about production numbers. The DDI's staff kept (and regularly distributed) extensive statistics on the types and quantities of intelligence production, leading in turn to considerable rivalries and only thinly veiled competitions between offices for winning production numbers. The "bean count" remained paramount even after Gates rescinded a guidance on the average number of major papers (like IAs and RPs) he expected from each analyst per year. Some managers interpreted this guidance as a rigid requirement that each analyst produce that number—two. The message had been passed. A factory production floor ethic that more is better entered the DI culture; the word "production" itself came to be the goal to be reached through the means of analysis. Incongruously, however, no corresponding interest in sound production management followed. After an initial flurry at Gates' insistence in the early 1980s, there was no longer any significant interest in making analytic quality, as opposed to stylistic rigor or production numbers, job 1. This was particularly true after Dick Kerr became DDI in 1986.

Management largely ignored objective measures of quality or questions of whether DI judgments were accurate or useful for several reasons. Printed papers by definition meet Agency quality standards; they satisfy managers paid to make such decisions. There are no standard measures to objectively compare a short piece on the military prospects of Afghan rebels over the next month with a lengthy assessment of the long-term consequences of AIDS on African elites, for example. The accuracy of forecasts cannot be judged for varying and sometimes considerable periods of time. Moreover, any criticism of papers would be implicit attacks on the office directors and DDIs who approved them—dangerous acts for employees in, or on rotations from, those same production offices. Style, or "packaging" as it often is known, became still more important, reducing further the relative importance of quality analysis.

Two potential DI institutional checks on quality, and thus on politicization, evaporated on Gates' watch. In one of his first moves as DDI, Gates persuaded Casey to remove from the DI the Senior Review Panel—created in the late 1970s as a body of distinguished elders to advise management part-time on analyses.[66] The SRP became an intelligence community-level asset reporting to the DCI and the chairman of the National Intelligence Council. Gates ultimately did not replace it or its function. His haste to get rid of the SRP early in his tenure as DDI suggests that he viewed it as a threat of some sort; certainly these retired, respected men, all old enough to be his father, were unlikely to be as easily intimidated as ambitious young DI personnel.

In its stead, Gates announced in his introductory speech to DI employees, the creation of the Product Evaluation Staff, a part of the DDI's staff. It, Gates claimed, would be charged with "reviewing specific DDI products, categories of production (e.g., current intelligence publications), office publications, and so forth. Their reports, accompanied by comments from the head of the component producing the evaluated material, will be forwarded to ... me."[67] The Product Evaluation Staff initially carried the acronym PEST (pronounced as a word) in much of the DI, but quickly demonstrated that it intended no potentially annoying (to the production offices) quality control mission. Reassured that a potential threat had not materialized, the DI as a whole dropped the last letter of its acronym. I never heard of a single evaluation by PES (spelled as letters) of the quality of a specific DI product—as opposed to general comments about aggregates.[68] Even if it did review papers behind its closed doors, its lack of feedback meant that it had no practical effect on the primary producers of intelligence—analysts and first-line supervisor/reviewers.

The DI reorganization of October 1981 sharply reduced the chances that coordination between offices would act to halt poor or extreme judgments, particularly by office directors.[69] The reorganization, which ostensibly improved analysis by placing analysts of various backgrounds following the same country under one office roof, reduced the ability of other offices to offer meaningful alternative judgments or to match the bureaucratic power of the responsible office director. Thus, efforts to make the system more "efficient" and timely had the effect of reducing the amount of internal "competitive analysis"—the reason for multiple intelligence agencies and the thrust of recurrent recommendations for intelligence reform. These institutional changes thus gave office directors relatively free hands to inject their views into analysis by giving them primary review responsibility for analyses. Earlier reorganizations eliminated other potential brakes on politicization; the Board of National Estimates died during the 1970s.

Robert Gates both politicized some analysis and severely damaged the long standing mechanisms for ensuring that the process of genuine review works to purge biased analyses. He did this through massive overconfidence in his own abilities and his denigration of the views of others. In testimony given to the SSCI on October 1, 1991, former vice chairman of the NIC Harold P. Ford said:

> "Many will share my view that Bob Gates has often depended too heavily on his own individual analytic judgments, and has ignored or scorned the views of others whose assessments did not accord with his own. This would be OK if he were uniquely all-seeing. He has not been."[70]

Gates in essence confirmed such criticism in remarks to Senator Bill Bradley during his confirmation hearings in

September, 1991. In an exchange over charges of politicization of an estimate on Iran, Gates said, "the analysts weren't excluded from involvement in the estimate. They simply did not have their views accepted."[71] This recurrent attitude constitutes rejection of methods of effective policing against bias and questions the logic of having analysts—as opposed to research assistants—in the DI at all. It reflects bad judgment and an overwhelmingly presumptuous attitude that he alone is capable of determining sound analysis.

Gates exacerbated the problem by encouraging his office directors to display the same kind of intellectual arrogance within their own fiefdoms. The extreme concentration of power over DI analytical judgments placed in the hands of five office directors with regional responsibilities and the heads of OGI/RTT and OSWR, means that poor personnel decisions about single individuals can have devastating effects on the ability of entire offices to provide warnings of serious threats and to do more mundane analysis. In many important respects, analysts in some offices have become but research assistants and drafters for the single analyst in the office—the director. According to a SOVA analyst, the director of SOVA in the late 1980s and early 1990s pointedly told his office he became SOVA's senior analyst when he assumed his position. In essence, he declared his ability and intention to analyze by fiat. This attitude remained in several DI office directors' suites long after Gates went to the White House in 1989.

Reliance on a small number of "senior analyst" office directors to cover the planet would be worrisome enough if they were renaissance people, but some lack training, experience, and the common sense to know their limitations. Some of these people's intellects are widely disrespected within their own organizations. For example, the director of the Office of Global Issues—whose office followed some world-wide generic political issues—declared to an OGI branch chief repeatedly in early 1990 (prior to OGI's reorganization into RTT) that the topic of insurgency was no longer of intelligence interest because the Cold War was over.[72] He clearly indicated his belief, despite the plethora of insurgencies over a host of issues, that Moscow was the root cause of all insurgencies in the entire world. Other analysts and managers simply shake their heads in disbelief at this man's lack of understanding of major issues that his office follows.

A former ALA and OGI director who prospered greatly in the Gates years illustrated his own ignorance in a report to his analysts on his trip to Brazil in the mid-1980s. According to an analyst present, the director described how he and a US Embassy officer got lost while driving and stopped to ask directions. After receiving them, he expressed his thanks with an "A-okay" hand expression which, unknown to him until then, in Brazil is an obscene gesture. Unhappy, the Brazilian began to scream at the Americans in a language that the office director described as "Brazilian," evidently oblivious to the fact that most Brazilians speak Portuguese.

A former director of the Office of African and Latin American Analysis would not accept the judgment of his analysts and subordinate managers that a relatively well-known African rebel group had a poorly developed political agenda and was motivated primarily by its simple opposition to the government. D/ALA continued, according to a former ALA analyst, to ask for this non-existent political program after repeated explanations. He killed several papers on the rebel group because his people would not manufacture such a platform.

Similarly, the director of the Office of Soviet Analysis indicated to a SOVA economist in 1990 his unfamiliarity with the elementary difference between real and nominal prices—at a time when inflation and other price issues threatened *perestroika* and political stability in the USSR. Other SOVA analysts comment simply on his ignorance of economics. A SOVA analyst's critique of management using the medium of an anonymous (for good reasons) spoof of Tom Clancy's *The Hunt for Red October*—featuring recurrent hero Jack Ryan this time as a junior, GS-9 SOVA analyst—characterized the office director as unconstrained by a sense of proportion.[73] Another

SOVA employee was still more critical in *The Ballad of Bad King Georgie* (see figure 3).

Former SOVA analyst Jennifer Glaudemans recounted to the SSCI her views of a director of SOVA—a demonstration that Gates' methods of operations extend to lower ranking officials and outlived his 1982-89 tenure as a senior officer at CIA. In discussing the internal US government debate over Soviet President Gorbachev's political prospects, Glaudemans wrote:

> It was also in March of 1989 that Mr. Kolt became director of SOVA. In all due respect, I cannot tell this story without bluntly stating that everyone I know in SOVA, including myself, believes that Mr. Kolt was Mr. Gates' choice for head of SOVA and that Mr. Kolt has used SOVA's analysis to support Mr. Gates' position in this debate. (Having also worked in the State Department, I can tell you that this perception also exists outside of SOVA.) For example, I recall that Mr. Kolt, in a personal memo to the director, warned that Gorbachev could well be overthrown at the April 1989 plenum. Again that summer when the coal strikes first began, he was predicting the end of Gorbachev. He also said, at a briefing at the State Department which I attended, that there was a better than even chance of this at the September 1989 plenum."[74]

Glaudemans, speaking to the senators, added a biting additional comment about SOVA management: "As you all well know, the perception that analysis is politicized widely persists in SOVA to this day."[75]

Gates' managerial appointees institutionalized the altered personnel evaluation criteria and promotion processes to enable the office directors to ensure politicization. They gradually mandated quantity of "production" as a key employee performance criterion, while leaving enough fudge room to allow either the rapid promotion of favorites or, at the other extreme, the vindictive punishment of individuals the office

Figure 3

The Ballad of Bad King Georgie

Anon.

[by a SOVA employee, 1991]

To the tune of any fraternity drinking song or English rugby theme.

Georgie once had birdies upon his suit of blue
But as time passed he saw it was the best that he could do,
And so he said that if I seek to climb above just this,
I'm going to have to find myself some bigger buns to kiss.
— And so he said that if I seek to climb above just this
I'm going to have to find myself some bigger buns to kiss.

So Georgie came upon the NIC, his fortune for to seek,
And showed he knew to heed the strong while bullying the weak,
Now milit'ry intelligence may not get much respect,
But it certainly will teach you at which gates to genuflect.
—Now milit'ry intelligence may not get much respect,
But it certainly will teach you at which gates to genuflect.

Then Georgie went to EURA and imposed his iron hand.
The royalty all lived it up and thought that life was grand,
But the common folk were so oppressed; the gentry they arose,
And made it plain for all to see: the Emperor had no clothes.
—Yes the common folk were so oppressed; the gentry they arose
And made it plain for all to see: the Emperor had no clothes.

Next Georgie went to SOVA and surveyed his new domain,
Said George: I'll need some flunkies to help keep things in train.

Men of no great principle who'll always answer yes,
So he got Grey and Stevie K. and so began the mess.
— Men of no great principle who'll always answer yes,
So he got Grey and Stevie K. and so began the mess.

The Lord sent His Son to Earth two thousand years ago,
But Georgie said Christ's reappeared as Yeltsin, don't you know.
From drunken slob to Son of God, that's quite a leap he took.
That's no problem, Georgie said, we'll simply cook the books.
—From drunken slob to Son of God, that's quite a leap he took
That's no problem, Georgie said, we'll simply cook the books.

Slowly and Sadly

So things have really changed here since the days of Douggie Mac.
SOVA makes her living now by lying on her back.
Her golden gown integrity lies tattered, torn, and limp;
Poor SOVA is a prostitute and Georgie is her pimp.
— Her golden gown integrity lies tattered, torn, and limp,
Poor SOVA is a prostitute and Georgie is her pimp.

NOTES: Georgie was a career Air Force officer who reached the rank of colonel, and who took a rotational assignment to CIA headquarters as an Assistant National Intelligence Officer. During the tenure of Robert Gates as chairman of the NIC, as well as DDI, he became a full NIO—a position normally reserved for major generals. After deciding to retire from the Air Force, he took his first CIA job in 1986 as director of the Office of European Analysis. I was in EURA at the time and refer to Georgie and some of his sycophants in my letter of resignation; he ordered that my letter not be distributed within SOVA—a source of both amusement and additional interest in it. Georgie took Stevie K. and two other similar EURA managers with him to SOVA. Douggie Mac is SOVA's former director and a man with many detractors; the nostalgic reference to Douggie is a good measure of the author's severe unhappiness with Georgie.

directors disliked. This was and is possible because of the extensive powers the office directors alone wield over the careers of most analysts and junior managers.[76] The increased emphasis on quantity by the mid- to late-1980s almost completely reversed Gates' 1982 statement to DI personnel, "You and your supervisors will be evaluated and promoted on the basis of the quality of your work. ... Quality, not quantity, will be the basis of evaluation."[77]

Most analysts learn quickly that the surest avenue to "success" is emulation of superiors—both intellectually and personally. A director of the Office of East Asian Analysis made the point explicitly when he told a conference of his office's employees that the best way for analysts to prosper was to be like him. According to a participant of the conference, his subordinate managers dutifully agreed, while none of the assembled analysts offered an objection. I repeatedly have imagined Kim Il-Sung saying the same thing to an assembly of both loyal and fearful North Koreans.

DI management periodically tries to figure out what kind of person makes the most successful analyst—by definition the "best" analyst. It has passed the word that "getting along with others" is the premier success determinant—other than the useless observation that good analysts are good at analysis. This is particularly telling because most analysts work most of the time on individual assignments; management regularly claims that it cannot adequately assess the work of individuals who work on teams. The "getting along ..." observation thus refers primarily to analysts' obsequiousness during the review process, with smaller emphasis on analysts' ability to work smoothly through the process of coordinating drafts with other offices.

At the other end of the spectrum, one of the most fatal accusations is a variant of "failure to accept criticism" or "failure to accommodate the views of reviewers." It is a major mechanism by which some office managements seek to ensure intellectual orthodoxy. Management not infrequently regards analyst discussions and rejoinders to managers' views during the review process as evidence of unacceptable combative behavior—a punishable offense. These may reflect honest differences in judgment, divergent views on style and format, or disagreements about specific language. They may indicate analyst concern that his reviewers' comments reflect ignorance, political bias, laziness, simple factual error, or poor judgment. They also may reflect analysts' obstinacy or shoddy work.

But because discussions for all of these reasons are bureaucratically dangerous for analysts—as numerous and widely known instances attest—virtually all analysts are constantly on guard during the review process. Note taking, rather than discussion, became a far safer approach to take when receiving the comments of reviewers. In particularly badly managed offices and divisions, many analysts simply came to accept docilely the comments of reviewers and hope that the intellectual damage is minimal. In SOVA in the late 1980s and early 1990s, analysts mused ruefully that the office needed fewer analysts but more secretaries; they take better notes.[78] Sherman Kent, I expect, would be appalled.

A newly-appointed OGI division chief made clear the relative importance of sound analysis versus packaging when he declared in early 1990 to his assembled division that analysts perform two functions: analysis and writing. In his view, anyone could do analysis, but only especially gifted individuals could write to DI standards; these individuals would prosper in his division. Similarly, a deputy office director once simply said that accuracy of forecasts does not matter and is not a high priority in judging the performance of an analyst.

Senior managers periodically become personally peeved at analysts (and junior managers) and become sometimes blatantly vindictive. Most analysts who have been in the DI for more than a short time know of at least one case, reinforcing the incentive to be docile. A particularly egregious case occurred in the mid-1980s in the Office of European Analysis, when the deputy office director ordered a branch chief to write critical performance appraisals of two analysts. When the branch chief responded that the analysts were doing good work, the deputy office director in essence said that the branch chief would write critical evaluations or should expect to receive a poor one himself. The branch chief capitulated. Within a fairly short time, all three victims left the DI.

Analysts widely regard management's use of its powers to reward as capricious as well. In a particularly poorly managed office like the Office of European Analysis, for example, large numbers of analysts once expressed the view in a survey that they would rather see the program that grants modest cash awards for ostensibly good performance terminated than see yet more given to brown-nosers.

Gates' advancements of individuals possessing the characteristics described above fundamentally changed the character of management and were so numerous that the culture is now self-sustaining. Gates' proteges and theirs now occupy most senior managerial offices in the Directorate, while practitioners of older values appear to be declining in number and influence.

Gates' elevation to Deputy Director of Central Intelligence (DDCI) in April 1986 allowed him to institutionalize further the changes he had made. He supported a kindred spirit as his replacement as DDI—his Associate DDI Richard J. Kerr. As DDCI, Gates could protect and enhance the changes he had made in the DDI as: a DDCI with Casey's confidence in 1986-87; as Acting Director for several months in late 1986 and early 1987; and as a powerful deputy to intelligence neophyte William Webster in 1987-89. When Gates moved to the White House as deputy national security advisor in early 1989, then-DDI and Gates protege Richard Kerr became DDCI. For the first time, DI careerists who became DDIs had become consecutive Deputy Directors of Central Intelligence. It was a major victory for the DI in the Agency's internal bureaucratic battles.

Kerr's role as protector of the current "DI culture"—as it has come to be popularly known in the Directorate—is critical for two reasons. First, he tapped many of the DI's current managers and shares with them personal interests and bureaucratic objectives. Second, as an experienced deputy to a DCI who remained a novice at foreign affairs and intelligence, Kerr like Gates before him appears to many to have been de facto DCI over analytical as well as many other intelligence community matters during the Webster years (1987-91). It is arguable that even DDI John Helgerson was powerless to make significant changes in his own Directorate—if he was so inclined.

DI employees widely viewed Dick Kerr as a consummate bureaucrat—personally pleasant, eager to avoid controversy, and always protective of the DI's interests. Even as DDCI—an intelligence community as well as CIA position—Kerr pushed DI bureaucratic prerogatives at the expense of the National Intelligence Council. Casey actively used the members of the Council—the National Intelligence Officers—as personal advisors on analytic matters.[79] When Kerr became DDCI, the Council lost influence, members, and access to the DCI. Kerr also eliminated positions on the NIC Analytic Group—a handful of capable analysts that prepares NIC memoranda and sometimes drafts NIEs—reducing the ability of the NIC to compete against the DI. Kerr's pro-DI views were so well known to NIOs—and were such a concern—that then-NIC Chairman Fritz Ermarth repeatedly addressed the implications for the NIC of Kerr's promotion at NIC staff meetings just before and after Kerr assumed his new position. (Moreover, the appointment of some National Intelligence Officers who were DI managers on rotation helped ensure that the NIC would not be too independent of the DDI and Kerr, and would thus not be significant alternative sources of analytical judgment.)

Kerr, who retired in early 1992, was very protective of the DI in narrow bureaucratic terms as well. He looked for silver linings to gray clouds. For example, as DDCI he once rationalized as good work what many within CIA headquarters believed to be a failure to discover a major arms proliferation case until well after it was too late to stop by diplomatic means, even though information long existed to suggest development of a very unusual international relationship. Junior analysts in the Office of East Asian Analysis and another intelligence agency suspected what later proved to be the case, but were unable to convince their managers of their suspicions. Kerr also was unwilling to accept that the DI has significant problems that need to be addressed; he repeatedly suggested to Agency employees that either problems are minor and can easily be worked around, or that individuals with concerns about the management of the Agency should find employment elsewhere.[80]

As a bureaucrat averse to conflict and controversy, Kerr after 1986 also completed the abandonment of many of Gates' better initiatives—those that initially served the valuable functions of disrupting complacency and asking for better quality. Kerr continued to sterilize and bureaucratize Gates' program, destroying many of its better points and leaving much of the worst of it. Gates seemingly either did not notice or did not care during the period 1986-89 when he was DDCI, Kerr was DDI, and their offices were but a short walk apart.

Kerr only finished the job Gates' own inattention had started. Gates regularly failed to ensure that his good initiatives were implemented successfully. In one of his better early efforts, for example, he directed that a "Product Review Record" accompany each paper through the review process that would convey two basic series of data: who approved the paper; and, when review commenced and was completed at each level. Gates' stated intent was to prod reviewers to act quickly; he, as final reviewer, would be able to see who had held the paper for "too long." Reviewers, however, concerned that Gates might see them as slow, simply tore up incriminating Product Review Records and directed that analysts submit new ones with later analyst submission dates. During Gates' tenure as DDI, I noted this action several times by managers in the Office of European Analysis—involving the work of several analysts, including my own.

Judge Webster's appointment as DCI with the principal mission, many Agency people believed, of keeping the Agency off the front page of Washington newspapers reinforced the trends of the DI he inherited.[81] Controversy and complaints were to be minimized. Consumers were to be satisfied. Webster left the DI to its own devices and Gates' and Kerr's oversight. In the day-to-day lives of most DI analysts and managers, he may as well not have existed except as the protagonist of some new humorous anecdote.[82] Thus, despite rampant complaints by analysts and some managers about poor management and the basic conduct of analysis, senior DI and Agency executives were clearly uninterested in recognizing, let alone addressing, the problems of the DI. They were solid, and sometimes stolid, bureaucrats.

Keen DI observers of Gates' initiatives of the early 1980s and their consequences believe his initiatives have had devastatingly negative effects. While commendable in many of his ostensible goals, Gates appointed subordinates to implement them who altered them into procedurally rigid forms that have hurt, not helped, his objective of better, more useful analysis. Insecure subordinates changed his missive that managers do better jobs and take personal responsibility into procedures that are inefficient and allow the injection of personal opinion in the name of taking responsibility for "quality." Gates made personnel choices that many in the DI regard as very unfortunate; moreover, many of these appointees are relatively young, meaning that they have years to further entrench their views, proteges, and ethical standards. His procedural changes added another level of review—that of the DDI—that is expensive in time and effort, and provides an opportunity to lower the common denominator of review further; however, it arguably serves little positive purpose other than informing the DDI about the activities of his offices to offset these costs.

Ultimately, Gates failed to fulfill his own directive that managers should ensure quality by properly supervising the implementation of his program (see figure 4). Key specific elements of his initial program fell by the wayside over time. Gates' initial success in ordering "hard-hitting" analyses turned by the mid-1980s into the same "mush" designed to avoid controversy that he had criticized only a few short years before. His order to bring analysts closer to both policymakers and outside experts—an initial success in some ways—by the late

1980s was completely reversed and DI analysts were quite isolated from outside contacts. He first directed more papers, then decided that he had asked for too many, while not rescinding the personnel management system's bias toward rewarding quantity.

Gates failed to improve the responsiveness of CIA analysis to the informational and intelligence judgmental needs of the policy community and concentrated on satisfying that community's wants. On his watch, CIA executives compromised the integrity of the institution by bringing it too close to policy wants. He and his appointees denigrated the service of national intelligence needs to satisfying the wants of policymakers and the bureaucratic interests of those officials and the Agency itself.

Gates' failings as DDI and as DDCI with major supervisory responsibilities for analysis seem to me very similar to those alleged about his role in the Iran-contra affair. In Iran-contra, the public record indicates that Gates has told Congress that he did not know of events, and only picked up unsubstantiated rumors prior to being informed by Charlie Allen of his suspicions. During his 1991 confirmations hearings Gates admitted that he might have asked a few more questions. Still, critics find it hard to believe that he could not have known of events when DCI Casey, Deputy Director for Operations Clair George, a number of other DO personnel, then-Assistant Secretary of State Elliott Abrams, and others were involved and well-informed. They argue that such ignorance is hard to believe given Gates' close relationship to Casey and his well-known practice of hard work and close supervision of Agency activities. In the view of some observers, thus, either Gates did not tell the truth or he suffered an extremely uncharacteristic lapse in attentiveness at a crucial time.

To account for the problems of CIA analysis during his tenure, I propose a similar set of alternatives. Either Gates purposefully politicized Agency analysis—a view many DI personnel hold—or he ignored or condoned subordinates' significant changes in his ostensibly well-motivated directives

Figure 4

Gates' Record: A Gatesian Scorecard

Gates' Claim	Source	Performance/status
"We are more candid now with our readers about the level of our confidence in our judgments and the reliability of our sources."	(1)	Clearly not, or criticisms about "waffling" would not be so strong
"The Agency has elaborate procedures for reviewing to filter out individual bias…"	(2)	True for analysts, untrue for senior reviewers.
"We now evaluate past CIA assessments and national estimates to see how they have held up over time."	(1)	Never common. Now all but non-existent.
"The directorate has for the first time its own independent evaluation staff."	(1)	It never could be independent in evaluating work Gates approved. It now is useless.
"We require all CIA analysts to have outside training every two years."	(1)	Abandoned.
"I expect analysts to know their subject, past, present, and future."	(3)	Largely abandoned. Certainly a lower priority than in 1982.
"Finally, perhaps the best guardians of the integrity of the process are the caliber and honesty of the people involved."	(1)	True. The cause of the bitter opposition to Gates and the internal struggle.
"We must give the highest priority to ensuring a lively intellectual atmosphere, a questioning and creative spirit, and above all a sense of adventure."	(4)	Gates and his successors did the opposite—quashing creativity and curiosity in favor of intellectual orthodoxy.
"Each office will be required to develop an aggressive program of contacts, conferences, and seminars on important subjects."	(5)	Active at first, abandoned by Kerr and Helgerson.

Sources:

(1) Robert M. Gates, "Is the CIA's Analysis Any Good?," The *Washington Post*, December 12, 1984, p. A25.

(2) Robert M. Gates, "The CIA and Foreign Policy," *Foreign Affairs*, Vol. 66, No.2, Winter 1987/88, p. 222.

(3) Robert M. Gates, Speech to the Directorate of Intelligence, January 1982, recounted in United States Senate, Transcript of Proceedings Before the Select Committee on Intelligence, Nomination of Robert M. Gates to be Director of Central Intelligence, Morning Session, October 3, 1991, p. 21.

(4) Robert M. Gates, "Remarks to DDI Analysts and Managers," 7 January 1982, p. 14.

(5) Ibid., p. 11.

over a period of seven years. Each of these possibilities is unflattering; either Gates lacked intellectual integrity or he was a miserable manager. Or both. Gates himself discussed a variant of the charge in comments to the SSCI on October 3, 1991:

> "Indeed, charges as have been made by at least one person before this Committee of a systematic, years-long effort to politicize and corrupt the analytical process imply that former Deputy Directors Admiral Inman and John McMahon, the current Acting Director, Dick Kerr, the heads of all the other intelligence agencies and hundreds of analysts and managers in CIA, either acquiesced to it, ignored it, somehow missed it, or joined it. And that's ridiculous."[83]

It is not ridiculous. Bobby Inman can be excused by dint of his short tenure as DDCI while Gates was DDI—less than six months—at a time when his relationship with DCI Casey was deteriorating.[84] McMahon had an operations background, despite a short stint as DDI before Gates, and appears to have had little authority over analysis because Casey had such confidence in Gates; and, as Gates well knew, the heads of other intelligence agencies have never been responsible for the DI. Kerr clearly was a willing colleague who bears similar responsibility for what happened to the DI. The 1991 confirmation hearings, periodic Inspector General reports, the mid-1980s complaints of ALA's "Gang of Four" about politicization of analysis on Nicaragua, Tom Barksdale's comments directly to Gates and his follow-up memo, and DDI Helgerson's June 14, 1991 letter to DI employees indicate clearly that large numbers of Agency employees were well aware of just such systemic changes by Gates and his immediate subordinates. Many of them opposed the changes for the best of reasons—concerns about intellectual integrity of CIA analysis and the well-being of the nation. Many analysts and managers took the opportunity the hearings presented to break from their apparent "acquiescence"—at considerable personal bureaucratic risk—to make those concerns known to the Senate and the American people.

Moreover, Gates received written notice from DI managers that significant numbers of DI personnel were concerned about his politicization at least as early as July 1985. In a now declassified critique of DI production concerning the attempt to assassinate Pope John Paul II in early 1981, Ross Cowey and two other DI managers wrote to Gates about the controversial April 1985 assessment on the attempt:

> "But the perception of upper-level intervention was compounded by the pressure from on high to produce that paper quickly and from the resulting shortcuts in, if not circumvention of, the usual review and coordination process for such papers. We found no compelling reasons to rush this paper to completion without benefit of all expert views. Our interviews have not unearthed any reason except management's desires to finish it quickly. Moreover, nearly everyone we talked to who was involved in the review and coordination process views the shape and tone of the Key Judgments, and the deletion of the explanatory Scope Note, as having been inspired, if not directed, by the seventh floor."[85]

The "seventh floor" is the floor where the DDI, DDCI, and DCI have their offices. It thus is a euphemism for senior Agency management.

The evaluation team summed up the problem in its seventh "key finding:"

> *Senior management may want to take some steps to dispel the perception in some quarters that the issue has become politicized*, along with some measures designed to redress the organizational problems that we have identified in the following review (emphasis added)."[86]

The Bob Gates who helped create a climate of politicization showed no meaningful recognition of it or genuine concern about its consequences. He apparently did not respond to the Cowey recommendation, or those of anyone else, in any way. Former SOVA branch chief Wayne P. Limberg wrote to the SSCI of his experiences in the mid-1980s:

> "Nor did Mr. Gates work to ease the atmosphere of fear and intimidation that gripped the directorate. Contrary to his testimony, during my years in SOVA, he never met with analysts or managers, despite the fact that he knew he had problems in that office. He also let it be known that he suspected SOVA and that its work was subject to special scrutiny. The result was that morale fell, production declined, and analysts, rightly or wrongly, began to censor themselves. More than once I had to argue with analysts to do a piece because they were convinced 'Gates will never let it out.' More and more attention was paid to the 'packaging' of our product and to long-term research rather than current intelligence because it was 'safer.' In short, Bob Gates' leadership (sic), we became less creative analysts and more cautious bureaucrats."[87]

Gates incongruously expressed frustration about concerns about politicization in testimony to the SSCI. He admitted that he repeatedly heard of concerns from more than one office but fatuously claimed he looked for "evidence" in the papers themselves and never did anything but "worry" some:

> "Again and again, Inspector General reports and studies by the Directorate's Product Evaluation Staff found pockets of perceptions of politicization. More often in the Soviet Office than elsewhere. But [they] searched in vain for evidence of slanting in our products. Evidence of politicization was always elusive but the perception was always a worry. I'd ask analysts ... if their work had been distorted... [T]he answer was virtually always no. But they had heard that had happened for sure in the next branch over."[88]

The personal staff of DCI Webster knew of problems of politicization early in Webster's tenure, and so possibly did the Judge, yet he also did nothing about it. One of Webster's staff officers, Mark Matthews, conducted what veteran analyst Carolyn Ekedahl called in a sworn statement an "informal investigation" into politicization in 1987 (see Appendix B).[89] She wrote that she talked with Matthews for several hours, "trying to explain the culture and the corruption of the process which had occurred under Casey and Gates. On my way in and out of his office, we both were careful to prevent my being seen by Bob Gates..." whose office was nearby.[90] "This reflects the atmosphere of paranoia that pervaded the place by that time."[91] Matthews told her that the Judge was "very aware of the problem of politicization," and that he was aware of passing references (contained in a single paragraph) about politicization contained in a report of the Inspector General.[92]

While Ekedahl indicated that Webster once knew of politicization, I doubt that he ever understood its significance, and may have forgotten about such charges. Webster, in over four years as DCI, appears never to have learned much about the organization he headed.[93] His faults were those of ignorance, lack of caring, and lack of supervision, not the slanting of a process he did not understand and judgments about which he showed little interest. His de facto mental absence let Gates, then Kerr, run the DI with little interference from a man whose much ballyhooed personal integrity was irrelevant to the deterioration of integrity in the DI.

Despite periodic references to politicization, the Office of the Inspector General (OIG) long has been generally unresponsive to management problems, including politicization. It has been, in the view of many DI people, part of the problem. It never has demonstrated consistent usefulness for solution of other than minor problems. Even OIG staffers note that when OIG sees a problem, DI office directors can and do ignore its "recommendations" at will. I know of no instance in which an Inspector General has addressed seriously a major DI management problem to the DCI. Analysts often assume that serious complaints about management will return to haunt them via IG communication to office managers, despite continued OIG promises to the contrary. Other employees, either understandably fearful or convinced that discussions with OIG officers are simply a waste of time, avoid the periodic IG "inspections" of DI offices. A director of OGI was uncharacteristically blunt when, after an unfavorable inspection of his office in 1982, he passed the word fairly directly to his personnel that they should not go to the Inspector General to complain about management.[94]

An analyst's complaint about the management of one DI office is a case supporting the conventional wisdom. In July 1989, the analyst charged office management with directing politically slanted papers, incompetence, violations of Agency Equal Opportunity regulations involving denial of rights of a pregnant analyst to work on a part-time basis, simple dishonesty, and more. The analyst provided the names of corroborating witnesses on separate sheets of paper to try to protect the cited individuals. In a conversation with the Agency's Deputy Inspector General for Special Investigations, he asked for discussions with the investigator(s) assigned to the case to clarify and elaborate points.

In January 1990, the analyst received a copy of a portion of the formal OIG rejection of his charges from two individuals he had not met until moments before. The investigators, on the basis of their admitted discussions with the management targets of the analyst's complaints, found that the charges were groundless. They added that they felt no need to talk with any of the witnesses listed in the complaint because they knew thoroughly the state of the office even though neither had ever been assigned to any DI office and the last full IG inspection of the office was before the management team the analyst complained about assumed their positions.

Amazed, the analyst appealed to then-Inspector General William F. Donnelly. The IG, however, backed the conclusions of his "investigators" and claimed that initial discussions with the Deputy IG—when the written complaints were delivered—

constituted the requested discussions. Agency procedures at that time held that any complaint to the DCI about any Agency component, including the IG, would be handled by the Office of the Inspector General—thus effectively ending the complaint and appeals process.

The OIG persistently has ignored its responsibilities to root out politicization. My own complaints during inspections of the Office of European Analysis had no effect at all. More damning, an inspection of the Office of Soviet Analysis in 1987-88 shows a clear pattern of irresponsibility that reached to the highest levels of CIA.

During the course of a periodic inspection of SOVA, OIG personnel received a series of reports from numerous analysts and managers about politicization, including directives from Robert Gates to alter analyses in ways that many SOVA officers considered politically motivated. The charges were specific and lengthy, according to SOVA personnel. They were so potentially explosive that the senior OIG investigator, a former deputy director of the Office of European Analysis, decided to brief then-DDI Dick Kerr on most of her findings, instead of the usual practice of including them in a written report. In the view of one former SOVA officer privy to the report, some 90 percent of the accusations presented to the inspection team were excluded from the final written report. The senior OIG official, in her comments to SOVA managers on her findings, admitted that the OIG had skewed its findings to place blame for the politicization it recognized on SOVA managers, not Gates; this revelation unsurprisingly did not sit well with those SOVA managers. DCI Webster, in a letter to the SSCI, recalls seeing a report "about June 28, 1988" concerning the "routine" inspection of SOVA that "contained two recommendations designed to improve the quality and flow of intelligence, both of which were approved."[95]

The senior OIG official abdicated a basic responsibility. She implicitly condoned politicization by both failing to act to stop it and by covering it up. She contributed to the intellectual prostitution of the Directorate of Intelligence. To my knowledge, no Agency officer, including Kerr, took any remedial or punitive action as a result of the "inspection."

The Office of the Inspector General appears to have been chronically disinterested in exploring management deficiencies for at least four reasons. First, the IG himself for most of the Agency's history has been an appointee of the DCI alone, who could use loyalty and discretion as key criteria in his selection. Second, many on the rank-heavy IG staff either have been managers themselves or have been in the Agency long enough to accept the status quo and to be uninterested in major critiques. Third, the bulk of positions on the staff are rotations, meaning that staffers will return to line offices at the pleasure of their home office management and have their careers managed by those offices while they work in the Office of the Inspector General; they thus have real incentives not to make waves. Fourth, the OIG has had no real power. It can only recommend changes. It is foolish for an OIG official to spend his bureaucratic capital on an issue like managerial politicization when the very targets of such findings can simply ignore them.

The Congressional mandate of a statutory Inspector General confirmed by the Senate—the first, Frederick P. Hitz, took office in November 1990—will do little to change the IG's legal, regulatory, or policy treatment of DI mismanagement. Vigorously opposed by the Agency in any form, the final legislation, modified by compromises, authorized new responsibilities to review operational matters, not mere allegations of management problems. Presumably an outsider with Congressional backing will feel less intimidated by Agency personnel policies, but personality and not regulation or law will drive any increased investigative vigor. On the other hand, a more conscientious IG would quickly stimulate bureaucratic protective instincts throughout the Agency, and his continued reliance on Agency careerists on rotations to his Office would hinder efforts to move aggressively.

Inspector General Hitz's changes by the spring of 1992 appeared limited, probably reflecting in part the problem of relying on old CIA hands in his staff. The analyst who made the complaint cited above resubmitted it to Hitz, with an additional request—that he take steps to prevent repetition of OIG's previous misfeasance. Hitz, however, passed the request to the very same Deputy IG who handled the earlier complaint. She not surprisingly found no cause for additional investigation. The analyst resubmitted it to the Deputy IG's replacement in mid-1991, without apparent effect.

Hitz's OIG continues to be extremely conservative in its approach to alleged wrongdoing. OIG officials in 1991 told me that the OIG continues to require what I consider an extreme legal standard of "proof" before it reaches any conclusions—despite the obvious fact that it is not conducting criminal proceedings and does not have to adhere to the "beyond a reasonable doubt" standard for any conclusion. (This seemingly is the same kind of "evidence" that Gates claims to have looked for regarding complaints of politicization and which, not at all surprisingly, he did not find.)

The OIG continues to provide massive protections for bureaucratic offenders. Deputy Inspector General for Special Investigations Americo R. Cinquegrana—a lawyer Hitz brought in from outside the Agency—told me in August 1991 that the OIG was not in the business of "public hangings" and would continue to protect the privacy of offenders—the very sort of attitude that fostered the loose standards of integrity that plague the DI. By so doing, CIA grants far more rights to accused than the United States Constitution grants criminals, and conducts its equivalent of trials and punishments in thorough secrecy. Cinquegrana confirmed to me that the OIG still may not even confirm to those who complained that it has investigated their charges, and will not divulge its findings or recommendations. He told me only that his office was continuing to look at spin-offs of the complaints I made in my letter of resignation, even as its failure to find "proof" of my concerns had given DDI Helgerson the narrow grounds to declare in his June 1991 letter that my charges were unsubstantiated.

Even the accused object to the OIG's procedures. Douglas MacEachen, director of SOVA during the 1987-88 inspection of SOVA, told the SSCI:

> "But it's right out of Franz Kafka. Because once you are accused, the Inspector General will never come back and say you're absolved. You will never be definitely acquitted. They will say we found no evidence to substantiate it. Charged but not indicted. Ostensibly acquitted."[96]

Oversight organizations have been equally irrelevant to the conduct of the daily operations that are so crucial to the overall performance of the DI. Bureaucratic details clearly have generated even less excitement in the President's Foreign Intelligence Advisory Board—a body of respected citizens who serve without compensation and may be worth little more in the area of detailed oversight than they are paid. PFIAB head Bobby Inman in late 1991 indicated clearly, by his comments in exorbitant defense of Gates' management of analysis, that he has no idea how DI analysis is conducted. The PFIAB shows no sign of rousing itself. The President's Intelligence Oversight Board is concerned with legal and proprietary issues, not with managerial competence and integrity.

The Congressional intelligence oversight committees' staffs did not learn in the 1980s how the organization really works, preventing them from making accurate assessments and, concomitantly, critiques and reform proposals. In significant part, according to a senior SSCI staffer, this reflected an unwillingness on the Hill to "micro-manage" intelligence. This would have been a good attitude if the Agency had been able to manage itself.

Notes to Chapter 4

1 As quoted by a senior DI officer who dealt with Robert Gates fairly regularly when Gates was DDI.

2 A frequent Gates phrase that other senior DI officers picked up and used periodically, quoted from an officer who heard Gates say it.

3 For a very personal and jocular account of the early years of the DI, see former DDI Russell Jack Smith's book The Unknown CIA, *(McLean, Virginia: Pergamon-Brassey's International Defense Publishers, Inc., 1986). Smith left the Agency in 1974. His DI is long gone.*

4 Gates was appointed DDI on January 4, 1982. Previously, he served as Casey's executive assistant and had additional staff responsibilities.

5 Gates entered his January 7, 1982 speech entitled "Remarks to DDI Analysts and Managers" into the record at his confirmation hearings in October 1991; see pp. 2-3. See also Haynes Johnson, "For CIA, Hearings' Legacy Could Be A New Beginning or Deeper Schism," Washington Post, *October 4, 1991, p. A8. See also, United States Senate, Transcript of Proceedings Before the Select Committee on Intelligence, Nomination of Robert M. Gates to be Director of Central Intelligence, Morning Session, October 3, 1991, pp. 17-18.*

6 Robert M. Gates, "Remarks to DDI Analysts and Managers," 7 January 1982, p. 2.

7 Robert M. Gates, "Is the CIA's Analysis Any Good?," Washington Post, *December 12, 1984, p. A25.*

8 Gates, "Is the CIA's Analysis Any Good?"

9 Gates' personal ambition is legendary in the DI. In one of the stories, Gates, near the end of his stint as a National Security Council staffer in the late 1970s, returned to CIA headquarters to look for a job. He reportedly called on the director of the Office of Political Analysis (OPA), which followed political events around the world, and asked for a job as a division chief. The director noted that he had never been a branch chief and declined to give him a division. At about the same time, he made a similar request of the Director of Strategic Research (OSR), which followed military developments around the world. Gates got the same negative answer.

Gates, however, persevered and returned to CIA headquarters with significant staff and National Intelligence Council responsibilities. When he assumed the position of DDI, he had never been a branch or division chief, or an office director or deputy director.

The director of OPA who reportedly rebuffed Gates lost her office director's job shortly after the reorganization of 1981 and had staff responsibilities throughout Gates' tenure as DDI and DDCI. Many DI employees viewed her case as an example of the cost of crossing Bob Gates. In January 1992, only two months after DCI Gates returned to CIA, this woman again lost her job. The director of OSR retired shortly after Gates' alleged request to him.

10 Joseph E. Persico, in a biography of William Casey, viewed the relationship similarly, claiming, "Casey loved young Bob Gates." See Persico, Casey *(New York: Viking Penguin, 1990) p. 292.*

11 Gates' Ph.D. from Georgetown University is in Russian and Soviet history.

12 Persico, Casey, *p. 294. Gates told Persico that he "protected" Meyer, arguing that "... you need people who push, ask hard questions. He served this purpose..." My own experience with Meyer was a challenge to an assessment I had done on an East European country's economy. Meyer suggested strongly that I was wrong because my views differed from those of contacts he had made at* Fortune *magazine. He did not respond to my detailed, point-by-point rejoinder, but left an impression on me as shallow, policy-motivated sniper who, rather than asking "tough" questions, was a loose cannon who in this instance required me to provide for him alone some basic groundwork on centrally planned economies.*

13 Ibid., p. 319. Menges also had a reputation as being a genuinely odd man.

14 Ibid., p. 354.

15 Ibid., p. 496.

16 John Hibbits, "Statement of John Hibbits before the Gates Hearings, 2 October 1991," p. 2.

17 Hibbits, "Statement," pp. 2-3.

18 My source heard this officer say he felt the pressure. I consider the source to be highly reliable.

19 Gates, "Remarks to DDI Analysts and Managers, 7 January 1982, pp. 12-13.

20 Ibid., p. 13.

21 Glaudemans, "Written Statement of Jennifer Lynn Glaudemans for the Senate Select Committee on Intelligence," September 25, 1991, p. 7.

22 George Lardner Jr. and Walter Pincus, "Chairman to Back Gates as CIA Chief in Panel Vote Today," Washington Post, *October 18, 1991, p. A4.*

23 Ibid.

24 The Reagan and Bush Administrations regularly certified Pakistan until October 1990, when aid was cut off. By that time, evidence of Pakistani nuclear efforts was clear. In addition, Soviet forces had left Afghanistan and the country was no longer a major element in US/Soviet competition.

25 102nd Congress, 1st Session, Senate, Exec. Rept. 102-19, "Nomination of Robert M. Gates to be Director of Central Intelligence," October 24, 1991, p. 184.

26 Ibid., p. 185.

27 Ibid., p. 171.

28 Elaine Sciolino, "Slanting of Intelligence Becomes Issue for Nominee," New York Times, *September 19, 1991, pp. A1 and B10.*

29 Ibid., p. B10.

30 Elaine Sciolino with David Johnston, "In Rebuttal to Senate Committee, C.I.A. Nominee is Truthful but Incomplete," New York Times, *October 13, 1991, National Section, p. 24.*

31 Ibid.

32 Senate, Exec. Rept. 102-19, p. 131.

33 Ibid., p. 127.

34 Ibid., p. 128.

35 Ibid.

36 Ibid., p. 155.

37 Ibid., p. 109.

38 Ibid.

39 Persico, Casey, *pp. 286-288.*

40 Senate, Exec. Rept. 102-19, p. 109.

41 Ibid., p. 110.

42 Elaine Sciolino, "Slanting of Intelligence Becomes Issue for Nominee," New York Times, *September 19, 1991, p. B10.*

43 Papal Task Force (Ross Cowey, John McLaughlin, and Christine Williams), "Review of DI Production on the Attempted Assassination of Pope John Paul II," July 12, !985, p. 13.

44 Charles R. Babcock, "Gates Admits Deficiencies in Note on Papal Shooting," Washington Post, *October 4, 1991, p. A8. See also the declassified cover memorandum for then-Vice President George Bush from DDI Gates that accompanied the assessment.*

45 See, *for example: "War by Another Name,"* Washington Times, *November 26, 1986, p. D1; and "What's Going on in the Soviet Union?," Freedom at Issue, No. 104, September/October 1988, pp. 5-9.*

46 Robert Gates, "War by Another Name," Washington Times, *November 26, 1991, p. D1. Gates gave a speech with the same title in Los Angeles in November 1986. The article was based on the speech.*

47 Ibid.

48 A portion of the speech was reprinted as a Washington Times *article entitled, "War by Another Name," November 26, 1986, p. D1.*

49 Glaudemans, "Written Statement," p. 3

50 Senate, Exec. Rept., p. 156.

51 Glaudemans, "Written Statement," p. 3.

52 Ibid., p. 8.

53 Ibid., p. 6.

54 Charles R. Babcock and Walter Pincus, "Gates's Intelligence Management at the CIA Becomes an Issue," Washington Post, *September 27, 1991, P. A10.*

55 Elaine Sciolino, "Slanting of Intelligence Becomes Issue for Nominee," New York Times, *September, 19, 1991, p. B10.*

56 Harold P. Ford, "Statement to the Senate Select Committee on Intelligence, 1 October 1991, concerning the confirmation of Robert Gates as Director of Central Intelligence," p. 3.

57 In his "Remarks to DDI Analysts and Managers" speech of 7 January 1982, Gates wrote on page 5: "As most of you know, until recently the DDI and then NFAC's response to most criticism—particularly in the political intelligence arena—was to make fairly circumscribed organizational changes. We also know that those successive reorganizations made little real difference in the way we do our business."

58 Glaudemans, "Written Statement," p. 9.

59 Ibid., pp. 9-10.

60 Melvin A. Goodman, "Testimony of Melvin A. Goodman to the Senate Select Committee on Intelligence," pp. 11-12.

61 Thomas M. Barksdale, memorandum entitled, "The Iranian Imbroglio: Implications for the Intelligence Process," p. 3.

62 Ibid., p. 1.

63 Ibid.

64 Ibid., p. 3.

65 Walter Pincus and George Lardner Jr., "Gates's Role in Iran Reports Questioned," Washington Post, *October 1, 1991, p. A8.*

66 Gates announced the transfer immediately after he became DDI in his initial speech to the Directorate, "Remarks to DDI Analysts and man-

agers," p. 9. He told the SSCI that he persuaded Casey to move it out of the DI. See *U. S. Senate, Exec. Rept. 102-19, "Nomination of Robert M. Gates to be Director of Central Intelligence," October 24, 1991, p. 187.*

67 Robert M. Gates, "Remarks to DDI Analysts and Managers," 7 January 1982. Initially classified, the speech was declassified and released to the public by the SSCI in October 1991.

68 A declassified note to the DDI (Robert Gates) entitled "Review of DI Production on the Attempted Assassination of Pope John Paul II" ostensibly is a PES product. In fact, three DI production office managers—Ross Cowey, John McLaughlin, and Christine Williams—conducted the study.

69 A hypotethical example may serve to illustrate the point; evaluation of a report that a Middle Eastern country plans a massive military buildup over a five-year period with the intent of conquering a neighboring country it long has claimed. Under the old organization, the Office of Strategic Research would have examined the military feasibility of the reported plan, the Office of Politcal Analysis would have assessed the reasons and plausibility of motives and goals, and the Office of Economic Research would have had responsibility for calculating resource requirements and costs. Any substantial divergences of views among the offices would have triggered inter-office discussions about inconsistencies and required development of a collective view (subject to the periodic exceptions of uncoordinated views clearly identified as such). Under the current organization, NESA has sole responsibility for such assessments, which thus rely heavily on the good sense and integrity of NESA's director.

70 Harold P. Ford, "Statement to the Senate Select Committee on Intelligence, 1 October 1991, concerning confirmation of Robert Gates as Director of Central Intelligence," pp. 6-7.

71 Walter Pincus and George Lardner Jr., "Gates's Role in Iran Reports Questioned," Washington Post, *October 1, 1991, p. A8.*

72 This ridiculous observation may have sprung, in good bureaucratic fashion, from Gates' declaration in his January 7, 1982 speech that the DI would examine insurgency because of his concern about instability in the Third World and Soviet efforts to exploit it. See Gates, "Remarks to DDI Analysts and Managers," p. 10.

73 This spoof used the forum of what might have been the real CIA analytic setting for a Red October*-type development to comment on the management of SOVA in 1990. It specifically stated that any apparent references to real people were intentional. It devoted much ink to the review process, noting the propensity of the review/edit process to bring out the worst in some people. It followed the frustrations of Jack Ryan as he sought to get his message heard through the review and coordination processes. He finally settled on the venue of a stylistically rigid current intelligence form, where an editor changed his word submarine to its synonym* hoagie, *for example. The editor noted that his objections reflected the propensity of analysts to be overly defensive about their prose—a common comment by reviewers that, while valid in some cases, has become an excuse for reviewer politicization or incompetence. A few references to technical intelligence collection led the author to classify the work, keeping it within*

Agency vaults. This is regrettable because the spoof provides a good glimpse of analyst life in a poorly-run DI office. The author's decision to remain anonymous was wise, given SOVA management's track record of vindictiveness.

74 Glaudemans, "Written Statement," p. 11.

75 Ibid., p. 10.

76 DI offices, or "career services," hold regular career boards or "panels" composed of office managers. These boards discuss the performance of employees and rank individuals of the same pay grade. However, the office director, as head of the career service, has complete control over promotion decisions for most analysts.

77 Gates, "Remarks to DDI Analysts and Managers," 7 January 1982, p. 8.

78 See United States Senate, Transcript of Proceedings before the Select Committee on Intelligence, Nomination of Robert M. Gates to be Director of Central Intelligence, Evening Session, September 25, 1991, p. 91 (sanitized).

79 Several NIOs have told me that it was not uncommon for Casey to simply call to discuss issues that wandered into his imagination, and sometimes to order them into his office immediately for impromptu meetings. That NIO role virtually ceased when William Webster became DCI.

80 I once spoke with Dick Kerr one-on-one after a series of analysts and branch chiefs had talked with him—mostly in complaining terms—for over an hour at a conference. I noted that several of my colleagues had expressed serious concerns about DI management. He shrugged off the comments, noting that he had always been able to work the system to get around problems. I persisted, saying that I believed my colleagues' concerns were genuine and deep. He responded, in essence, that the solution for anyone who has a problem with the Agency is for that person to leave the Agency. At the time, it was a conversation stopper. I now believe that his statement reflects de facto DI management philosophy and personnel policy. Kerr's comments to me were consistent with his statements over years to many other Agency employees.

81 Webster's apparent prime bureaucratic directive appeared close indeed to that of DCI George Bush, who in 1976 took the helm of an Agency torn by controversy and Congressional criticism.

82 During his tenure, Webster was a source of recurrent funny stories. These usually involved his ignorance of world geography, foreign affairs, and intelligence topics, as well as his allegedly less than robust work ethic. The simplicity of his speeches, apparently in part a result of his lack of coordination with appropriate DI offices during their drafting, also was a periodic source of cringes.

83 United States Senate, Transcript of Proceedings Before the Select Committee on Intelligence, Nomination of Robert M. Gates to be Director of Central Intelligence, Morning Session, October 3, 1991, p. 14. The "one person" about whom Gates referred was Melvin A. Goodman.

84 See Persico's Casey, *various entries.*

85 Formerly classified note to Robert Gates from Ross Cowey, John

McLaughlin, and Christine Williams entitled, "Review of DI Production on the Attempted Assassination of Pope John Paul II," July 12, 1985, p. 19.

86 Ibid, p. ii.

87 Senate, Exec. Rept. 102-19, p. 103. In fact, Gates did visit with analysts during weekly "brown bag lunches" early in his tenure as DDI, when Limberg worked at another government agency. These were staged affairs, with division- and branch-level managers prepping analysts prior to meetings. Gates sometimes had catered lunches from the Executive Dining Room, according to participants in some of these lunches, while analysts ate their cold sandwiches, adding to the awkwardness. Gates soon abandoned these regular meetings and thereafter, to my knowledge, made no significant effort to regularly meet middle- or lower-ranking Directorate personnel.

88 Senate, Exec. Rept. 102-19, p. 104.

89 Carolyn McGiffert Ekedahl, Statement to the Senate Select Committee on Intelligence entitled "CIA POLITICIZATION," September 30, 1991, p. 6.

90 Ibid.

91 Ibid.

92 Ibid.

93 Webster maintained a very modest work schedule. Even in the first few months of his tenure—in mid-1987 when he might have been expected to dive into a new job he was little trained to handle—his schedules featured short work days punctuated by extensive social and tennis commitments. He made his schedules available to his NIOs for a time, then withdrew them, possibly because their contents generated so much disdain. In his early days as DCI, Agency personnel quizzed acquaintances at the FBI about Webster. They heard that many Bureau personnel viewed Webster as "lazy"—a label that soon was common at Langley as well.

94 This man later became director of the Office of Security, which for several years at least used alleged security concerns to harass internal critics of DI management. This irresponsible activity helped prompt at least one law suit against the Agency.

95 Exec. Rept. 102-19, October 24, 1991, p. 166.

96 Ibid., p. 207.

CHAPTER FIVE

LESSONS OF THE 1991 GATES NOMINATION FOR DCI

President George Bush's nomination of Robert Gates to be Director of Central Intelligence on May 14, 1991, and the nearly six month process to confirm him, provided a good look at the strengths and weaknesses of Congressional, and particularly Senate, oversight of intelligence. The process also showed how the Agency moves to protect its interests—in this case by supporting the nomination. I believe CIA came close, at the very least, to overstepping its bounds as an executive branch agency simply serving the will of a president.

The Senate Select Committee on Intelligence began its preparations for confirmation hearings with the legacy of Gates' abortive 1987 nomination in mind. Gates withdrew his name from consideration after hearings began, when questions about his involvement in, and knowledge of, the Iran-contra affair provoked significant Committee opposition to him. The Bush Administration clearly believed that because no new Iran-contra revelations had surfaced, Gates had a credible record as a White House aide, and Gates had been actively courting senators to "rehabilitate" himself, the proceedings would go smoothly. Bush himself declared he had "no qualms at all" about reopening old questions; of preliminary talks with SSCI members, he declared himself "very, very pleased with the way they have gone … All will be well."[1] SSCI Chairman David L. Boren, who backed Gates in 1987, immediately declared him "an extremely able and non-partisan professional in the intelligence field."[2]

The White House and Senator Boren made two misjudgments, however. They failed to account for the possibility of new information from former operations officer (and head of the Agency's Central American Task Force) Alan D. Fiers about Iran-contra. Fiers on July 9 pleaded guilty to two misdemeanor charges of lying to Congress and promised to cooperate with prosecutors, which precipitated a recess in the Gates hearings during the summer.[3] They also did not anticipate the flurry of charges leveled about Gates' performance in senior positions at CIA, most by his former subordinates in the DI. These charges, and the press attention given them, threw the Committee off its planned schedule. By late September a staffer, who claimed he represented the views of his senator, said, "The process is no longer under control in any way."[4]

The SSCI staff began its preparations even before the nomination formally reached the Senate and the Committee on June 24. The staff asked Gates some 80 questions, to which he responded on June 28. For a month, according to staffers, the Committee had little except vague stories about Gates' role in politicization of analysis. By mid-June, however, former employees began to come forward with specific accusations, particularly Gates' handling of analysis on the Soviet Union, and general criticisms of his management of the DI. Some of these people provided details on politicization—including some of those in chapters 3 and 4—and provided names of Agency employees who could corroborate the charges.

Consistent as they were with the rumors it had heard, the staff began to investigate the allegations. Staff members called CIA employees and requested testimony from a former SOVA office director and a National Intelligence Officer. The staffers indicated that they were available for comments from employees; by late August, according to a reporter with contacts on the SSCI, over two dozen current and former employees voluntarily had stepped forward to criticize Gates. The *Los Angeles Times* in August quoted separate backers of Gates as saying, "They've come out of the trenches screaming," and that CIA employees said Gates told Soviet analysts "to write a certain way, especially on the Soviet Union."[5] The *Times* quoted a senior Committee source as saying, "We are looking at all of the allegations, but those (the allegations of slanting analyses) are the ones we are taking most seriously because they go to the heart of the nature of the intelligence institution."[6] According to a *Los Angeles Times* source, "Gates' use of his office for policy purposes is documented and broader than what has been brought to light so far."[7] By late July, according to a staffer, the SSCI staff had largely completed its investigation of politicization and the larger question of intellectual integrity; maneuvering by both sides continued, however, through the start of hearings proper.

The hearings began on September 16 and initially went well for Gates. He had prepared well and offered a series of apologies for fairly minor failures like not asking enough good questions soon enough as the Iran-contra scandal was unfolding. These *mea culpas* clearly satisfied a number of senators to the point that Senator Howard Metzenbaum declared on the evening of September 16 that Gates had the votes to carry the Committee and by extension the full Senate.[8] His prognosis was good. The Iran-contra issue faded further when Alan Fiers offered but weak criticism of Gates and did not implicate him in any Iran-contra activities. Other witnesses repeated earlier testimony about when and under what circumstances Gates was informed of Iran-contra activities.[9] To this point, Gates appeared secure.

On September 25, the Committee held closed door hearings on allegations of improprieties concerning the sharing of intelligence with Iraq in the mid-1980s, and charges that Gates politicized intelligence.[10] At the conclusion of the latter, which included the charges of Mel Goodman, Jennifer Glaudemans, and Hal Ford, the Committee decided to discuss the politicization issue openly. The testimony had been explosive and the Committee decided to air the charges publicly.

Thus, on October 1, the Committee again met in open session and heard from Mel Goodman, Graham Fuller, Hal Ford, and NIO for Strategic Programs Larry Gershwin. On October 2, Jennifer Glaudemans and Doug MacEachen testified; late in the day, the six who had testified about the politicization issue, for and against Gates, sat in a panel before the senators. Gates returned for public responses on October 3 and the morning of October 4, and met the Committee one last time in private on the afternoon of October 4. The SSCI met again on October 18, voting to report the nomination favorably and recommend confirmation.

The full Senate began its debate on the Gates nomination on November 4. Senator Sam Nunn said he would vote for Gates with some reluctance. Senator Arlen Specter, a sharp Gates critic in 1987 scheduled to return to the Committee as ranking Republican in January 1993 (if re-elected in 1992), remained quiet. When the votes were tallied on November 5—nearly 6 months after his nomination—Gates was confirmed 64-31 in the most divided vote ever for Director of Central Intelligence. Bush's partisan pressure was effective; all 42 Republicans present voted for confirmation, including Specter.

The Gates confirmation process offers some insights into the nature and effectiveness of Congressional intelligence oversight. Some are reassuring to me, some are not comforting. The observations of the next 20 paragraphs spring from thoughts and information based on my own experiences with the Committee, those of current and former DI employees, published reports, journalists' observations, and the comments of current and former Congressional oversight committee staff members. The Committee's staff directors decided not to grant my request for a discussion of the confirmation process.[11]

The personal role of Senator Boren was pivotal to Gates' confirmation. Senate Majority Leader George Mitchell, in announcing his opposition, said that, if approved, Gates "will owe that confirmation to one person, and one person only, and that is Senator Boren."[12] By numerous accounts, Boren was a personal champion of Gates; his enthusiasm, again by many accounts, reflected the development of a strong personal relationship with Gates. New DCI Gates acknowledged Boren's special role in his confirmation ceremony remarks, saying Boren "spared no effort on my behalf."[13] Thus, once again, Robert Gates' ability to impress and befriend people who could do him good was instrumental in securing a promotion. It is a powerful lesson in bureaucratic politics.

Gates began to court Boren at least as early as 1985, when it became clear that Boren probably would soon be the ranking Democrat on the Committee and remain so for six years. Boren's Democratic seniors on the Committee were in line for leadership positions—and chairmanships after the Democrats regained control of the Senate in 1986—on more prestigious committees. Gates made a point of courting Boren at hearings—making special greetings and chit-chatting before and after sessions—and called Boren regularly with flattery and tidbits of intelligence information. These calls continued while Gates was DDI, DDCI, and deputy national security advisor at the White House. Boren responded by inviting Gates to social events attended by the socially and politically powerful in Washington. Some of my contacts speculated that Boren may have wanted to atone somewhat for his abrupt withdrawal of support for Gates in 1987 after Iran-contra concerns blossomed. In any case, by 1991 the relationship was solid; Gates' "recruitment" of Boren—the word of one of my Congressional sources—was complete.

By the spring of 1991, when Judge Webster finally stepped down, Gates' rehabilitation through service as a hard-working White House staffer was well underway and President Bush found a willing Gates supporter in Boren. With Bush able to count on the Committee's Republicans, and the chairman on board, the nomination was off to a good start. Boren and Vice Chairman Frank Murkowski, working through the staff directors, began the process of confirming Gates.

Staff directors George Tenet and John Moseman moved to expedite the confirmation in at least two ways: by picking staffers to do the investigative leg work who were at least somewhat sympathetic to Gates; and, by increasing strictures on releases of information about Gates and the proceedings to the press (and thus to me as well). These efforts did not constitute a white-wash, however, and I believe the staff ultimately did some good, objective work.

The confirmation process indicated clearly that SSCI oversight long had failed in a key respect: prior to the testimony of former and current analysts specifically related to the Gates nomination, much of the Committee membership and staff had little idea of how CIA analysis is produced and thus little understanding of how politicization could occur. They thus were in no position to identify it, let alone move to correct it. Some staffers demonstrated this ignorance by actions, questions, and attitudes—some simply presumed that politicization occurred regularly and thought it was normal business—while others candidly admitted ignorance. Of some 25 SSCI professional staffers, about 10 had any actual experience working in any agency of the intelligence community.[14]

While they started from a surprisingly poor knowledge base many staff people, especially the dozen or so staffers committed as a "core group" to the confirmation proceedings, seem to have done a decent job.[15] They interviewed "hundreds" of witnesses and reviewed "thousands" of documents.[16] Qualitatively, many of them also appear to have done well; my discussions with people with whom the staff spoke yielded reports of professionalism and objectivity, although a minority view is much less charitable. By October, many of the staffers seem to have acquired a much better understanding of both the processes and problems of DI analysis than they had in May. The staffers, including "designees" representing specific senators, also were in substantially greater general agreement about the meaning of their findings than their masters, although some sharp differences remained.[17] Some staffers of Republican senators were much less supportive of Gates than their bosses, for example.

Some of the staffers, however, appear to have acted as

advocates as well as investigators—not unlike the senators themselves. At least one former DI employee is convinced that some staffers quickly passed the details of accusations by former analysts, including the names of people who could corroborate the charges, directly to Gates and later to the Agency. The value of this is clear. It allowed Gates and his partisans at Langley to prepare responses in advance; it gave Agency officials opportunities to monitor prospective witnesses still with CIA and prepare warnings that employees should not be cooperative. Such activity was not new; it was consistent with SSCI practices during Gates' 1987 confirmation hearings, when Boren himself reportedly passed accusations to Gates prior to the hearings. A major aim of Gates' rehabilitation campaign in 1987-91 presumably was to assure such help again.

The process revealed a SSCI membership not particularly devoted to intelligence oversight. The state of ignorance caused by this lack of dedication continued to the end of the proceedings in the view of several of my interlocutors, and was a source of some staff frustration. I heard variants of essentially three reasons for a level of ignorance and disinterest substantially greater than that of the Committee's staff; these go well beyond the obvious one that senators are busy people with many responsibilities who have staff experts for just that reason. First, SSCI membership is not a "politically profitable" assignment and does not, on narrow political grounds, justify the expenditure of time and energy members need to become effective. According to this reasoning, many voters "outside the [Washington] Beltway" do not care about such matters; the letters to members concerning the nomination of Clarence Thomas to the Supreme Court, which occurred entirely within the period of the Gates confirmation process, were substantially more numerous.

Second, some members find intelligence matters uninteresting. While there usually is a substantial number of applicants to Senate leaders for assignment to the "select" committee, some senators who gain membership anticipating exotic secrets find the work and products of intelligence fairly mundane, and thus lose interest.[18] Clearly there are exceptions to this generalization; some senators have maintained lively interests and acquired considerable expertise.

Third, directly concerning the Gates nomination, the members were tired of Iran-contra. The issue had been covered extensively, and they did not want to rehash it. The Committee staff uncovered additional Iran-contra information during its Gates investigation, according to one of my contacts, that the senators did not want to see for this reason. According to another source, the Committee had access to an extremely sensitive intelligence document, which Gates also received prior to his alleged notification of Iran-contra by Charlie Allen, which raised questions about Gates' memory or truthfulness about what he knew of the operation.[19] According to someone who has read the document, it also suggests a good possibility that senior US government officials, contrary to stated policy, were content to maintain American hostages in Lebanon as a justification for continued arms sales to Iran, which generated the funds that went to the Contras. In essence, according to this conspiracy hypothesis, very senior government officials decided to let the hostages rot to keep money flowing to the Contras. The senators may not have wanted to address a possibility that had potentially dire implications for the Bush Administration.

Whatever the reason, at least two Democratic senators apparently were quite uninterested in the politicization issue until as late as September. Newspaper accounts of staff research, not so much the staffers' efforts themselves, prompted the senators' interest; the leaks, and publication of SSCI information, were the catalysts for increased attention. Senator Alfonse D'Amato was absent from the hearings much of the time; he largely restricted his interest to the Agency's coverage of the 1981 attempt to assassinate Pope John Paul II.

Additionally, the president's extreme pressure made the final tally less a vote on Gates than one for George Bush. If the vote actually had been on Gates, in the very similar words of two of my Congressional contacts, the outcome would have been much different. With the decision foregone for some senators, there was no point in examining the evidence.

The list of witnesses called to testify before the senators themselves indicates a group decidedly pro-Gates. This presumably was part of the Boren/White House effort to "rig" the testimony, as one of my Congressional contacts described it, to confirm him. Of the dozen or so witnesses, only three were known in advance to be anti-Gates: Tom Polgar with an Iran-contra focus, and Mel Goodman and Jennifer Glaudemans with concerns about analysis. Bobby Inman was an unabashed cheerleader for Gates. John McMahon was unenthusiastically supportive. Graham Fuller was a Gates fan, linked to him at the hearings at least by Goodman's criticism of both concerning their handling of the 1985 SNIE on Iran; Fuller could defend his own reputation by defending Gates. Current Agency employees had conflicts of interest that should have rendered their testimony suspect; Charlie Allen, Dick Kerr, Doug MacEachen, and Larry Gershwin would have to work for Gates if, as seemed likely from the beginning, he was confirmed. The Committee clearly expected Hal Ford to support Gates and must have been very surprised when he changed his opinion.

The Committee focused on aspects of Gates' qualifications that related only to his own specific words and deeds. They thus ruled out any broad investigation of the effectiveness and general implications of Gates' management or mismanagement. They appear to have done this for several reasons. The main ones related to the inability to attach to Gates specific responsibility for the actions of his subordinates; the SSCI thus declined to hold him, as a man once firmly in charge of the DI, at least, to any "bottom line" accountability for the continuing problems of CIA. Another was that any such assessment would require a thorough understanding of the management aspects of the Agency, which the SSCI did not have and was in no position to develop quickly. The Committee thus largely ignored a major part of the complaints of Gates' critics from the DI. It seemed content to place the recognized troubles of the Agency in the 1980s on the gravestone of William Casey alone.

Committee members displayed varying levels of enthusiasm

for real cross-examination of Gates, and allowed him to avoid responses to sharp attacks; he virtually ignored Jennifer Glaudemans' comments in his 20-point response to his critics, for example. They also allowed Gates to select evidence carefully to make his points while ignoring potentially damaging documents.[20] In my view, only Senators Metzenbaum on Iran-contra, and Bradley on politicization, displayed real energy in their questioning.

Despite the additional knowledge gained, and Gates' own call for restoration of a sub-committee devoted to analysis, there appears little chance of fundamental changes in the institutions of oversight that could better identify or redress current or future problems in CIA analysis or intelligence generally.[21] SSCI spokesman Zach P. Messitte and House intelligence committee spokesman Mike Sheehy told me their committees planned no significant new procedures or initiatives as a result of the hearings.[22] Presumably some of the same considerations that led then-Chairman David Durenberger to eliminate sub-committees in the SSCI in 1985 still apply. At the top of the list is the fact that they dilute the power of the chairman. The HPSCI, by contrast, has sub-committees and arguably a more involved membership. Similarly, there appears to be no interest in increasing day-to-day tracking of the Agency's conduct; the long aversion to "micro-management" seems to be intact.

Boren and the Committee won clear acceptance from Gates of the principle of oversight. Gates commented, for example:

> "I think that it's clear that people [CIA employees] have to be completely forthcoming with the Committee because if you are not willing to go beyond the question that is asked, then you are going to get the kind of crises that took place ... in the first half of the 1980s where tremendous misunderstandings occurred and there really is no confidence."[23]

Boren repeatedly cited the importance of Gates' acceptance of oversight, listing it as a critical reason for his support in his message to the full Senate after the SSCI vote to recommend confirmation.[24] The Committee's concern stemmed heavily from repeated half-truths and periodic lies by CIA officers that mislead the Committee about issues it considered important. These concerns continued well after Casey's death, were not stopped by Webster's coterie of lawyers at Langley, and obviously continued through late 1991 in Boren's mind.

The confirmation process, in sum, revealed warts about oversight generally, and the confirmation process in particular, as well as about Gates himself. The Committee's leaders seemed determined to have their way in advance, but were forced largely by the charges of analysts—reported by the press and a relatively objective Committee staff—to make the process look at least fairly open. The partisanship, and uncharacteristic behavior like Senator Warren Rudman's shrill personal attacks on Mel Goodman, nevertheless leave the Committee looking less than completely successful at attending to the "people's" business. The SSCI, nevertheless, certainly fared better than the Judiciary Committee after its nearly simultaneous handling of Anita Hill's sexual harassment charges against then-Supreme Court nominee Clarence Thomas.

Will Congressional oversight of CIA, Gates, and intelligence generally be any better for the confirmation process? I expect the improvement to be modest. Gates' promises of commitment to oversight may help, but his history of trying to satisfy those who can help or hurt him remains; Gates has a president to satisfy as well. Gates can say pretty words while doing little to change the long standing distrust of Congress in CIA—especially in the DO but in the DI as well. The revelations did not persuade the oversight committees to do their business in fundamentally different ways.

The education of the staff, and its increased sensitivity to the issue of politicization, cannot but help, however. The process also provided information to the HPSCI and should be somewhat beneficial for it as well. This may be the most important plus of the process. Some institutional memory will remain over time, even as regular turnover and frustration with

SSCI work take their toll. The education process may have a long-term benefit if Gates opponents Howard Metzenbaum or Dennis DeConcini take the chairmanship after Boren's six-year term as chairman (and his tenure on the Committee) ends in late 1992. Moreover, open testimony revealed much of how the DI actually works, and a more informed citizenry cannot help but improve oversight of the oversight committees themselves.

* * *

CIA officials moved quickly after Bush announced the nomination to support Gates actively in several ways. In June, apparently after learning that the SSCI was talking with DI personnel about their experiences with Gates—a reflection of information provided to the SSCI by former and perhaps current Agency employees—DDI John Helgerson reportedly wrote a letter to DI personnel informing them that they could, but did not have to, talk with SSCI staffers. This less than full cooperation with a Congressional committee had to have been read instantly by people long experienced at reading management nuances as a warning not to talk to the SSCI. It constituted, I believe, overt interference with the Committee's work.

For a time, this message appears to have been somewhat effective in stifling employees' cooperation with the SSCI. The Committee's investigators initially encountered reluctance among current Agency employees to talk about Gates, according to SSCI spokesman Messitte, and only got much greater cooperation after the media reports about charges of politicization; these presumably made clear to employees that the issue was prominent and that charges came from several sources, offering some hope of insulation against retribution.[25] Eventually, the Committee talked with approximately 80 current and former DI employees with analytical backgrounds.[26] Of these, about 30 were former employees and roughly 50 were then-current CIA officers.[27] The current employees who stepped forward were from SOVA, RTT, NESA, ALA, and EURA, at least. Late in the process, the initial early stream of negative comments from current and former employees became more balanced—that is, more favorable commentary reached the Committee. The Agency evidently began to appreciate the damage done to Gates' cause by these communications, and apparently decided it could play that game as well by encouraging some employees to make what amounted to off-setting calls.

At least one Agency office began preparing information for use by Gates himself almost immediately after the nomination in May. Senior managers of the office indicated that their work was designed to help prepare Gates for the confirmation hearings; many Agency observers of his testimony before the SSCI in 1987 regarded his performance as poor when he was asked questions he had not expected. This office's management could not have decided to do this preparation on its own; given Agency practices, the work almost certainly was approved by the head of the directorate and either DCI Webster or DDCI Kerr, or both.

According to several sources, DI people in very large numbers worked to help Gates defend himself against charges of politicization during early October. Their work involved searching for documents and writing papers to help Gates draft his 20-point rebuttal, in particular; they thus were not doing their normal work and were supporting a nominee then working for another component of the government—highly unusual behavior. The Agency selectively declassified documents designed to buttress Gates' position—including two reprinted in this volume—and appears to have acted with varying speeds to make available to the SSCI documents the Committee requested—undoubtedly to hurry favorable documents to the Committee and delay less helpful or harmful ones. It sent attorneys to the hearings. In addition, the National Intelligence Council, under the control of Acting DCI Dick Kerr in October 1991, supported Gates' arguments by forwarding NIEs to the Committee.

Stanley Moskowitz, CIA's senior Congressional liaison officer as head of the Office of Congressional Affairs and a former senior DI manager, actively worked for Gates before and during the hearings.[28] Moskowitz reportedly passed information on testimony to Gates directly, and since mid-summer regularly read Committee documents outlining the course of the investigation and, thus, the nature of the charges against Gates. This practice raises questions in my mind about both the conduct of CIA's Congressional liaison function and the propriety of the SSCI's actions as well. (Certainly this policy is consistent with Boren's favorable view of Gates and his eagerness to gain a confirmation vote, but does it indicate a degree of on-going cooperation that compromises the principle of oversight?)

According to a DI employee, the head of the PDB staff told White House interlocutors during the first week of the hearings—when Gates appeared to have addressed most SSCI concerns about the Iran-contra affair—that CIA employees were "ecstatic" at Gates' good showing. It is hard for me to believe that this was anything but a deliberate lie intended to deceive the White House staff, and thus Bush, about the depth of the antipathy toward Gates within the Agency. Some intelligence officers might call this comment "disinformation."

The Public Affairs Office chimed in, in mid-July, with a description of Gates as "uniquely qualified." Spokesman Peter Earnest told the *Washington Post*, "He'll be an outstanding DCI and we need him."[29] I was surprised by this overt partisanship and called the Public Affairs Office for clarification; another PAO officer, after talking with Earnest, confirmed the accuracy of the quote.

During the hearings, former DCI Webster and his aide Mark Matthews denied sworn statements by Carolyn Ekedahl and Mel Goodman that Matthews had conducted an "informal investigation" in 1987 into charges that Gates had politicized analysis.[30] Matthews wrote a letter to the SSCI saying that he had indeed met with two analysts about problems in the DI but that, in essence, they were inconsequential:

> "... Judge Webster never in any way, at any time, asked me to conduct an investigation of the DDCI and

accordingly, never asked me to keep any such investigation secret from the DDCI.

"With respect to the alleged investigation, I believe that Mr. Goodman is referring to an incident in the late spring or early summer of 1988, when I met a Soviet analyst named Jennifer Glaudemans. During ... conversation, the subject of the DDCI came up, and Ms. Glaudemans related some concerns about the DDCI's objectivity within the Soviet analytical division and alleged personnel changes designed to further the DDCI's analytical views. ... Neither prior to nor during my meeting with Ms. Glaudemans did I consider the meeting an 'investigation' of the DDCI.

"I also recall another brief meeting in my office on this same topic to which Ms. Glaudemans brought another Soviet analyst... During that meeting, the other analyst expressed concern about the DDCI learning of the meeting, and I assured her that I would keep their names to myself. Perhaps this is the genesis of Mr. Goodman's testimony about something being kept from the DDCI. Mr. Goodman also states that I made calls, including one to him. I do not remember making any such calls or ever speaking with or meeting with Mr. Goodman. (I suppose it is possible that I had a very brief conversation with him if a particular allegation needed to be clarified or if Ms. Glaudemans or the other analyst indicated that he wanted to speak with me.)"[31]

The opposing positions were very different indeed about rather simple matters of fact—whether there was an inquiry or not, and in what year the conversations occurred. It seems rather clear that someone either was lying or extremely forgetful. Webster and Matthews had to deny the charge or obfuscate—or risk delivering a major blow to Gates' credibility at a critical time in the hearings. While I cannot determine the truth of the matter, the Ekedahl/Goodman version, Goodman's comment that Jennifer Glaudemans could speak about Matthews, and Goodman's statement that he had discussed the matter with someone in the Office of the Inspector General, lend it plausibility.[32] So does the historical pattern of dishonesty by senior CIA managers about the foibles and attributes of other senior managers. The SSCI apparently chose to ignore these inconsistencies in its late deliberations; nor did it ask what, if anything, Matthews did with information of serious charges about the character of the Deputy Director. And why or why not? I suspect that the truth of the competing claims may be relatively simple to establish.

These actions, both early and late in the confirmation process, indicate that senior CIA officials actively supported Gates' candidacy. They took actions beyond those normal for government officials passively supporting the decision of a president about a nominee to lead their department or agency. These CIA officials assumed roles beyond the norm, apparently on their own initiative. Their actions arguably constitute a conflict of interest.

Why would Agency officers so strenuously back Gates and risk charges that they lied or injected the Agency into a domestic political debate—a potential violation, in an extreme case, of the Agency's charter? I believe there are at least four major reasons. Agency personnel, remembering Gates' past practices of rewarding people he liked, wanted to be on record supporting him. Others, also remembering those practices, feared that inaction would be perceived as a lack of support punishable by new DCI Gates or his zealous supporters. Some—if my survey is right a small minority—genuinely supported Gates. Finally, those senior officials who had collaborated actively with Gates—like Kerr and several of the office directors—needed to support him to protect their own personal interests. Especially after the integrity-related charges surfaced, a Senate repudiation of Gates would have meant a slap at them as well—one that presumably could have led to remedial action including dismissals by another DCI. The personal stakes for these senior miscreants thus became great.

During the Gates hearings' third week, Agency managers may again have acted to protect Gates, this time by stifling employees' criticism of the nominee. In early October, as the scope of inquiry shifted increasingly to Gates' management style and charges of politicization, passions flared. On October 3, Senator Warren Rudman publicly accused Gates' critics, particularly Mel Goodman, of "McCarthyism, pure and simple."[33] That same day, ABC News reported that it had received word "from someone who had been warned not to come on our broadcast" that CIA employees John Hibbits and Carolyn Ekedahl had been told by superiors that their careers were "over" for contacting the SSCI with comments critical of Gates.[34] The SSCI reportedly investigated the report and found that it was false, but Senator Boren reassured Ekedahl that he would not permit retribution.[35] An ABC official later confirmed the network's report, however, and added that a prominent former CIA officer backed out of an appearance on Nightline after being warned by superiors at another government agency that he should not appear on the show.[36] Later, Boren praised "the courageous analysts" who cooperated with the committee and promised to intervene on their behalf "at the slightest hint of retribution."[37] On the day Gates was confirmed, Boren again made the point that as long as he remains in the Senate he would "intervene on their behalf at the slightest hint of retribution."[38]

The word nevertheless had been passed again by Agency managers that critics were subject to sanctions.[39] This kind of threat is consistent with managerial behavior toward "problem" employees who fail to toe analytical and bureaucratic lines; it would be surprising if vindictive Gates allies do not retaliate against such "disloyalty" in the future, regardless of Boren's assurances. Senator Boren, so strong in his defense of Gates and so incongruously redundant in his expressions that Gates' CIA better not retaliate against Gates' opponents, should be held strictly to his promise of protection.

Notes to Chapter 5

1 Ann Devroy and Tom Kenwothy, "Gates Nominated To Head the CIA," Washington Post, *May 15, 1991, P. A1.*

2 Ibid., p. A4.

3 Former Deputy Director for Operations Clair George, Alan Fiers' boss, later was indicted on Iran-contra charges by the office of independent counsel Lawrence E. Walsh. The charges against George played little role in the Gates hearings.

4 Elaine Sciolino, "Gates Almost a Side Issue in Hearings," New York Times, *October 1, 1991, p. A19.*

5 Douglas Jehl and Michael Ross, "Some in Agency Oppose Gates as CIA Chief," Los Angeles Times, *August 2, 1991, pp. A1 and A22.*

6 Ibid, p. A22.

7 Ibid.

8 Metzenbaum made his comments on ABC's Nightline program.

9 On September 19, the Committee heard from: Fiers; John McMahon, DDCI from 1982 to 1986; and, Tom Polgar, a retired operations officer who worked for the Senate committee investigating Iran-contra. The Committee recessed until September 24, when Dick Kerr and former NIO for Counter-terrorism Charles E. Allen testified on Iran-contra.

10 For a chronology of the nomination in the Senate, see Senate, Exec. Rept. 102-19, October 24, 1991, pp. 1-3.

11 On November 8, 1991, I asked press spokesman Zach P. Messitte for discussions with staffers. The next day, he told me that majority staff director George Tenet and minority staff director John Moseman had decided not to grant my request. Messitte explained that the Committee staff does not, as a matter of policy, grant interviews about process—a statement I later learned is incorrect.

12 Walter Pincus and George Lardner Jr., "Senate Confirms Gates as CIA Chief," Washington Post, *November 6, 1991, p. A4.*

13 CIA Employee Bulletin Number 2146, 18 November 1991, p. 3.

14 Press spokesman Zach P. Messitte provided these figures in telephone conversations on November 15 and 21, 1991.

15 According to SSCI spokesman Messitte, these dozen or so were most fully committed, but virtually all of the rest of the staff also participated to some extent in the Gates process.

16 Senate, Exec. Rept. 102-19, p. 2.

17 Professional staffers consist of two general types: long-term staffers and those designated by Committee members. These latter are known as "designees."

18 As a select committee, the SSCI receives its members on the basis of the selections of the party leaders, not via the normal committee assignment process.

19 The sensitive nature of the intelligence document makes it necessary to write somewhat obtusely in this paragraph to gain passage of even the concept of Gates' potential indiscretion through CIA security officers.

20 The press covered this issue in some detail. See, for example, Elaine

Sciolino with David Johnston, "In Rebuttal to Senate Committee, C.I.A. Nominee Is Truthful but Incomplete," New York Times, *October 13, 1991, p. 24.*

21 In point five of his 8-point reform program contained in his 3 October rebuttal comments, Gates said, "I encourage the [oversight] committees to consider re-establishing something like their old analysis and production subcommittees that can focus oversight on the analytic process."

22 Messitte commented in a phone conversation shortly after the confirmation vote. Sheehy commented in a February 3, 1992 telephone conversation, in which he also said the HPSCI was then conducting a study of the intelligence production process that was unrelated to the Gates hearings.

23 Senate, Exec. Rept. 102-19, October 24, 1991, p. 196.

24 Ibid., "Additional Views of Senator David L. Boren," pp. 200-211.

25 Messitte made these points in a telephone conversation on October 30, 1991.

26 Ibid. See also Senate, Exec. Rept. 102-19, p. 4.

27 SSCI spokesman Messitte provided these data in a telephone conversation on November 21, 1991.

28 Elaine Sciolino, "Gates Almost a Side Issue in Hearings," New York Times, *October 1, 1991, p. A19.*

29 Walter Pincus and George Lardner Jr., "Panel May Place Gates in Confirmation Limbo," Washington Post, *July 12, 1991, p. A16.*

30 See Ekedahl's Statement, p. 6, and Goodman's oral testimony contained in United States Senate, Transcript of Proceedings before the Select Committee, Nomination of Robert M. Gates to be Director of Central Intelligence, Evening Session, September, 25, 1991, p. 35. See Richard Grenier, "Intelligence Intermission," Washington Times, *October 9, 1991, p. F4. See also George Lardner Jr. and Walter Pincus, "GOP Senators Grill Gates Critics,"* Washington Post, *October 3, 1991, p. A31.*

31 Senate, Exec. Rept. 102-19, p. 167. See also George Lardner Jr. and Walter Pincus, "GOP Senators Grill Gates Critics," Washington Post, *October 3, 1991, p. A31.*

32 Ekedahl, "Statement," p. 6. See also Senate, Exec. Rept. 102-19, p. 166.

33 Walter Pincus and George Lardner Jr., "Gates Strikes Back At Critics in CIA," Washington Post, *October 4, 1991, pp. A1 and A8.*

34 Reported by Ted Koppel on the "Nightline" program. See also Benjamin Weiser, "Monolith or Bickering Analysts? Hearings Peel Back CIA's Veneer," Washington Post, *October 6, 1991, p. A23.*

35 Ibid.

36 Nightline producer Dan Morris on October 31, 1991 called ABC's source reliable. A former Agency employee told me cryptically that ABC may have misunderstood the communication; also according to this source, the Agency began an investigation but stopped when it realized that no one had charged that it tried to influence former employees.

37 George Lardner Jr., "Committee Approves Gates at CIA," Washington Post, *October 19, 1991, p. A12.*

38 Walter Pincus and George Lardner Jr., "Senate Confirms Gates as CIA Chief," Washington Post, *November 6, 1991, p. A4.*

39 Ingenious senior Agency bureaucrats can and regularly do find many ways of punishing less than pliant subordinates in ways that ostensibly are related only to job performance. These can include a range of subjective assessments about the "quality" of work, inexact comparisons to other employees with similar assignments, inherently imprecise judgments about "potential," and so on.

CHAPTER SIX

IMPLICATIONS OF CURRENT PRACTICES

The implications of DI practices and trends, especially in poorly managed offices, are extensive and negative. These deficiencies compromised the ability of the Central Intelligence Agency to perform its mission in the 1980s and continue to pose a threat to national security. They are financially and intellectually wasteful. They also abuse capable, conscientious employees, including good managers, who deserve much better.

While elements of the DI do very good work, an appreciable amount of product is notably poor. This has led to a continuing series of negative remarks and attitudes within the corridors of government, as well as the public critiques. The lack of respect for and confidence in DI reports lead policymakers to simply ignore CIA papers or, like then-Secretary of State George Shultz said in 1987 at Congressional hearings on the Iran-contra affair, "come to have grave doubts about the objectivity and reliability of some of the intelligence I was getting."[1] The *New York Times* quotes aides to Shultz as saying that the Secretary's concerns included both Casey and Gates.[2] The State Department's intelligence arm—the Bureau of Intelligence and Research, or INR—has become so unhappy with CIA analysis that for years it routinely refused to coordinate on *National Intelligence Daily* articles.[3]

DI analysis sometimes is biased, and even senior Agency

officials sometimes admit it. A director of SOVA in the late 1980s and early 1990s claimed his predecessor had politicized SOVA analysis. Robert Gates also recognized obliquely that politicization existed in his own organization. In his 1988 *Foreign Affairs* article, discussing bias in analysis, Gates wrote, "More serious is the accusation that an institutional bias affects CIA's work. I believe there probably is bias in some areas, in a broad sense."[4] He did not, however, follow up the comment with an explanation or a proposal for remedial action.

DI analysis often fares poorly in government officials' comparisons to other sources of news and analysis. For example, several then-current and former National Security Council staffers have told me that they prefer INR's publications to CIA products. Some executive branch and Congressional oversight committee personnel say they prefer good local and national newspaper analyses over the Agency's. Senator Patrick Leahy, a former SSCI member, repeatedly has said that the major difference between the NID and the *New York Times* is that the *Times* has a crossword puzzle.[5] (Some DI people would argue that the comment insults the *Times*). Others fault intelligence for providing comparable news later than the press—a dysfunction of the multi-layered review process. Cable News Network has become the standard for current intelligence reporting among many US intelligence organizations and is usually on in watch offices at CIA, throughout Washington, and in military command centers. Moreover, readers of CIA analysis often fault its literary style—the object of so much time, effort, and misguided internal pride. Some prefer INR's more personal style while finding Agency products overly encumbered with rigid formats and phrases like "we believe ..." and "according to a generally reliable source ...." At the same time, they complain that the coordination process pushes judgments toward blandness, leaving them unsure of the message of papers—just what Gates claimed in 1982 he wanted to end.[6]

The enormous effort at cultivating consumers, at so much cost in terms of slanted analysis and missed opportunities, still fails to impress key constituencies. A senior Congressional intelligence committee staffer told me in June 1991 that, of all the elements of the intelligence community, only CIA's Directorate of Operations does a worse job of representing its interests to his committee; DO officers, he believed, transparently treated committee staffers as potential agents to be recruited. Another oversight committee staffer in July 1991 called the leadership of Webster and Kerr "weak." Consumers unhappy with the politicized and often poor work of the Office of Soviet Analysis turned in the late 1980s to the Office of Leadership Analysis for assessments of Soviet political affairs; an LDA manager confirmed to me in 1990 that the office was responding favorably despite SOVA's ostensible responsibility for Soviet politics and policies while LDA's mandate covered only the makers of the policies.

These consumer attitudes reflect damaged credibility of DI analytical work on a daily basis, but they are potentially devastating to the ability of the Agency to provide warning of a serious threat to the nation. The history of Pearl Harbor and other disasters demonstrates clearly that good information and sound analyst judgment are not sufficient to elicit significant government responses. Warnings must be clear and persuasive if they are to generate action. The Agency's reputation for mediocre daily performance and recurrent, serious concerns about its objectivity hinder its ability to produce convincing warning messages about a genuine threat. I believe the debilitating effects of a lack in confidence by policymakers in the integrity and relevance of CIA analysis are hard to overemphasize. These are far more important, in my view, than any general popular feeling about the "standing" or "good name" of CIA.[7]

The Agency's propensity to avoid controversy means that it is likely to be conservative in sending warning messages until a potential threat is more apparent—and the value of warning is thereby reduced. Managers at each level are prone to ask, "Are you sure?" for bureaucratic as well as intellectual reasons before passing prospective warnings up the chain. On a daily basis, this accounts for the much complained-about tendency of DI analysis to make tentative judgments and forecasts or, as Eliot Cohen puts it, "to weasel."[8]

The hierarchical nature of analysis (including review) and strong bureaucratic incentives for analysts simply to accept intellectual instructions has a chilling effect on creativity—with major implications for the quality of CIA analysis. Analysts have resigned specifically citing the lack of opportunity for initiative and creativity.[9] Work is assigned. Too many of those who remain labor under varying degrees of intellectual orthodoxy—with acceptable bounds of inquiry and judgment established by office directors and enforced by middle managers driven primarily by bureaucratic imperatives. Mid-level managers committed to their bosses' opinions, for either ideological or bureaucratic reasons, enforce the primacy of those views with varying forms of intimidation.

The tendency of senior managers to micro-manage and micro-edit also means that they have comparatively little time to spend developing strategic visions for their units—a standard mission of senior executives. Often unwilling to solicit or to accept input from their subordinates, they tend to react to comments from their seniors, to outside queries, and to external criticism. DI offices' organization and research programs thus, in important respects, lag the development of both foreign events and government officials' reactions to those events.[10] They thus are hard pressed to anticipate or convincingly warn.

The urge to address immediate issues and to publish leaves sometimes gaping holes in coverage of topics that could explode in the future. For example, bureaucratic squabbling between SOVA and EURA in the mid-1980s left a gap in DI coverage of Warsaw Pact defense capabilities that happily now is harmless. The issue involved coverage of low priority defense activities that were of relatively modest concern and did not generate papers, but which took analyst time to track. Each claimed the other had responsibility, so both ignored the issue. When SOVA decided to drop coverage, it simply delivered files to a EURA division, whose management promptly directed that the files be destroyed. Most were. Analysts who recognized that they might one day be helpful squirreled away the rest.

Separately, EURA for years ignored the militaries of two countries in a volatile corner of the continent—Yugoslavia and Albania—being content to devote modest analysts' time to the way the military of Yugoslavia entered domestic political battles. Repeated analyst observations over the course of years about the oversight to both EURA management and the Office of the Inspector General stimulated no remedial action of any kind. Yugoslavia became violently unstable and dissolved in 1991-92. EURA's years of neglect undoubtedly hindered the DI's ability to address elementary aspects of the federal military and those of the break-away states like order of battle, doctrine, equipment, logistical stocks, and so on. Managerial incompetence, not poor analyst performance, is ultimately responsible for any intelligence failures stemming from CIA's lack of understanding of the Yugoslav military.

The basic intellectual conservatism of management contributes to what probably is a very common intelligence failure—the failure to alert policymakers of opportunities to exploit. No one knows how frequently these occur. The opposite of warning of the threats, this intelligence function gets relatively little press or academic analysis.[11] Nevertheless, intelligence information and judgments can provide opportunities to win foreign friends, head off undesirable foreign alliances, to avert misunderstandings, to overcome obstacles to trade pacts, and so on. The list of potential opportunities is very long. It is limited largely by the imagination of intelligence professionals (as well as the legal bounds and policy guidelines they work within). The inherently difficult intelligence task of divining the meaning of mysteries before they become histories is still harder when management tacitly or explicitly discourages imagination and creativity.

Management has little incentive to redress such failures. They are bureaucratically safe. No Congressman or oversight committee is likely to complain about the lack of warning about a situation he/it does not know existed. On the other hand, a botched policy initiative to exploit such intelligence information could lead to blame of the Agency, threatening bureaucratic and personal interests. Moreover, might not such creativity and initiative invite a new round of criticism that the Agency is running amok and making its own foreign policy?

The attrition of analysts is cutting expertise and threatening the quality of analysis. While low by the standards of fast food restaurants and the roughly eight percent annual level of other government agencies, DI attrition is higher than attrition in the other directorates and has led periodically to concerns even within DI management about shortages of expertise generally and some specific skills. Attrition tends to be particularly high in poorly managed offices, while vacancies for positions in the better-run units usually are filled internally.

Poorer managers generally reacted to attrition in the 1980s by stepping up recruiting rather than taking steps to redress grievances. They thus did a disproportionately large share of recruiting, staffing their offices with relatively inexperienced people happy to have jobs. Once these people understood their bosses' deficiencies, established a modest track record, and learned of other DI job opportunities, many perpetuated the situation by wisely moving on. The behavior and demands of these poor managers placed sometimes huge strains on these new employees when they were most vulnerable, and very early demonstrated the bureaucratic value of conformity to the detriment of the Agency's mission. There was and is little a job applicant or new employee can do to avoid these pressures.[12]

Poor management thus is often compounded by analyst inexperience, leaving the DI with a patchwork of units of widely varying talent and experience. Because position description by definition confers expertise and rigid turf rules guide the assignment of responsibilities, the DI may staff crises with groups of comparatively inexperienced personnel while truly expert individuals tend comparatively innocuous chores in other offices. The personal enmity that may have driven an experienced analyst to leave an office reduces further the odds that the management of that office will tap his expertise when it really is needed.

Attrition, driven in part by analyst unhappiness about management, affected negatively the ability of the Office of Near East and South Asian Analysis (NESA) to perform during the Persian Gulf war. Between the summer of 1989, when a new chief took over the division following the Gulf region, and the Iraqi invasion of Kuwait on August 2, 1990, over half of the division's analysts left. Some normally would have rotated, but the biggest impetus for many, according to a former NESA analyst who also left, was the poor management of the new chief. By the time of the allied counter-offensive Operation Desert Storm in early 1991, NESA was seriously short of experienced Persian Gulf analysts. It had lost half the analysts responsible for the Iraqi military; none of those remaining had followed the Iran/Iraq war, which ended in August 1988. The division also had lost a senior Iraqi political analyst, all its senior Iranian political analysts, and several political and military analysts following countries of the region that joined the allied coalition. Meanwhile, an experienced former Iraqi military analyst tended to other chores within NESA.

Years of poor management in the part of the Office of European Analysis responsible for Eastern Europe helped account, I believe, for CIA's lack of warning about the demise of communist regimes in much of the region in 1989. Turnover long was way above normal; analysts enjoyed, in ironic sorts of ways, comparing divisional rosters from year to year—calculating percentage turnover rates that ran well into three digits. In the wake of an IG inspection, a new office director fired three managers for cause in 1986 only to replace them with still worse managers, in the view of most division employees. Meanwhile, considerable expertise on Eastern and Central Europe is scattered throughout the Agency, wasted.[13] A somewhat similar situation is true of Latin American analysts. Mel Goodman told SSCI in 1991 of such losses of expertise on the USSR during the 1980s.

Ironically, this attrition has helped ameliorate one of Robert Gates' purported concerns about the Agency. Discussing the Directorates of Operations and Intelligence in a 1986 article, he wrote, "There is—unfortunately in my view—little flow of people serving in one directorate to positions in the other."[14] The increased flow in recent years—unfortunately in my view—has been largely to the DO and motivated strongly by escapism.

The often strict definition of analysts' duties and the rigors of the coordination process encourage narrowly defined intelligence products that may be of limited use to policymakers. The personnel management and rating system encourages solitary work, while job descriptions and turf concerns limit individual responsibilities. Hence, the organization itself encourages the lack of relevance in intelligence products to broad policy questions that critics often blame on analysts' flawed vision.

This problem is potentially more severe in offices following important intelligence topics; the very priority of these issues means larger allocations of personnel and correspondingly narrower individual responsibilities. Many analysts thus study trees while few watch the forest; they feed their analytic pieces for assembly into broad judgments by senior managers whose real expertise, if it ever existed, may under the best of circumstances have been current years ago when intellectual fashion potentially was very different. Former SOVA Director Douglas J. MacEachen put the issue similarly in trying to explain to the SSCI in October 1991 how the Agency had miscalled events in the turbulent Soviet Union of the late 1980s. He said the DI never approached the Soviet Union "as a society, and therefore, I think we were really not ready for the way to deal with the reactions when finally the lid did come up."[15]

The review process too often is not so much a real "review" process as it is a "rewrite" process. The basic management purpose in some cases is not to ensure overall standards of quality but to pass on specific thoughts and language. It thus becomes a censorship process as well, done in the name of ensuring quality; at its worst, it ensures the primacy of the personal views of a relative handful of senior managers.

The heavy emphasis on review is unaccompanied by significant management concern on the "production process" by which papers are conceived, researched, analyzed, and drafted. Indeed, there is no such commonly used term. While there is some training (heavily on DI writing style) and mentoring that most usefully conveys institutional knowledge, many managers normally assign projects and simply tell analysts to sink or swim on their own. False starts, delays, and frustration are common, especially among new analysts working on a major project for the first time. Teams are rare—despite their ability to provide assistance to junior analysts, boost quality, and improve the timeliness of projects—because managers claim that they cannot assess the work of individual members of teams.

The current production/review process is enormously wasteful of the considerable talents of analysts and the taxpayers' money. Essentially useless editing called review consumes vast amounts of time, and analysts often sit idle as papers wind through the review chain. The lack of real management of DI resources hurts analytic quality, timeliness, and the volume of papers printed even as it surely wastes millions of dollars annually.

Many analysts feel that managerial constraints on the kind and focus of acceptable analysis have atrophied their technical professional skills. In their view, management's emphasis on production—even if that means sitting around waiting for a reviewer—reduces analysts' ability to regenerate their intellectual capital, diminishing their ability to do their jobs. This fosters in some analysts the idea that they are trapped at CIA.

The personnel system's tendency to reward sameness and loyalty up (but not necessarily down) has severely negative implications for the Agency's ability to recruit and retain the diversity of background, experience, and even opinion that any good intelligence agency needs. Instead, DI preference for "team players" who "get along ..." perpetuates a similarity of background and world view. Some offices' active discouragement of real intellectual inquiry and open discussion of issues will contribute mightily to the intelligence failures of the future.

DI management's preference for sameness clashes with its recognized bureaucratic need to attain "cultural diversity" in the DI—defined as acquisition and maintenance of acceptable numbers of minority and women employees throughout the Directorate (and the Agency as well). Ever keen on appearances, the DI hired a retired black general officer who once commanded one of the Army's best known divisions to join its "multi-cultural" program. This man has talked with many Agency personnel who, he told me, believe that the entire program is little more than a shield to deflect criticism of the DI's demographic statistics. Ostensible DI efforts to increase real diversity, as well as the bureaucratic imperative to attain politically correct racial and sexual percentages, seem doomed when the Directorate is disinterested in intellectual diversity among even its male WASP employees. I believe the Agency's advertising efforts ostensibly designed to boost recruitment of minorities are similarly motivated.[16]

The DI's concentration on the short term has had negative consequences for intelligence collection, and thus the long-term abilities of analysis as well. Analytic offices provide sometimes significant guidance on priorities for both human and technical intelligence collection agencies. Because these organizations' resources are limited, efforts by analytic offices to satisfy immediate but transient policy community interests may preclude the development of information collection programs that are essential to the ability of the intelligence community to address key enduring questions, as well as those that will emerge over time.[17] Good examples relate to the abilities of potentially unfriendly countries to produce and field nuclear, chemical, and biological weapons. These development programs take years, are capital and construction intensive, and often involve technical contacts and contracts with foreigners. They may be much more vulnerable to monitoring when in development than after they are operational—when they receive the greatest policy community concern. Failure to maintain a modestly long-term time horizon when setting priorities for collection thus may diminish the abilities of the entire intelligence community for years.

The only major institutional check on this myopia and conservatism in analysis of all issues—the National Intelligence Officer for Warning—since 1988 damaged his personal credibility and that of the warning function generally by making a series of outlandish forecasts and by regularly displaying an unnecessarily combative demeanor.[18] At the same time, the NIO/W foolishly tried to compete with analytic offices to cover breaking current intelligence issues, thus abandoning his warning mission as described in a special, formal DCI Directive (or DCID, pronounced D-skid) on warning.

The Agency's increasing tendency in recent years to place intelligence advisory responsibilities in the hands of managers alone (without analysts' backup) has damaged the quality of intelligence provided to senior government officials. While anecdotes are numerous, I experienced one that shows both the method and consequences of shallow analysis. In the fall of 1988, the DI prepared a classified book for use by DCI Webster in his briefing of Democratic presidential candidate Michael Dukakis—consistent with similar intelligence briefs in earlier campaigns. The objective was to give Dukakis information on developing foreign events that could trigger political debate during the campaign; it aimed to level the political playing field by reducing the opportunity for a seasoned foreign policy insider like then-Vice President George Bush to exploit foreign developments.

Despite its knowledge of Webster's preference for simple briefings, the DI prepared one so lengthy and detailed that the Judge rejected it and turned instead to the NIO for Warning. I, as a senior analyst on the NIO/W's staff, helped prepare a new briefing. Recalling Webster's concerns, the NIO directed us to prepare a loose leaf book composed of discussions of 15 or so issues that might develop by early 1989. Each was printed in "bullet" style—short, sentence-length points placed on a single page—whatever the complexity of the issue. Each had a map on the facing page in deference to the Judge's well-known weakness on geography, as well as to provide the additional data—such as dates, figures, and short analytical judgments—that were printed on many of the maps. Intra-staff observations that the individual briefs were shallow and too short were irrelevant; the DCI's preferences and our marching orders were clear. After some long days, we completed our job on a Saturday afternoon prior to Webster's departure the next day. He thus had a fair amount of time to review our material, but to my knowledge did not talk to NIO/W or anyone on our staff as part of his preparation. When the Judge returned after the briefing, he passed his thanks and we went on to other things.

Much later, I learned how the briefing went from someone present at the meeting. Dukakis brought foreign policy and other campaign staff advisors. Others also attended. According to my source, the Judge stumbled badly when asked questions that our sheets did not cover explicitly, and the Dukakis camp assessed the briefing as poor. If Webster talked only from our book, I suspect it was indeed poor. I can think of no reason to believe Webster's performance was normally much better. This quality of work may help explain why Webster was not a major intelligence advisor to President Bush during the 1990-91 Iraq/Kuwait crisis and war, and why then-White House staffer Bob Gates played such a prominent role.

The sometimes haphazard oversight by Congress and willingness by executive branch departments to give CIA considerable latitude in determining its activities explains much of both the Agency's problems and consumers' unhappiness with CIA. I believe these consumers are at least partly to blame for the inadequacies of CIA analysis. Sherman Kent years ago warned of the dangers of a disinterested policy community or inadequate guidance by consumers to intelligence producers:

> "... the want of sharp and timely guidance is chief contributor to the worst sickness that can afflict intelligence. This is the sickness of irresponsibility. Intelligence loses the desire to participate in the thing to be accomplished; it loses the drive to make exactly the right contribution to the united effort. It becomes satisfied with

> dishing up information without trying to find out what lies behind the order for them, without trying to make sense out of what appears senseless. When intelligent and sensitive men reach this stage they are no longer either intelligent or sensitive; they begin behaving as dumb and unhappy automatons who worry, if at all, about the wrong things."[19]

Echoing Kent's concerns of the late 1940s, Robert Gates wrote in the 1980s:

> "For many years the CIA has struggled, largely in vain, to get policy officials to devote time to intelligence issues other than those directly related to a crisis. Agency officers work hard to ascertain what is required of them: what policymakers' priorities are, what issues or problems the CIA should address, how the CIA can help the Administration."[20]

Yet the same consumers who have on occasion provided too little guidance often hold intelligence to unusually high standards of accuracy and prescience. Indeed, critiques of intelligence "failures" are common, even when data that went into construction of the judgments are few and inconsistent, and forecasting horizons are long. Kent wrote:

> "... intelligence is bound to make mistakes. Some of the questions it is required to answer demand a divine omniscience; others demand more painstaking work than can be accomplished in the time allotment; still others can be had only with the most elaborate sort of undercover preparations which have never been made. But let intelligence make a mistake or come up with an inadequate answer and all too often the reaction of consumers is on the uncomprehending and bitter side: 'I wouldn't ask those geniuses to tell me how many pints there are in a quart.' ... For good reason or bad, an

> intelligence failure seems to rankle out of proportion to its importance, and to tend to justify the consumer in doing his own intelligence henceforth."[21]

The DI's severe sensitivity to criticism, eagerness to please, and tendency to deny even obvious failures stem in large part, I believe, from such consumer attitudes in combination with personal and bureaucratic insecurity of senior CIA officers.

Ironically, some of the DI's most insightful critics contribute to this problem. In the 1991 Gates confirmation process, for example, Senator Bill Bradley repeatedly was critical of Gates' failure to more aggressively pursue reports of Soviet economic problems, particularly those alleged by Soviet emigre economists. Perhaps Gates should have been more aggressive and perhaps SOVA should have been more receptive to these reports. There undoubtedly was room for improvement among the economists. The fact is, however, that the issue was a major topic of legitimate research, and many DI economists used the data available and a series of other techniques to acquire the best understanding they could of Soviet economic problems and prospects. This issue was an inherently difficult problem. Responding to such criticism, Gates properly noted that reasonable people could and did disagree. Senators Bradley and Daniel Patrick Moynihan—a former SSCI vice chairman and frequent critic of specific CIA judgments—encourage the Agency's propensity for intellectual conservatism by attacking specific judgments, rather than the systemic bureaucratic problems that lead to consistent biases and judgmental errors.

The DI's rigorous adherence to stylistic doctrine imposes significant substantive as well as administrative and financial costs. In ostensible efforts to present terse, understandable analyses to busy consumers, the DI too often makes style more important than substance. Sherman Kent also knew the substantive and psychological dangers of forced brevity:

> "The imposition of a word limit forces the intelligence producers to be clear in their thought and precise in their

> presentation, and it enables the hurried consumer to consume while he runs. But the result, while necessary, is by no means an unalloyed good. There is such a thing as a complicated idea; there is such a thing as so complicated an idea that it cannot be expounded in 250 words... The consumer who insists that no idea is too complicated for a 300-word summary is doing himself no favor. He is requiring the impossible and is paying heavily for it. He is paying in two ways: he is kidding himself in his belief that he really knows something, and he is contributing to the demoralization of his intelligence outfit. The intelligence people who spend weeks of back-breaking work on a substantive problem and come up with an answer whose meaning lies in its refinements are injured at the distortion that may occur in a glib summary from which all real meaning has been squeezed. Next time they go at such a problem they will have less enthusiasm for exhaustive work, will turn in a poorer study with a still poorer summary tacked on the front. This is not a plea for the harassed consumer or man of action to read all the hundreds of pages that come his way, but it is a plea for him to realize that there is a middle position and that as he lets it be known that he will read nothing longer than one single-spaced page, a good many of his most loyal and hardest workers are going to lose some of their fervor in serving him."[22]

DI management clearly has ignored Kent's pleas. Its stylistic requirements largely preclude policymakers from making format, length, and other requests even if they are so inclined. I once was assigned to prepare a written "briefing" for a senior intelligence community official that was not to exceed four typed lines in length. DI attrition figures indicate that a large number of hard working people have already lost fervor and left.

Many of those remaining who share the values of Sherman Kent are fighting an intense bureaucratic war with the proteges of Gates—the partisans of politicization and bureaucratic expediency who occupy so many of the senior positions of the Directorate. Those disturbed by the trends of recent years do the best they can to preserve standards of objective analysis and informally share anecdotes of poor management and politicization; they hope to catch managers in especially egregious misconduct, while having little faith that positive change will come soon.[23] The poor managers know they have enemies, and try to root them out and ruin careers where they can. The sides battle for the hearts and minds of fence-sitters and new employees. Suspicion is often great; loyalties often are suspect and transient. This internecine bureaucratic warfare is unpleasant and, at minimum, is not conducive to the concentrated cooperative effort needed for good intelligence analysis.

The demise of the Cold War, with its relatively simple conceptual (although not practical) nature, and the development of a host of new intelligence issues in areas like the proliferation of high-tech weaponry and economic rivalries among traditional Western political allies, for example, makes DI analytical myopia even more dangerous. According to the first director of the Office of Resources, Trade and Technology (RTT), the reorganization of the Office of Global Issues into RTT in June 1990 was a reaction to, rather than an anticipation of, policy concerns. Senior officials of the Intelligence Community Staff—a composite organization that mainly conducts coordination, planning, and collection management functions for the intelligence community as a whole—have expressed to me in recent years frustration with the lack of vision of the community led by Webster and Kerr. These officials properly note that the development of both human intelligence (HUMINT) and technical intelligence collection capabilities require long lead times, and that capabilities are most efficiently developed when they are designed to meet potential needs of policymakers, hopefully as identified in part by analytical offices, not only those of adventurers and engineers.

Time will tell if the Agency's claims that it is re-assessing itself amount to much more than a reaction to a Congressional recognition that the world is changing, and Congress' questions about what the Agency is doing to respond. I am skeptical that meaningful change was underway prior to the arrival of DCI Gates in November 1991. The "planning directorate" begun during the Webster years initially was but a renamed part of the DCI's staff. Gary Foster, the Deputy Director for Planning and Coordination, formerly headed an office in the Directorate of Administration—hardly the part of the Agency that sharpens one's ability to see intelligence requirements over the horizon.

I see nothing better at the DI level. For example, an assessment for the DDI of economic issues the Directorate is likely to face in the 1990s, prepared in 1990 by a group of mid-level DI managers, could have been snipped from mediocre financial press articles. Typically, it was of predetermined length and prepared within a tight deadline. It was the bland, uninspired work of a committee composed of individuals from offices with sometimes competing bureaucratic concerns.

The ultimate result of the DI's many problems is that the quality of DI analysis has suffered and probably will continue to deteriorate unless there are significant changes. This deterioration is concentrated in those areas requiring sophistication, technical proficiency or education, and in-depth analysis—where deteriorating analyst skills and the review process are most destructive. The damage is smaller in current intelligence publications, which are reporting media. Damage also is less in those areas relying heavily on technical means of collection because even very self-confident DI managers are reluctant to "review" imagery, for example. More importantly, the Office of Imagery Analysis has not suffered from the kind of poor management ravaging some of the regional offices and RTT. Thus, the objectivity of imagery analysis generally has been maintained.

The "DI culture" thus features many of the worst characteristics of a university department and the hierarchical structure of the military, with few of the advantages of either. The petulance, back-biting, and slow review of academe are common, while intellectual freedom is rare and intellectual integrity is sporadic. At the same time, imperious managers have military-like authority over ideas as well as legitimate management prerogatives. However, they too rarely have the propensity for leadership and the awareness of responsibilities, as well as command rights, that professional military organizations usually insist their leaders possess and practice.

These problems, as well as the attrition in NESA, undoubtedly contributed to General H. Norman Schwarzkopf's unhappiness with CIA support during the Persian Gulf war. Schwarzkopf on June 12, 1991 told the Senate Armed Services Committee, "I would tell you very candidly that based on some of the analysis that we were getting, we'd still be sitting over there waiting if we were dependent on that analysis."[24] Analyses were so "caveated, disagreed-with, footnoted and watered down" that they were useless.[25] Schwarzkopf added:

> "There were so many disagreements within the intelligence community ... so many disclaimers that by the time you got done reading many of the intelligence estimates, no matter what happened, they would have been right. And that's not helpful to the guy in the field. It really isn't."[26]

A key area of disagreement between Schwarzkopf's command and CIA (along with the Defense Intelligence Agency) was bomb damage assessment. Schwarzkopf's assessments of damage inflicted by air strikes came from pilots' eyes, gun cameras, and theater-level technical collection means. CIA and DIA relied heavily on national-level technical collection assets, and interpreted data much more conservatively. Because Schwarzkopf deemed considerable damage to Iraqi forces a prerequisite to launching the ground attack, he told the senators that if he had relied on Washington assessments he would "still be over there waiting."[27]

Intelligence generally performed poorly during the war. The fact that surprises were positive does not diminish the magnitude and importance of the errors. Intelligence agencies grossly overestimated Iraqi capabilities despite knowledge of Iraq's performance in a major war with Iran in 1980-88. Casualty forecasts ran up to tens of thousands for American forces alone; the Iraqis managed to kill a maximum of 113 Americans.[28] Newspaper accounts cite communications problems.[29] Classified military after-action assessments list more intelligence deficiencies.

These failures came despite a near-perfect intelligence operational environment. Intelligence officers had: the legacy of the Iran-Iraq war to study; generally good weather and favorable terrain; unopposed technical collection systems; an enemy that obligingly deployed largely static defenses using essentially the same doctrine employed against Iran; unjammed communications; a rear area fairly secure except for an occasional SCUD missile attack after fighting began; and, over five months to prepare before US forces joined combat—an unprecedented luxury.

The severity of the problems of intelligence, despite these advantages, suggests that the intelligence community and the Defense Department need a fundamental re-assessment of the community's ability to support American military forces in the field. These deficiencies could have far greater consequences next time. We cannot count on having such a favorable situation in the future. Bob Gates, in a convoluted rendition of CIA's long-time, partial military support mission, admitted a need to do better to the SSCI—in essence also admitting his previous managerial shortcomings:

> "CIA has basically been considered a fundamentally peacetime organization... But war ... was defined as something like global thermonuclear war ... what the Gulf War showed, unlike Vietnam ... was that in this intense, very large conventional war, we had something in between ... peace and full-scale war.
>
> "We really didn't have, I think, very good procedures particularly for CIA support for military

> operations of that scale. I think that is one of the areas we need to look at... We discovered some real problems during the course of the war ... in terms of the transmission of our information to local commanders, to the commanders on the ground."[30]

I believe that CIA's poor performance also resulted in part from a general lack of interest in supporting the military. In part, this reflects bureaucratic squabbling stemming from the fact that each service has its own intelligence arm and the Defense Department has the Defense Intelligence Agency and the National Security Agency in tow. However, it also reflects an often thinly disguised disdain for the military and a belief that, as operators and not decisionmakers, the military services are less important consumers of CIA intelligence than senior civilian policymakers at the White House, the NSC, State, and Treasury, as well as DoD's civilian leadership. Because of such beliefs—and some similarly parochial military opinions about civilian intelligence people—liaison relationships are not well developed. Thus, CIA's collection and analytic capabilities, long focused on strategic military questions, purposefully are not structured to meet tactical- or operational-level needs like those of General Schwarzkopf.[31]

True to its normal knee-jerk defensive form, however, CIA defended its conduct during the war and rejected the General's concerns. In the words of the *Washington Post*, Gary Foster, head of the Agency's so-called planning, or "fifth," directorate, "recognized the frustrations of field commanders, but defended the conservatism practiced in Washington. A pilot and his gun camera may both attest to hitting an Iraqi tank, but if the turret remains on the tank, Foster suggested, it deserves another hit."[32]

Foster's attitude demonstrates massive ignorance of the capabilities of modern anti-armor weapons and a blatant disregard for logistics, targeting priorities, and the judgment of military commanders and their intelligence officers. It cannot but further damage what is already an often strained relationship between military and civilian intelligence people.[33]

Reality is that CIA management has taken little effective action to redress the chronic criticism of DI analysis—and seems disinterested in such action. Management, while offering small inducements like modest cash awards for language proficiency and noting that foreign travel is a good idea, has made no fundamental effort to improve the analyst corps' expertise or its propensity to think conventionally. Indeed, the opposite appears to be the case. Training courses ostensibly intended to improve analysts' skills are given by the Office of Training and Education (OTE)—a non-DI organization. Its offerings often are not well appreciated by DI employees and it has no power to ensure that its teachings find practical use. Other courses under discussion include "deprogramming"—the word of one DI manager—new employees from their university educations to better mold them to DI stylistic and intellectual preferences. Prohibitions and restrictions on contacts with non-Agency people are insulating the average analyst more that he was a few years ago. Moreover, the commonly used phrase "DI culture" indicates the existence of a sub-culture with all the attendant mores and prejudices the concept implies. This very dominant culture cannot but interfere with analysts' abilities to understand foreign perceptions, motives, and abilities.

The Agency's own employees sometimes act to circumvent failures caused by poor DI management. A common ploy is to aim publications for policy officials at the deputy assistant secretary-level, or below, because such papers need not be reviewed by the DDI.[34] A DO officer told me that in 1987 that the DO division responsible for the Soviet Union and Eastern Europe decided to deny both EURA and SOVA some of its reports because it thought that DI managers would distort them in DI papers; instead, it sent the reports directly to the State Department, at least.[35] A former analyst, according to the *Washington Post*, says that some analysts, fearful that Gates would thwart their efforts and judgments, went secretly to State Department colleagues and helped those counterparts work their views into State's positions. "The emphasis came on how do you get it past Gates. How do you package it? What subterfuge do you use to get your votes out?"[36] This kind of action is extreme, but my experience is that analysts sometimes tell consumers that they are less that satisfied with the work that bears their names, if that is in fact the case, and offer verbal clarifications of their actual judgments. These actions, and the problems that spawned them, do not boost consumers' confidence in CIA generally.

The DI has no mechanism to recognize and counter abuse, incompetence, politicization, venality, or myopia in the ranks of its senior officers, meaning that these characteristics thrive. The linkage of the review and managerial chains means that officials with biases or sycophantic tendencies can order, via the review process, slanted analysis and have power through the personnel system to punish subordinates who protest. Combined with the ineffectiveness of the Office of the Inspector General, the unwillingness of senior executives to consider the possibility of management problems, the protective shroud of secrecy that limits employees' recourse to the press and Congress, and spotty Congressional oversight, this system means that analysts and junior managers have no practical route of complaint and redress. The DI thus is a "closed system" that is vulnerable to chronic systemic problems, whatever the merits of individual allegations, complaints, or analyses.

The Directorate relies heavily on the competence, dedication to public service, and integrity of its leaders. Yet history shows that confidence that people with such characteristics will always rise to the top is likely to be disappointed eventually. The Founding Fathers had generally positive assessments of human nature, but nevertheless established the three branches of the United States government to provide checks and balances to guard against possible excesses by any of them. The DI was not organized with such wisdom.

I believe that much of the Agency's senior management, Gates' and Kerr's claims notwithstanding, cares little for the quality and usefulness of its analyses—only consumers' reactions to them. These are harsh words, but they are consistent with the words of some DI managers and the actions of many more. The attitude of the head of the PDB staff—that it did not matter what happened in Moscow in 1991, CIA had forecast all possibilities and thus was "covered"—reflects an attitude that the welfare of the Agency itself is the reason for many of its activities. By trying to satisfy consumers, senior Agency officers hope to further its bureaucratic interests. This attitude strikes me as similar to that of a stockbroker who for a while does well by randomly recommending shares to his clients, but whose fortune wanes when those clients see poor performances from his recommendations and come to suspect that he is more interested in generating fast trades than in giving good advice and prospering along with them. American policymakers and the Congress have only noticed some of their losses.

With time, the propensity of Gates and some of his immediate subordinates to produce analysis that satisfied specific consumer wants has evolved into a culture that no longer consistently values objectivity. Slanting need not be directed; it occurs normally during the course of intelligence production and review. The values of Sherman Kent are dying out, and a new one of self-service and bureaucratic self-interest is ascending. Once entrenched, such attitudes are enormously difficult to root out even in a much more open environment than that of CIA.

The DI's deficiencies are thus systemic, and can be expected to recur. These failings probably were partly responsible for the black eye the Agency received in the wake of the scandal following the seizure of the Bank of Credit and Commerce International (BCCI) by banking authorities around the world in the summer of 1991. In another public relations debacle, CIA managed to garner public blame both for dealing with BCCI through its operational activities and failing to provide either reporting or analytical warnings about BCCI's alleged international involvement in narcotics, terrorism, and money laundering, and its allegedly illegal activities in the United States. The latter included money laundering and the unauthorized acquisition of First American Bankshares, Inc., a bank holding company based in Washington, D.C.

DDCI Dick Kerr explained the Agency's actions to a group of high school students in early August 1991. Kerr said the Agency was "very aggressively collecting information against BCCI, as a target of intelligence, because ... from the early '80s, it was quite obvious it was involved in illegal activities ..."[37] Kerr claimed CIA's years-long use of BCCI for operational purposes was "absolutely legal."[38] At the same time, Kerr said that the Agency issued reports on BCCI well before 1986; according to a source of the *Washington Post*, these were "quite a few and quite a number of very interesting ones."[39]

If CIA was so good, how could the Justice Department have failed to notice BCCI's activities for years? Why did the Federal Reserve Board not know of BCCI's connection to First American? Kerr in late October explained to a Senate subcommittee that CIA made just a little "honest mistake" when it failed to notify the Fed of BCCI's First American connection in 1985.[40]

How could CIA manage to generate major criticism of both operations and analysis yet again? I believe normal operating practices can explain relatively easily this real life episode. CIA's lack of credibility probably is a major reason why the large number of reports that it sent to consumer agencies produced so little action; it thus provides an explanation for Senator John Kerry's lament:

> "An awful lot of information was being given to people... It just seems that nobody wanted to respond... Somewhere in this process you would have thought somebody would have leaped up and said there's a major problem with this bank."[41]

I do not know the actual details of CIA's performance and offer the following as a likely scenario given regular CIA practices. The Agency in recent years has been concerned to a considerable extent with the issues of narcotics and terrorism, and established special centers composed operations officers and, to some extent, analysts to track such events.[42] In such work, it would have identified financial institutions that facilitated such activities. This information may have been passed in part to analysts in the Counter-narcotics and Counter-terrorism Centers and the Office of Global Issues—which handled international financial events. The DO would not normally, for security reasons, have passed on information on its dealings with BCCI or other financial institutions to the DI.

Meanwhile, analysts in OGI would have had DO and other information on BCCI, and the office would have written about developments it deemed news-worthy. Its publications on such issues normally were short and restricted narrowly to the issue at hand. Its analyses normally did not recall events of months or years earlier in order to place current events in context. Nor would the analyses have pointed to actions that other US government agencies might take in response to the information; this would be undue intrusion into the policy realm. OGI's articles on BCCI-related financial matters might have been stashed in publications featuring articles on other, unrelated topics, leaving the intelligence liaison personnel at consumer agencies to divine what might be important to their principal officers. Normally conservative analyses—tending toward blandness, not the right wing of the political spectrum—would have made that task more difficult. OGI's general prohibition against analyst contacts with consumers would have discouraged analysts from phoning policy officials to say something like, "Hey Mike, did you see my recent article? No? I suggest you take a look at page six. You guys might be able to use that information. Call me back if you need anything more." Even economic analysts, moreover, normally consider the Federal Reserve to be an organization with few intelligence needs; they often scratch the Fed from papers' computer-generated distribution lists.

The tendency of OGI's director to order analysis, rather than encourage initiative and creativity, would have limited the freedom of analysts to offer comprehensive analyses if they noticed a trend. The director's palpable tendency to react to both his CIA superiors and to consumers, rather than to demonstrate initiative, would also have weighed against either a written or oral warning to consumer agencies that action might be desirable. Analysts, distant from consumers, could only wonder why Justice or the Fed took no action against BCCI. Certainly they would have had no invitation to ask their managers why.

This pattern of compartmentation, analyst isolation from policymakers, DI managers' bureaucratic conservatism, and waffling short analyses that do not put a whole picture in a useable context are recurrent events. These are likely to continue to negatively affect the performance of CIA generally.

While the costs of most of the Agency's ethical problems are subjective and difficult to measure, a controversy over relocating CIA offices indicates one tangible measure of the cost of its willingness to please a powerful sponsor—up to $1.2 billion. In June 1991, Director Webster announced a plan to move 6,000 Agency employees using rented facilities in the Washington area to Prince William County, Virginia and Jefferson County, West Virginia—a plan sponsored by West Virginia Senator Robert Byrd, former majority leader and chairman of the Appropriations Committee. Byrd already had managed to move the FBI's 2,000-person fingerprint laboratory and part of the Treasury Department, among other federal agencies, to West Virginia. Webster decided not to discuss the move with the House intelligence committee before announcing the move, miffing chairman Dave McCurdy, among others. The plan provoked massive opposition on Capitol Hill and ultimately was killed—a rare defeat for a Byrd pork-barrel project.

After the controversy broke, Inspector General Hitz investigated the plan. He concluded, in a 73-page report, that Agency officials knew that a move to West Virginia would be more expensive than one to nearby Prince William County, but they believed that West Virginia had a "political, funding edge" and that these factors were the "only ones that count."[43] In essence, Hitz accused both Webster and DDCI Kerr, who had publicly defended the plan, of dishonesty. Gates killed the plan to move in March 1992, concurring with the IG's report, but characteristically argued that mounting expense was the real reason for his decision.[44] The Agency's employees cannot have failed to notice management's cavalier willingness to disrupt the lives of 6,000 of their colleagues (if not their own) and waste their tax money solely to curry favor with a powerful senator.

Nevertheless, it would be unfortunate indeed, in my view, if the Agency's chronic, systemic problems, lead to stronger demands that it be dismantled or diminished instead of reformed. Intelligence community partisans long have struggled over budgets and responsibilities, in both absolute and relative terms. The United States military's victory in the desert in early 1991 may give it more clout to move on CIA bureaucratically. I see nothing to be gained by stronger intelligence services supporting the Joint Chiefs and the Secretary of Defense if a central intelligence organization dedicated to meeting the needs of all of government languishes. A far better solution, in my view, is a rejuvenated and reformed CIA.

* * *

Robert Michael Gates' confirmation as the fifteenth Director of Central Intelligence on November 5, 1991 has a number of prospective implications. Few of them appear appealing to me. The SSCI and Gates himself made clear during Gates' confirmation hearings that they expect significant organizational changes for CIA and different priorities for the intelligence community that reflect changes in the world. But concerns about internal problems and Gates' role in fostering them were not major elements in the modest discussions about organizational changes.

Neither Gates nor the senators much discussed internal procedural changes either, despite testimony late in the hearings from Hal Ford, Mel Goodman, and Jennifer Glaudemans that attacked Gates' integrity and managerial skills. This is not entirely surprising, given the larger importance of the issues of whether or not Gates was involved directly with Iran-contra and politicization, which consumed much of the hearings. The question of how Gates would fix the mess could not arise if the existence of the mess itself was still in doubt.

Nevertheless, obviously stung by some of the criticism,

Gates addressed internal change at the end of his rebuttal remarks:

> "... what has emerged here in these hearings is clear evidence that the perception of politicization in some areas remains real and must be addressed by the next Director. What is needed then is a set of measures to assure that the integrity of the process is protected. That one or another person's views do not inhibit the diversity of analysis and that analysts need not play it safe with upper management through self-censorship.
>
> "And yet to accomplish these objectives while maintaining and further improving the quality and intellectual toughness of the product. To change an atmosphere, a tone is a tall order. And in the real world, probably never perfectly attainable.
>
> "Even so, there are measures that can be taken. First, if confirmed I would candidly and quickly address these issues for all analysts. I would stress the importance of integrity and objectivity of the product. The importance of insuring that divergent views are heard and conveyed to the policymaker. And emphasize to all managers that analysts are to be encouraged to speak their minds openly. And that there should be incentives for doing this.
>
> "In short, we should try to codify that professional ethic that Mr. MacEachin described and make it part of our daily work.[45] In this connection, I would also tell all agency employees my door is open to those with concerns about this and other issues.[46] And that I intend to reach out to them as well.
>
> "I also would ask for a restoration of collegial civility that acknowledges that honest people can and

will disagree and that we must not attribute base motives when disagreements are involved.

"Second, I believe all managers of analysis should have as a part of their own performance evaluation, an appraisal of how well they encourage the above principals (sic) and values in their organizations.

"Their openness to alternative views and their willingness to support their analysts up the line once they've approved the analysis themselves.

"Third, if confirmed, I would direct the office of the Statutory Inspector General to pay special attention to problems of analytical process and to serve as a focal point for analysts and analytical managers concerned about process and the integrity of the product.

"Fourth, I believe issues relating to integrity of analysis, relationships with policy makers, and managing different points of view should be made a part of every training course for analysts and their managers.

"Fifth, this committee and its house (sic) counterpart for the past decade have focused especially on budget and clandestine activities. I encourage the committees to consider reestablishing something like their old analysis and production subcommittees that can focus oversight on the analytical process.

"This also could help the DCI better deal with analytical problems such as you have heard the last few days.

"Sixth, if confirmed, I would ask the President's foreign intelligence advisory board for its help and ideas in this area.

"Seventh, if confirmed I would consider creation of an analysis council of retired former senior officers that could advise the DCI and DDCI and the Deputy Director for Intelligence about the problems we are discussing.[47]

"Suggest possible, additional, remedies and perhaps serve also as ombudsman to hear and evaluate analyst complaints and concerns.

"Eighth, and finally, if confirmed, I would solicit from the analysts, and the managers of analysis themselves, their own ideas on how to rebuild morale, ensure integrity, and independence. How to avoid self-censorship, and deal with the perceptions of politicization."[48]

What a damning admission of failure! Robert Gates, of all people, is responsible for the problems he proposed to solve. He is the man who created the atmosphere and tone. He is the man who Ford, Glaudemans, Goodman, John Hibbits, and Carolyn Ekedahl attacked in testimony and statements. He made the issues of integrity and objectivity important. He is the man who told the Directorate in January 1982 that it was broken and needed to be fixed—and who "fixed" it all right. He is the man who once promised regularly to meet with analysts and then quit doing it. He could have implemented altered performance rating criteria and could have asked OTE to include in its courses references to the importance of integrity, but he did not. He chose not to do so during seven long years of developing, deepening problems. He thus implicitly admitted that his program and management caused major problems. It must have been a bitter pill to swallow.

Rhetoric to the SSCI aside, Gates' record and his legacy of 1982-89 suggest a few likely trends during his tenure as DCI. Gates is likely to move quickly to make organizational changes that will necessarily entail personnel shifts. These will allow him to place loyalists in the new, important positions. Gates' record of extremely poor judgment in picking individuals with tendencies toward sycophancy suggests that these new senior executives will be no better that the ones he tapped in 1982-89—and may in many cases be the same people. Because most of these men and women are likely to come primarily from intelligence positions, they will carry with them the ethics they practiced in the 1980s.

Gates demonstrated great energy in the early part of his tenure as DDI and slowed down later, allowing some of his intitiatives to wither and others to be managed by underlings less committed to his policies. Gates in a position of still greater responsibility may again overextend himself, only to retrench later from fatigue; the merits of his choices for immediate subordinates will become clearer then.

By the spring of 1992, Gates indeed had acted in a number of cosmetic ways. He established a series of task forces to investigate a range of issues from excessive secrecy to politicization, which he finally admitted. In a March 16, 1992 address to employees in the Agency's auditorium, Gates noted that "over half" of respondents to a survey conducted by the task force he created to investigate politicization "said that forcing a product to conform to a view thought to be held by a manager up the chain of command occurs often enough to be of concern."[49] Gates declined in the speech to attribute responsibility for the mess. Earlier he created a politicization "ombudsman" who ostensibly would act to ensure analytical objectivity where management and the Office of the Inspector General previously had failed. He told employees in his March 16 speech that his door was open—similar to the promise he made in his first speech as DDI in January 1982 in the same auditorium—and blamed low employee morale on "poor communication."[50]

If he really intends to improve analysis, he can do some things. He can again introduce elements of his initial reform program that improved the speed of review and forced less waffling on judgments; these are now long abandoned. Such measures will help some.

But any reform package will be overshadowed by suspicion and some fear. This will not be the fear of change that he so regularly has evoked to explain the failings of analysis. Instead, I believe a better analogy is the fear present in police states when new dictators take power. CIA employees will search for hidden meaning, motives, and implications. It is axiomatic in some DI offices that those offices acquire some of the characteristics of the part of the world they analyze. If this approach is a any guide, the appropriate model of Gates' tenure as DDI and DDCI is Brezhnev's USSR—with its apparatchiks, orthodoxies, internal or external exile for dissenters, stifling bureaucracy, inefficiency, and ultimate failure. DI personnel can hardly expect that Gates—a classic apparatchik—will become suddenly a Gorbachev committed to genuine reform.

After Gates' March 16, 1992 speech to employees, in which he recognized problems, a DI division chief who heard the speech told a source of mine that DI employees are so cynical that no one in the Directorate believed Gates was committed to genuine reform. Indeed, several current and former employees separately told me that they believe Gates and five other then-current senior Agency officials committed "perjury" at Gates' 1991 confirmation hearings. I cannot confirm the beliefs, and repeat them only for their value as measures of employees' confidence in senior Agency management.

Gates faced massive opposition from within CIA and much of the rest of the intelligence community during his confirmation process and will have to deal with people who dislike and distrust him.[51] His slickness is well known and his *mea culpa* and proposed institutional changes themselves will sway few. His confirmation alone caused morale problems that could be substantially exacerbated by unusually bad decisions about key subordinate managers. His confirmation and the prospect of President Bush's re-election in 1992 may prompt a jump in resignations from throughout the Agency in his first year or two. Opposition to Gates runs deep for a variety of reason: analysts remember politicization and labor under his poor choices for office directors; operations officers generally view analysts as less than intelligence officers and will resent the ascendency of a DI officer to the DCI's suite for the first time; others think his management style is poor; still others regard him as a cold fish.

Even Gates' staunchest supporters recognize that he made mistakes at CIA, even as they claim he has learned from his mistakes and will do better this time. Former DDCI and Gates mentor Admiral Bobby Inman, for example, said Gates "broke some china" during his earlier stint at CIA, but added that Gates in 1991 was "older" and "maturity had been added."[52] Inman's faith clearly is not shared widely among Agency employees. Senator Warren Rudman, Gates' chief Republican backer on the SSCI, said he had been too heavy handed as DDI in dealing with junior analysts.[53] SSCI Vice Chairman Frank Murkowski said, "The question is not whether he did everything right in the early 1980s ... The question is whether he has grown and learned."[54] Murkowski answered in the affirmative. Chairman Boren repeatedly said Gates had "matured," indicating he felt that was sufficient.[55]

The issue of politicization will remain. President Bush's substantial personal efforts to gain Gates' confirmation will reinforce suspicions that Gates caters to the president's wishes. Gates came back to CIA from a policy position where he worked closely with President Bush. He is known to have strong views on policy issues and will need to demonstrate that he can put aside the role of policymaker for that of detached, objective intelligence advisor. No amount of verbiage will convince DI personnel of Gates' personal or intellectual integrity. He must demonstrate it. I believe he will have a hard time convincing DI personnel that he is in fact objective. These same suspicions among consumers will continue to negatively affect the Agency's credibility and thus its effectiveness.

In an evident effort to project a good image and rehabilitate himself politically, new DCI Gates repeatedly appeared before Congressional committees in early 1992 but quickly became ensnared in new controversies involving alleged politicization. After Gates reported that North Korea was on the verge of developing nuclear weapons, the State Department in early March took the unusual step of publicly disagreeing—prompting charges that Gates had taken an extreme view. In another case, Senator Joseph Biden publicly attacked his objectivity. The *New York Times* on April 2, 1992 ran an editorial entitled, "At C.I.A., Word and Deed — Still Slanted."

This continued skepticism of Gates' motives, the continued presence of his like-minded proteges in senior positions with review process responsibilities, and Gates' record of having strong views will tend to strengthen the tendency toward politicization by efforts to divine what Gates "really wants." Many such politicizers will be motivated by bureaucratic rather than ideological considerations. Recalling Gates' earlier tendency toward vindictiveness and the retribution meted out by his appointees, they will want to please the bosses who can reward or punish them.

This tendency will be strengthened by knowledge that the Defense Department and intelligence community budgets are in for reductions and that the Agency personnel cuts thus are on the way.[56] The *Washington Post*, the largest newspaper in the Washington area in terms of circulation, just before Gates' confirmation wrote that CIA planned a 15 percent personnel reduction over the next five to seven years.[57] Failure to be good "team players" thus could be personally damaging as the Agency reshuffles priorities and duty assignments, and could be especially costly if the Agency actually lays off employees on the basis of "performance."

Because of the public stink over DI politicization in 1991, practitioners of politicization are likely to be more careful to couch their changes in drafts as better analysis; those not "on-board" with the team will still be subject to criticism under the rubric that they really are bad analysts or managers. The Congressional oversight committees, which did a poor job of detecting politicization in the DI in the 1980s, seem less than likely to adequately detect or even understand more sophisticated variants that sharp Agency bureaucrats are more than capable of developing.

Gates' confirmation seems certain to be viewed by some as evidence that sycophancy and intellectual dishonesty are rewarded handsomely—a devastating message to pass to CIA employees for whom integrity is so important. It is a terrible legacy. Senator Sam Nunn was right on the mark when, after the SSCI voted 11 to 4 for Gates, he expressed worry "about the signal being sent to the men and women of the intelligence community about how you get to the top in this town."[58] This signal cannot but damage the will of honest Agency employees to maintain ethical and intellectual standards.

Gates told the Senate that he would curtail his public commentary on substantive issues to reduce pronouncements that his subordinates could interpret as statements of an official orthodoxy that they should follow. Such a policy—not implemented through the spring of 1992—is likely to be minimally effective because Gates daily will make written and oral comments on substantive issues that will perform the same function. Such a change in policy would help protect him, however, from public scrutiny of his analytic judgments.

Gates' continued comments that intelligence should better know policy in order to serve it, combined with his personal relationship with President Bush, will sustain suspicions within CIA that he does not have a personal commitment to objective analysis. This legacy must have been on the mind of at least one SOVA analyst who in December 1991, less than two months after Gates became DCI, received a phone call from Gates pointing out specific raw message traffic and ordering a NID article using the traffic.

The suspicion will remain that Gates is breaking the basic, long-held precepts—described by Sherman Kent and represented by the much-respected Hal Ford during his hearings—and bringing intelligence too close to policy. Referring to the process of producing intelligence analysis, Gates wrote in 1984, "... perhaps the best guardians of the integrity of the process are the caliber and honesty of the people involved."[59] In the same article, he added, "Perhaps the strongest cultural trait common to all CIA analysts is a very deep sensitivity to the dangers of politicization." While it is apparent that promotion to management sometimes helps erode that trait, many weary guardians seem sure to continue to distrust Bob Gates.

The distrust will be heightened by Gates' defense that, in essence, he did no wrong and that soft analysts could not take the heat he legitimately gave them for "flabby" analysis. He maintained an undertone of complaint that it was "whiners," malcontents, and people unable to adjust to ancient reorganizations who so savaged him. I believe very few DI people accept what he told the SSCI:

> "I believe there are several causes for this perception of politicization. It's usually greater, for example, when people up the line have strong views on substance. And I must say in the history of CIA that happens more often than not. When major changes in draft analysis come out of a review process it is understandable that analysts would be more inclined to blame them on an external source, such as political pressure, than on weaknesses of their own analysis or exposition.
>
> "No analyst who considers himself or herself to be the best informed person on a subject likes to be challenged. Analysts like to write on subjects they like, in the ways they like. And to be told that your specific subject, or the way you present it, is irrelevant to policymakers is hard to swallow. It was for me as an analyst and it continues to be for analysts.
>
> "The much maligned review process takes the analysis of a single individual, challenges assumptions, asks questions and hopefully scrubs out the biases of the analyst as well as others at all levels, thus turning the draft of an individual into the official view of the Central Intelligence Agency or the Intelligence Community. The process can be rough and tumble. Most analysts do well

> in the give and take. But some do not. And some see in this process political pressure. *And that's why we're here today* (emphasis added)."[60]

Gates will have to contend with severe concerns about his leadership style as well as his integrity and management abilities. His own persistent whining about the attitudes of his troops suggests that his generalship leaves much to be desired. He was in charge. He was responsible. Gates alone generated concerns about his integrity. They did not spring from the ear of Zeus. His continued unwillingness to accept personal responsibility for such failures reflects continued poor judgment.

The hearings damaged Bob Gates and CIA. Former NIO Graham Fuller, called to the hearings in support of Gates, said after one day's session, "There's a lot of blood on the floor. It dismays me."[61] This blood promises to have lasting effects beyond the attitudes of working CIA employees that probably will be mainly negative.

CIA's credibility in the policy community has been damaged further. The effectiveness of any intelligence organization is only as good as its ability to persuade. Persuasion will be more difficult for at least the medium term; consumers will wonder whether they are getting another Iran estimate or another case for Soviet complicity in the attempt on Pope John Paul II's life that Gates once described as "comprehensive." Senator Ernest Hollings told Gates he thought Gates would need four or five years to undo the Agency's problems, but added," ... we don't have that much time ..."[62] Senator Howard Metzenbaum told Gates, "You might get 51 votes, you might get 65 or 82. But I say that no matter how you slice it, the fact that so many have come forward with so many reservations and so many concerns, I believe, has put the image of the CIA in question."[63] As the SSCI voted to send the nomination to the full Senate, Hollings said, "right at this minute, the Central Intelligence Agency has got cancer," spread by DCI Casey and by implication Gates, "who resented anybody around the agency that didn't conform."[64] Senator Bill Bradley called Gates, "a man who apologizes for undeniable mistakes, who recalls possible mistakes only when questioned repeatedly in public, refuses to recall or forgets unproven mistakes, admits newly proven mistakes, and finally, who promises to prevent any more serious mistakes."[65]

Gates undoubtedly will try to resurrect his reputation. If history is any indication of his tactics, he will try to assuage individual opponents with apparent concern about their concerns. He is likely to maintain a high public image intended to show that he is an apolitical intelligence professional. He will keep close watch on the wishes of Congress and make efforts to at least appear receptive. By early 1992, word was circulating in some CIA offices that Gates intended largely cosmetic changes designed to appease Congress while making few fundamental changes—a view supported by some of early personnel decisions, including elevation of two former heads of the Office of Global Issues—repeatedly referenced elsewhere in this volume—to be the Associate DDI and Comptroller.

The hearings and votes indicate that, Boren aside, Gates has significant opponents among current and future congressional oversight committee leaders. The chairman of the House Permanent Select Committee on Intelligence (HPSCI, pronounced hip-see), Dave McCurdy, on October 2 called on Gates to withdraw his nomination if he could not disprove charges of politicization "convincingly."[66] Gates' opponents included the next likely SSCI chairman (presuming the Democrats retain control of the Senate)—Metzenbaum or Dennis DeConcini—after Boren leaves the Committee in late 1992. Gates may yet rue his statement in opening remarks to the SSCI on September 16, 1991:

> "I commit to you that should I be confirmed, whatever differences may develop from time to time between the Intelligence Committees and the Executive branch generally or CIA in particular, I would resign rather than jeopardize that relationship of trust and confidence."[67]

George Bush's decision to push so personally for Gates

injected partisanship clearly into the Senate debate. While always present, SSCI members generally have submerged partisan issues in deference to the national interest. President Bush's actions weakened that tradition. Bush couched his support in bald political terms, damaging relations between some senators, and causing somewhat less friction between the staffers who work together daily on relatively non-partisan bases. The White House hired a veteran Washington lobbyist to push for Gates. Bush also made a series of scurrilous comments in defense of Gates; in remarks to veterans of the Office of Strategic Services on October 23, 1991, he said he was "sick and tired of those in the political arena and, yes, in the media, who do nothing but carp, criticize and second guess."[68] How ironic that Bush should have chosen a gathering of OSS veterans to praise a man who had done so much to damage the fine traditions those very OSS people helped establish!

These actions and statements make it more difficult for Gates to convince anyone that he is an objective, ethically neutral producer and communicator of intelligence who is willing to give Bush intelligence he does not want to hear. Bush may have given Gates the job, but he made the work harder. Gates added to his baggage by invoking Bush's name at the conclusion of his testimony, "I can pull [the Agency] through this because of my relationship with the president ..."[69]

I suspect that the hearings will affect CIA recruiting efforts. While there still will be enough applicants to fill the desks, the severity of the charges of politicization will tend to repel the very individuals the DI needs most—independent thinkers with keen senses of personal and intellectual integrity who have no stomach for "self-censorship" or life as a "scared rabbit" writing for "the seventh floor." Those who do apply may be more pliant—"team players" in the worst sense of the term.

Foreign governments and intelligence services undoubtedly were watching with keen interest. US friends are likely to be less inclined to accept CIA judgments and even raw intelligence information, damaging our ability to influence foreign decisions. A lack of confidence in CIA's ability to process information objectively may also incline them to send us less. There are always trade-offs in intelligence exchanges: potential gains from receiving information; and potential losses from compromises in the security of sources and methods. If friendly foreign services cannot be sure of the quality of what they receive from CIA, they will be less inclined to share their information and assessments.

Potential adversaries may be emboldened. Probably due in part to foreign disinformation campaigns about alleged CIA predations around the world, the Agency's reputation has long towered above its abilities, in my view. Revelations that CIA is indeed a human organization will reduce its power to intimidate those who might wish to harm US interests—like terrorists, for example.

Over the longer term, some real good could come from the public release of information about DI operations and the controversy over politicization. The oversight committees may have learned that they had lots to learn, and the education may convince them that they need to do a better job of oversight in the future. Politicization has become a legitimate topic for discussion within CIA; it no longer is so wildly unthinkable that it is not of managerial and analytic concern. The Office of the Inspector General has a new base of public complaints of politicization from which to monitor the DI's work. Unless Gates changes his stripes significantly, however, his successors will need to institute substantial reforms to redress old problems. Moreover, the longer an un-reborn Gates and his proteges remain in power at Langley, the more formidable the reform task will be.

Notes to Chapter 6

1 Elaine Sciolino, "Slanting of Intelligence Becomes Issue for Nominee," New York Times, *September 19, 1991, p. B10.*

2 Ibid.

3 CIA produces the National intelligence Daily *and DI offices prepare the vast majority of its articles. The other major intelligence organizations—INR, DIA, and the National Security Agency—have opportunities to concur or ask for changes in texts during the "coordination" of articles.*

INR's decision to abandon its coordinatiion prerogatives indicates a general unhappiness with DI analysis and a conclusion that coordination battles are not worthwhile efforts.

4 Robert M. Gates, "The CIA and Foreign Policy," Foreign Affairs, *Vol. 66, No. 2, Winter 1987/88, p. 222.*

5 According to a former SSCI staffer who heard Leahy, the context usually was a complaint about the NID's inability to provide more news and insight than a good newspaper.

6 In his "Remarks to DDI Analysts and Managers" speech, Gates complained of "analysis that too often proved inaccurate or too fuzzy to judge whether right or wrong," p.3.

7 See Rhodi Jeffords-Jones, The CIA & American Democracy *(New Haven: Yale University Press, 1989) for such an argument. I find her case that "standing" is important to be unconvincing.*

8 Eliot Cohen, "The 'No Fault' View of Intelligence," in Roy Godson, ed., Intelligence Requirements for the 1990s, *(Lexington: Lexington, 1989) p. 74. Many analysts agree with this assessment. Cohen, as others, incorrectly attributes this failing to analysts and not the full production/review process.*

9 All such resignation letters I have seen have been classified, and thus publicly unavailable. Classification therefore eliminates development of a body of critiques that could be used to furthur public awareness of the DI's problems—and thus improve recommendations for reforms. My own experience with such a planned letter release was easy. Letters can be cleared before or after departure with the Publications Review Board. Names, numbers, and specific judgments, but little else, are off-limits. This represents a final way to serve the country, CIA, and remaining Agency employees.

10 The reorganization of the Office of Global Issues into the Office of Resources, Trade, and Technology is a good case in point. The reorganization in large part, according to RTT managers, reflected a DI response to questions the DCI was receiving about CIA coverage of issues long covered by the press and academe.

11 See Godson, ed., Intelligence Requirements for the 1990s, *pp. 6-7.*

12 An applicant clearly cannot be too demanding of a potential employer, but can make inquiries that may suggest a significant problem. The applicant should ask about the tenure of members of his prospective branch in that branch, not the Agency; a short average period will tend to indicate that analysts have voted with their feet by moving. Applicants often do not receive assignments they want or for which they feel they are most qualified; they can minimize this by eliciting promises from personnel officers, not just the DI managers they interview with. Applicants should take advantage of opportunities to talk to analysts in their prospective units if they are available; managers, especially poor ones, rarely feel so confident as to offer them, however.

Employees in their three year probationary periods face different but very difficult problems. Some managers use the threat of dismissal cavalierly in demanding drafts that "require" little review while they give little guidance on expectations. These managers also use their rating power to threaten to ruin a budding career if the new employee fails to meet sometimes impossible standards or seeks a new assignment too soon. This is especially damaging because analysts' reputations often are made very early in their careers. Once again, poor managers with weak senses of integrity and tendencies toward vindictiveness are most prone to this kind of behavior. I saw one new analyst in the Office of European Analysis reduced to tears over incredible management demands inconsistent with each other and those levied on even very experienced analysts.

The new analyst committed to CIA probably is best served by biting his lip and satisfying a poor boss within his bounds of integrity, getting a clear statement of management expectations, obliquely obtaining a definition of an acceptable initial tour in his office (usually publication of a major paper), and getting a transfer as soon as possible. Complaints in most offices to more senior managers are counterproductive.

13 Management clearly has cared little about this attrition or its causes. Inspector General William F. Donnelly in 1989 told an analyst that attrition was not a problem because the Agency's attrition was lower than that of other government agencies. The DI's staff, known as MPSS, in the mid-1980s warned in a memo that the loss of experienced analysts threatened to endanger the DI's ability to do its job, but then dismissed the problem with a favorite and incredible argument of Gates—that attrition in the mid-1980s was attributable to the failure of analysts to adapt to the reorganization of 1981. The MPSS report thus placed the blame on maladaptive analysts, who implicitly were better off elsewhere. Gates repeated a variant of the argument at his 1991 confirmation hearings; see Senate, Transcript of the Select Committee on Intelligence, Nomination of Robert M. Gates to be Director of Central Intelligence, October 3, 1991, pp. 15-16.

The Director of EURA decided in the summer of 1985 to commission an in-house, informal "IG Inspection" to assess employees' attitudes toward management. The results were devastatingly critical. D/EURA promptly forgot her promise to act on the "inspection's" findings and never, to my knowledge, acted on any of its recommendations. In early 1986, I spoke to her for over an hour about poor management in the division following Eastern Europe; at the end of our generally pleasant conversation, she informed me simply, "I don't believe you." Again, she did nothing.

14 Gates, "The CIA and Foreign Policy," p. 223.

15 Elaine Sciolino with David Johnston, "In Rebuttal to Senate Committee, C.I.A. Nominee Is Truthful but Incomplete," New York Times, *October 13, 1991, p. 24.*

16 See Paul Farhi, "Uncle Sam Says Come Spy for Me As CIA Begins Appeal to Minorities," Washington Post, *November 1, 1991, p. A23. Farhi's article said 10.1 percent of CIA's professional personnel then were minorities and that 6.4 percent were black. The article quoted Bob Garfield, the advertising critic for* Ad Age *magazine as saying he found "everything wrong" with the ad from its "anachronistic, scare-tactic headline" to "its condescending tone."*

17 In 1988 I participated in an internal discussion to determine CIA priorities for use of some technical collection assets in one part of the world. Virtually all of the DI (plus the two National Intelligence Officers who I represented) was arrayed against one office which maintained that its consumers most wanted steady reports on the status of a current issue, also regularly covered by the newspapers. The office argued that such collection could help. Representatives of the rest of the DI responded that they had consumer constituencies as well, that they had responsibilities to meet those consumers' long term needs, and that then-current priorities had permanently damaged their ability to provide intelligence support. In this case the majority won, but not until years after the issue in this one case had been joined and damage was done.

18 The incumbent in the late 1980s and early 1990s told me repeatedly that he felt he was not doing his job unless he "pissed off" people. He surely accomplished the latter.

One anecdote illustrates this man's tendency to be a "loose cannon." In the fall of 1988, NIO/W got the idea that the Soviet Union was trying to trick the United States and other countries about its activities in a sensitive part of the world. He felt that the Soviets had no intention of doing something that they had promised. He repeatedly made his points within the NIC. The National Intelligence Officer for the USSR indulged his views, granting that the issue fell within the bailiwick of warning, even though he disagreed with the NIO for Warning. One Sunday, however, NIO/W and one of his staff decided to push their view, which was also opposed by other members of NIO/W's staff. They wrote and disseminated a message to, among other places, the National Security Council staff and the White House. This message was not time-sensitive, it broke no new ground, and its conclusion was still opposed by much of the intelligence community; it stirred considerable excitement at the White House, however. On Monday morning, then-DDCI Gates called NIO/W to his office and directed him never again to send any such message out of the building without Gates' permission. Gates may have overstepped his authority somewhat, but NIO/W far exceeded the bounds of common sense, damaging his personal credibility and the function of his office in the process.

19 Kent, Strategic Intelligence, *p. 183.*

20 Gates, "The CIA and Foreign Policy," p. 226.

21 Kent, Strategic Intelligence, *p. 194.*

22 Ibid., pp. 176-177.

23 There is no formal organization of such people. Nor is there any conspiracy to do anything in this area.

24 Molly Moore, "Schwarzkopf: War Intelligence Flawed," Washington Post, *June 13, 1991, p. A1.*

25 George Lardner, Jr., "In a Changing World, CIA Reorganizing to Do More With Less," Washington Post, *July 5, 1991, p. A9.*

26 Ibid.

27 Ibid.

28 Of 148 Americans killed in action, the Department of Defense in August 1991 reported that 35 died from friendly fire. Others listed as KIA may have perished in plane crashes due to mechanical failures. See Barton Gellman, "Gulf War's Friendly Fire Tally Triples," Washington Post,

August 14, 1991, pp. A1 and A26.

29 Molly Moore, "Schwarzkopf: War Intelligence Flawed," p. A40.

30 Senate, Exec. Rept. 102-19, p. 194.

31 In military parlance, operations are divided into three general categories: strategic, operational, and tactical. While there are fuzzy dividing lines between them, strategic activities (and thus intelligence needs) focus on world-wide operations and include issues like nuclear weapons, and intercontinental ballistic missiles. Operational-level combat involves ground and air forces (and perhaps naval units) over a large but not global area. This definition is similar to the old concept of a theater of operations and was the level of operations during Operation Desert Storm. Tactical operations include combat involving units up to (in Army terms) divisional or perhaps corps size.

32 George Lardner, Jr., "In a Changing World, CIA Reorganizing to Do More With Less," Washington Post, *July 5, 1991, p. A9.*

33 Ibid. Foster also rejected the notion that the Agency was short of Arabic speakers during the war—a debatable point. He claimed that in-house language programs are strong and include "total immersion in whatever language you train in." In fact, immersion occurs only for short periods, and many DI personnel taking language courses do not get such immersion. Foster's comment thus as best is self-servingly half-true and at worst is a lie.

34 Reflecting largely its bureaucratic concerns, the DI has specific rules governing the level of DI management review required for each product. The higher the intended consumer, the higher the DI management review needed. Thus, to avoid review hassles—particularly if controversial judgments are involved—analysts and junior managers can specify that they intend their papers for low-level consumers. There thus is a clear tradeoff: the drafting of papers on major issues for key consumers usually is a lengthy and frustrating process, but may generate policy action and better "kudos;" on the other hand, papers for lower ranking consumers may survive review in better condition, but may not be noticed much by senior policy officials or DI managers.

35 DO officers were concerned that some EURA and SOVA units were taking snippets from reports derived from information provided by sources they regarded as somewhat suspect, while ignoring more voluminous reporting from better sources.

36 Benjamin Weiser, "Gates's Tolerance for Dissent at CIA Seen as Focus of Today's Witnesses," Washington Post, *September 25, 1991, p. A9.*

37 George Lardner, Jr., "CIA Probed, Used BCCI, Official Says," Washington Post, *August 3, 1991, pp. A1 and A12.*

38 Ibid, p. A12.

39 Ibid, p. A1.

40 Mark Potts, "CIA 'Mistake' Cited in Case of 1st American," Washington Post, *October 26, 1991, p. C1.*

41 Ibid.

42 These are known as the Counter-terrorism Center (CTC) and the Counter-narcotics Center (CNC).

43 Kent Jenkins, Jr., "CIA Cites Byrd Role in Move," Washington Post, *February 23, 1992, p. A12.*

44 Kent Jenkins, Jr., "CIA Cancels Its Divisive W. Va. Move", Washington Post, *April 1, 1992, pp. A1 and A6.*

45 Douglas J. MacEachen, former director of the Office of Soviet Analysis discussed his views of the role of the intelligence officer during Senate testimony in support of Gates.

46 Gates quickly in his tenure as DDI abandoned an early effort to get to know analysts and their concerns better—roughly weekly meetings with DI branches.

47 Note that this is essentially the same mission—advise to senior executives—with the same type of staff, as the Senior Review Panel that was transferred to the NIC from the DI immediately after Gates became DDI in early 1982.

48 United States Senate, Transcript of Proceedings Before the Select Committee on Intelligence, Nomination of Robert M. Gates to be Director of Central Intelligence, Morning Session, October 3, 1991, pp. 46-49 (draft).

49 Elaine Sciolino, "C.I.A. Chief Upset Over 'Politicization' Seen Within Agency," New York Times, *March 28, 1992, pp. A1 and A7.*

50 Ibid.

51 I doubt that the White House ever appreciated the depth of this feeling. Gates admirer Admiral Bobby Inman, a former DDCI and head of NSA, claimed publicly that only a few managers, worried about their positions, opposed Gates. Word reached DI analysts during Gates' confirmation hearings that the head of the PDB staff told White House personnel that CIA people were "ecstatic" about Gates' apparently good showing during the first week of testimony. This is a sharp man, well aware of his surroundings and the attitudes of people therein. I presume he decided simply to tell the White House people what he thought they wanted to hear.

52 Charles R. Babcock and Walter Pincus, "Gates's Intelligence Management at the CIA Becomes an Issue, Washington Post, *September 27, 1991, p. A10.*

53 Walter Pincus and George Lardner Jr., "Gates Strikes Back At Critics in CIA," Washington Post, *October 4, 1991, p. A8.*

54 George Lardner Jr., "Committee Approves Gates at CIA," Washington Post, *October 19, 1991, p. A1 and A12.*

55 Charles R. Babcock, "Gates Passed Panel's Test on Lessons Learned From Casey's Controversies," Washington Post, *October 19, 1991, p. A11.*

56 CIA's annual budget, according to Business Week *magazine, was $3.2 billion at an unspecified time presumably close to the fall of 1991. See "Should the CIA Start Spying for Corporate America?"* Business Week, *October 14, 1991, p. 96. The* Washington Post *cited a $3.5 billion figure in a George Lardner article entitled, "From Intelligence Estimates to Daily Newspapers," July 5, 1991, p. A9.*

57 Paul Farhi, "Uncle Sam Says Come Spy for Me As CIA Begins Appeal to Minorities," Washington Post, *November 1, 1991, p. A23.*

Whatever the case, CIA's budget is but a part of the overall US intelligence effort.

58 George Lardner Jr., "Committee Approves Gates at CIA," Washington Post, *October 19, 1991, P. A1. All seven Republicans on the SSCI voted for Gates: John Chafee, Alfonse D'Amato, Slade Gorton, Frank Murkowski, Warren Rudman, and John Warner. Democrats for Gates included Chairman David Boren, Alan Cranston, John Glenn, and Sam Nunn. Democratic nay votes were Bill Bradley, Dennis DeConcini, Ernest Hollings, and Howard Metzenbaum.*

59 Gates, "Is CIA's Analysis Any Good?"

60 Senate, Transcript, October 3, 1991, pp. 15-16.

61 George Lardner Jr. and Benjamin Weiser, "Spy vs. Spy: 4 CIA Veterans Criticize, Defend Gates," Washington Post, *October 2, 1991, p. A1.*

62 Walter Pincus and George Lardner Jr., "Gates Strikes Back at Critics in CIA," Washington Post, *October 4, 1991, p. A8.*

63 Elaine Sciolino, "Bush's C.I.A. Nominee in Counterattack at Senate Hearing," New York Times, *October 4, 1991, p. A15.*

64 George Lardner Jr. "Committee Approves Gates," p. A12.

65 Ibid.

66 Bob Woodward, "McCurdy: Gates Should Withdraw," Washington Post, *October 3, 1991, pp. A1 and A32.*

67 Senate, Exec. Rept. 102-19, p. 196. The passage is from the record of morning testimony of September 16, 1991, p. 119.

68 Donnie Radcliffe, "Intelligence Gathering," Washington Post, *October 24, 1991, p. C1.*

69 Elaine Sciolino, "Bush's C.I.A. Nominee in Counterattack at Senate Hearing," New York Times, *October 4, 1991, p. A15.*

CHAPTER SEVEN

RECOMMENDATIONS FOR REFORM

The DI needs a substantial package of reforms that cuts to the very heart of "DI culture." DI and many other Agency employees widely recognize as much and periodically recommend changes that reflect frustration and fancy as much as serious thought—usually because they see no prospect for meaningful reform. A common one long has been that Congress should cut the DI's budget in half. So the reasoning goes, DI management then would be forced to use its people more efficiently, streamlining the review process and improving the management of human and other resources. A variant is that cutting the budget in half would lead management to fire analysts while retaining the managerial superstructure; Congress would eventually notice diminished production and mandate changes.

Any genuine reform needs a series of steps that range from refocusing the DI's mission to improving the management of employees' day-to-day lives. I propose the following reforms. Some are essential to restoration of sound CIA intelligence analysis. Others offer approaches to take in engineering specific changes.

1. *The DI needs a restored sense of institutional integrity.* Managers and analysts need to know in certain terms that anything less than personal honesty and intellectual integrity is unacceptable and will be punished. A new DCI must back this message with a series of steps including altered training courses, changes in employee performance appraisal criteria, and, most importantly, internally well publicized punishment of offenders.

This reform is essential.

2. *The DI needs a restored sense of mission.* Senior management and the president need to make clear that the taxpayers buy intelligence analysis to serve the president and the rest of government—not to create sinecures by pandering to the perceived wishes of officials often condescendingly regarded as buffoons. This will not have occurred until analysts no longer believe they primarily write "for the seventh floor."

The DI needs, with the assistance of the rest of government and the knowledgeable public, a serious debate about what intelligence service to government means in practice. It needs better definitions of satisfactory performance of that service. Many low- and mid-level DI employees long have had both specific complaints and practical recommendations; their views should receive serious hearings. The DI's bureaucratic ossification has reached the point that its senior management cannot be counted upon to do the job alone.

3. *The review process needs fundamental overhaul.* The currently too common practice of judging papers against a moving standard of an office director's latest "I want..." statement is unacceptable. Review should become again a process whereby senior officials assure overall quality standards, while initially presuming soundness of analyst judgment and competence of junior reviewers. Review, as opposed to rewrite, can be a fairly quick process, enhancing efficiency. The presumably rare rejection of a paper by senior management for quality reasons *alone* should redound negatively on subordinate managers as well as the analyst author—a change from the general practice of blaming analysts for review problems while sharing credit for smooth review throughout the chain.

The office directors cannot maintain expertise on the topics their offices cover—no matter how capable or self-confident they may be—and need firm instructions to reduce their intrusion into the substance of analysis. These people ostensibly are managers who have many people, much money, long-term plans, and lots of meetings to worry about. They need to return to the attitude of a former director of the Office of Near East and South Asian Analysis who once said to me something close to, "At my level, I can't be a [substantive] expert on anything. What I try to do is gather good people and let them have at it." This elementary management concept and supportive attitude is foreign to too many DI "managers."

To assist in review, the DDI or the office directors could convene revolving or permanent bodies of experts to conduct substantive review, leaving editing chores to editors—not office directors. This practice could improve review, speed it, and introduce checks against injection of office directors' or other managers' partisan political views. It has precedent in the Senior Review Panel—a group of several retired, distinguished government officials, military officers, academics, and scientists—which examines drafts of national-level intelligence publications and was a part of the DI in the 1970s. The SRP comments on the scope, methods, and judgments of these publications to the NIO responsible for each, to the Chairman of the National Intelligence Council, and to the DCI.[1] The members of the SRP in its incarnations, however, have been part-time consultants with powers only to recommend; the DI needs a more formal body of career employees with institutionalized review powers.

The Directorate should experiment with competitive review chains. Under this scheme, analysts who believe a paper is ready to begin the review process could give the paper to more than one branch chief (or senior analyst) knowledgeable of the subject, each of whom is authorized to judge it acceptable. Because branch chiefs receive kudos for the successful publication of papers they review, they would have incentive to process a paper quickly but well; rejected papers are definite career negatives. Slow and incompetent branch chiefs would suffer; they also would be unable to make the now standard excuse that review by definition is taking time because the analyst prepared a poor draft. Analysts surely would be happy, review would be more efficient, and senior managers would have another tool to judge subordinate managers. This procedure also would tend to foster branch chief/analyst cooperation in pursuit of a common goal and reduce the current tendency toward confrontation. Branch chiefs now have captive crops of papers, and some enjoy opportunities to show how tough they are by "agonizing" over drafts.[2]

This approach has limitations and would not be universally useful. It is dependent on the availability of knowledgeable branch chiefs (or senior analysts) and the common sense of all in not having a dozen branch chiefs work simultaneously on one paper, for example. Nevertheless, in some cases it offers a solution for the chronic problem of slow, incompetent, and politically biased review. It also offers analysts a chance to implicitly review and rate the reviewers—a useful management tool for senior executives.

Any changes made should be accompanied by an explicit recognition that review entails costs—in time, money, and foregone analysis—that should be made only to the extent that papers are improved. At some point, the marginal returns to review fall below marginal costs, and sometimes may be absolutely negative as reviewers find ever lower common denominators and "weasel" words and judgments. DI "management" virtually never makes this elementary economic observation and basic management judgment.

4. *The DI should establish regular reviews of the accuracy of judgments and forecasts of papers to find lessons for improving analysis and to identify consistently poor performance in review chains.* These should not punish "errors." Predicting the future is inherently difficult and the most useful warnings occur when information is still sketchy and some false starts are likely. Indeed, good warning messages generate actions that head off the warned-about foreign events, leading to the appearance that the warning message itself was erroneous. Instead, the reviews should convey the message that the quality of analysis is important, and that production will continue to receive attention after the "bean" of publication has been counted. Particularly insightful analysis could be rewarded long after paper publication. This would tend to diminish the common current

attitude that publication and an entry on the ledger are the primary goals and are the end of any analytic exercise.

To be effective, these reviews must reach the authors and reviewers of each paper. Moreover, the Directorate should make internally public periodic assessments of the aggregate "accuracy" of entire DI units such as divisions or offices. The point is to make managers accountable—an initial and ineffective Gates directive in 1982—and give DI employees information with which to debate the reasons that some units do better than others; if they can find some good methodological or institutional reasons, they may be able to borrow successful methods. And, senior management would have another tool to evaluate subordinate managers.

Implementation of this proposal should be flexible, sophisticated, and handled by people who receive internally well publicized recognition that this review work is important. It would have to overcome at least two significant problems. First, there would be a tendency to use unsophisticated rating schemes or to reduce these reviews to simple decisions that papers were "accurate" or "inaccurate," for example. This would have a chilling effect on the bureaucratically inclined and would encourage insecure managers to make even more banal judgments in papers as defense mechanisms. Second, DI staffers doing this work would, under current administrative procedures, remain subject to office directors' anger if they worked too conscientiously. They need protection.

5. *Because the DI is unlikely to objectively critique itself without substantial incentives, Congress should consider legislative expansion of the authority of the Inspector General to include evaluation of the quality and conduct of intelligence analysis.* To ensure that Agency employees on rotation do not hinder his activities, the IG should have an adequate staff of personnel managed in a special career service of the Office of the Inspector General. Outsiders hired directly into the office would help ensure objectivity by reducing any tendency for OIG officers to curry favor with past and/or potential future bosses in the four main directorates.

The OIG at the same time needs better to understand its role as a protector of the institution and thus the nation. It must balance its extremely well developed sense of fairness toward accused miscreants with an urge to protect broader collective interests—such as institutional integrity, objectivity, fairness, effectiveness, and efficiency—and the Agency's charter to provide quality intelligence that policymakers respect, trust, and will use. Protection of these broader interests requires development of non-legal standards of assessment—ones related to performance.

To make him genuinely effective, and eliminate the ability of senior CIA managers to simply ignore his recommendations, the Inspector General should receive powers to mandate some remedial actions and to levy some punishments. He should have the ability to place findings and reprimands in the permanent records of personnel if appropriate DI managerial remedies fail. These documents might be the rough equivalent of non-judicial punishment under Article 15 of the Uniform Code of Military Justice. Receipt of an "Article 15" is often sufficient to stop an aspiring military officer's career in its tracks. The Inspector General should have similar power. This is an extreme proposal and has potential for OIG abuse, but that possibility seems remote and is dwarfed by the actual damage done by the lax managerial standards of the 1980s.

Because many DI officers view the OIG with such suspicion, Inspector General Hitz would do well to conduct an objective investigation of his own office, if that is possible. If necessary, the Agency could borrow IG personnel from other government agencies. The goals of such an inspection should be to identify more clearly the internal problems of OIG, methods for their correction, and how to restore employee confidence in the OIG's objectivity and commitment to integrity and sound CIA performance.

6. *The DI should stress more the importance of the "production" process, as opposed to the "review" process, and take steps to boost the ability of analysts to do sound work.* While some training in classroom settings may help, the most

important changes should be in the branches. Analysts need time to read and think without constant pressure to "produce." Teamwork and team projects should be encouraged. Where possible, new analysts should work initially as junior partners in teams. Management should judge analysts by their teamwork and ability to assist junior people; managers in most of the rest of the world are expected to do the same and seem to be able to do so with little difficulty. Managers should make clear that they are teachers and mentors as well as judges, diminishing the now common fear that any acknowledgement of a problem or a request for advise reflects a punishable weakness. In short, managers also should be teachers and leaders and should themselves be judged against standards of leadership.

7. *The DCI should create increased opportunities for genuine intellectual competition.* The primacy of responsibility of only one office for almost all issues means that an office can ignore or water down even vigorous dissent by another office with overlapping analytic duties—further increasing the danger of an opinionated or incompetent office director. In interagency intelligence discussions, the responsible office is the sole CIA voice, masking within the intelligence community sometimes major internal DI disagreements. The reorganization of 1981 eliminated a major institutional brake on biased senior review on developments within single countries or regions while only partially accomplishing its ostensible goal of more efficient and "cross-fertilized" work. Another look at DI organization is needed.

The competing analysis needs to be institutionalized, and might be housed in an organization outside the regular DI personnel management system to protect its integrity. This could be accomplished with a small staff that simply asks a lot of questions. It could be a larger staff of real experts. It could take other forms. An expanded version of the Analytic Group of the National Intelligence Council—a group of several capable senior analysts who draft NIC papers, sometimes draft NIEs, and perform a variety of other analytic functions for the chairman of the NIC—is a potential model. It must, however, be able to speak with analysts candidly; it should have access to their information, and original and edited drafts, free from management interference. Its must have entree for its findings to officials at the highest levels of CIA, at least. A presidential directive that this organization also have direct access to the president's national security advisor would be better.

This function is needed because the often claimed functions of competing analysis generally do not exist between intelligence agencies. While beyond the scope of this discussion, interagency jostling often represents bureaucratic combat over already decided positions, not intellectual competition. Because DI analysis covers a larger range of intelligence issues than do other intelligence agencies and has greater resources, sound inquiry in the DI is essential before the orthodoxy of "CIA position" is stamped on a judgment.

8. *The Office of Personnel, now a tool of senior Agency management, should receive a mandate to care for the interests of personnel as well.* Some senior OP officers know well that the DI has severe management problems and that many DI employees are unhappy. Some seem genuinely to regret it. They nevertheless typically take the Nuremberg defense for their actions and inactions: they claim they have no real power and are just following orders. The Office of Personnel should have some real authority to care for personnel and a requirement to perform better.

9. *The DI needs a substantially altered personnel management system for analysts and managers.* The DI should seriously consider reorganizing the missions of the directorate's personnel to emphasize the key role of the analysts and to reduce the role—and relative pay levels—of managers in the control of ideas. The DI needs to reduce the linkage of management functions and review functions, or possibly even to de-link them entirely. Management in think tanks and academe, which most closely resemble the DI office environment, function with far fewer managers with greatly reduced powers. Moreover, professors often view management as a chore, not a reward or a worthy aspiration. University department chair-

persons do not decide the worth of scholarly journal submissions; colleagues and referees do. Think tank researchers also have timeliness, target audience, quality control, and budget concerns yet do without the management overhead of the DI.[3] Similarly, research scientists at major corporations sometimes command far greater salaries and freedom than their immediate bosses because senior management realizes that they do the work that makes money. There is no mission in the DI, unlike the Directorate of Operations, for example, that requires a military-like hierarchical power structure that commands ideas as well as people and budgets.

Moreover, the managerial superstructure simply is enormously burdensome. It is financially costly and too often an impediment to sound analysis. Its meetings and interminable review consume with little benefit the talents of many capable people. Generally, the DI needs a thorough reexamination of the very nature of DI management requirements, methods, and needed skills.

Sound analysts should be encouraged to become better analysts, not poor managers, and the disincentives to remain an analyst should be reduced. Despite the existence of the "senior analyst" position, there are few pay or bureaucratic incentives to remain an analyst. The Agency can change this by providing greater pay opportunities for analysts while separating at least partially management and review functions. This would give analysts, or groups of analysts of demonstrated ability, responsibilities for blessing analytical judgments that now reside with even junior, incompetent managers.

Analysts also need assurances that they will not continue to be victims of capricious management for which they have no recourse but changing jobs. Even people willing to forego public praise in return for the opportunity to do good work at CIA need some reassurance and recognition. Just an occasional good word goes a long way. The lack of a figurative kick in the teeth does not suffice. The Agency needs to work much harder to demonstrate that it really appreciates what it claims are its greatest assets—its employees.

10. *To help make it clear where problem managers exist, the DI should institutionalize anonymous evaluations of branch- and division- level managers by analysts and secretaries; summaries of these should be a mandatory part of managers' performance appraisals.* These evaluations should focus on the role of managers in facilitating the production/review process. The premise behind this proposal is that analysts are capable professionals who indeed are the fundamental producers of analysis, and who need genuine managerial services; they are not day laborers to be bossed. More senior management is paid to be observant and make decisions and could decide if a determined band of bad apples was conspiring to attack unjustly a genuinely good but tough manager—an extremely unlikely event. Implementation of these evaluations would procedurally be extremely simple. The Agency already has forms that could be used for this purpose.

11. *The Agency needs the bureaucratic freedom and courage to encourage problem managers to leave the Agency, not just the DI.* The practice of shuffling poor managers through the Agency until retirement is wasteful and damaging to the institution and its mission. The Agency already is exempt from many Civil Service personnel protections and the DCI has fairly wide latitude to dismiss employees. Managers have few second thoughts about terminating new employees in their initial three-year probationary periods and should not discriminate by longevity or pay grade. The oft-made argument that terminated managers would be security risks is conspicuously absent when discussion turns to the fates of new employees with the same basic security clearances and similar access to sensitive information.

12. *The destructiveness of some managers' meanness, dishonesty, and lack of intellectual integrity is so great that significant numbers—including many senior officers—should be fired from the Agency.* Their behavior has been and is deliberate. They are adults whose established value systems are not likely to change easily. They have prospered under the current system and cannot be expected to support change. Moreover, the

example of a purge is needed to demonstrate clearly to all employees the determination of the DCI, the president, or Congress to improve the Directorate; skepticism of the Agency's interest in sound management is extremely high among DI employees. To use Deputy Inspector General Cinquegrana's term, there needs to be an institution known internally as a "public hanging."

This is an extreme proposal for so bureaucratic an organization, but it is standard practice in response to such behavior in much of the rest of American organizational life. It also is not a new proposal for observers of CIA. Angelo Codevilla, a member of the Reagan transition team working intelligence issues after the 1980 election, recommended blanket dismissal of senior Agency officers.

13. *The Agency needs a thorough review and modification of its procedures for selecting and training managers.* Selection now is largely hit-or-miss, reflecting a series of individual preferences. The Office of Personnel or another organization should be involved in assessing, ranking, and ratifying choices. Training should precede assignment to a managerial position. It should not come later as time is available. The view, attributed by some in the DI to Robert Gates, that the DI does not have the time to adequately train managers prior to assignment is preposterous and should be discarded as such. Even major crises demand the use of a relatively small proportion of DI personnel assets.

The Agency needs to boost its training in management and, particularly, in leadership. It needs to emphasize real teamwork, not cultivation of the mutual interests of a club of individuals wanting to avoid complaints by unwashed "employees." It needs to re-emphasize the meaning of management and clearly to distinguish that function from intellectual omnipotence. It needs most firmly to state the importance of personal and intellectual integrity—major components of many practical definitions of leadership.

14. *The DI needs a DCI who has three basic attributes: knowledge about intelligence, defense, or foreign affairs; an*

impeccable sense of, and reputation for, personal and intellectual integrity; and, excellent managerial skills. A lesson of Judge Webster's tenure is that amateurs at the intelligence game do not do well. A DCI need not be a career intelligence officer, but he should know something about the foreign policy community of the United States and be willing to make an effort to learn quickly about intelligence. Moreover, the personal integrity of any DCI is functionally irrelevant if he does not insist that his values are those of his organization as well, and does not take decisive action to remedy ethical deficiencies.

The DCI must be a good leader and a good manager. The Agency and the DI have suffered in recent years from a lack of both. The DCI as manager must be willing to make difficult decisions quickly, must hold his subordinates genuinely accountable, and must be willing to take effective remedial action when needed.

The DCI needs some other qualities. He should have a strong work ethic; there is much to learn and do. He should have an interest in the quality of analysis, while avoiding interference with its production. He should have a well developed sense of caring for his employees. The DCI needs, and should be perceived by his employees as having, a sense of mission beyond protecting the bureaucratic concerns of the Central Intelligence Agency. He needs vision, courage, and a strong sense of proportion.

The DCI is but one of a maximum of three people in the entire Agency not groomed in the Agency or selected by Agency managers; only the DCI, DDCI, and Inspector General are political appointees and in recent years the DDCI regularly has been an Agency careerist. CIA is a special organization and the president should be especially careful in selecting its director.

15. *The DI needs a larger infusion of ideas from outside the Agency and the hiring of larger numbers of outsiders in more senior positions.* The DI hires virtually no one directly into management. Most experienced professionals enter analyst ranks where, despite their expertise, they have little influence

until they demonstrate their mettle as intelligence analysts as defined by the DI culture. These people—employed on career, temporary, or part-time bases—also would be good candidates for staffing the alternative analytic organization discussed under proposal #7 above.

16. *Congress should make appointees to the position of Deputy Director for Intelligence and his deputy subject to Senate confirmation.* Even a vigorous DCI can devote only a fraction of his time to DI matters and the management problems of the DI require significant time and attention. Moreover, the DI has fewer of the organizational peculiarities that argue persuasively for Agency careerists to head the other directorates. Journalists, think tank researchers, authors, and professors all do analytical work; DI analysis is special in its use of sensitive information and its clientele, not its generic type. A DDI with a president's ear could help tailor the Directorate's organizations and programs to make them more policy-relevant.

The risk of an appointee's injection of political bias into analysis is acceptable. An appointed DDI's opportunities for politicization would be smaller than the office directors now have; the DDI has less direct control over analysts and analysis. Exploitation of opportunities to inject specific, politically charged language would be much more obvious than the insidious politicization of the entire review process through the quest to please bureaucratic superiors. Agency personnel alert to the suspected machinations of an outsider would be much more likely to blow a whistle on a political appointee than an Agency professional who could damage their careers long after the political appointee is gone. Besides, it would be more fun. Senator John Glenn, an SSCI member and chairman of the Committee on Governmental Affairs, has unsuccessfully proposed this in the past.

17. *The Congress should increase its supervision of CIA and authorize the oversight committees specific powers to mandate reforms as well as better monitor day-to-day activities.* This is an extreme recommendation that reflects the persistent inability

of the Agency to police itself and the persistent unwillingness of the executive branch to supervise adequately.

The oversight committees need to much better understand the organization they oversee and need to vastly improve their ability to communicate with rank-and-file Agency employees as well as with senior management. While there are many possible ways to accomplish this, they should consider the permanent posting of staff members at CIA headquarters. At least one should be assigned to the Office of the Inspector General. While there would be a tendency to isolate these people and monitor their contacts, these committee representatives would be much more accessible to CIA employees than the committees are now. This physical presence also is required, I believe, to educate the Congress about CIA practices and culture. It is clear to me that even long-standing members of the SSCI and HPSCI remain too ignorant of the routine of CIA that is so essential to understanding the strengths and weaknesses of the organization. This proposal could face formidable partisan political obstacles and possible Constitutional objections related to the separation of the legislative and executive branches of government, but oversight would improve if such difficulties could be overcome.

To ensure that management does not continue to deny the ability of employees to seek redress with the Congress, the Agency needs new protections for "whistle-blowers." Because of senior management's demonstrated unwillingness to entertain such criticisms in the past, new legislation is needed to assure such protections. Such statutes need special crafting to accommodate the special aspects of intelligence and to work to overcome the problems of similar regulations in other government agencies. The law should carry significant criminal as well as administrative penalties for Agency managers violating the statute.

The long-standing blanket requirement that Agency officers seek and receive permission before discussing Agency business outside CIA should be amended to exclude Congressional oversight committee personnel. The standard questions asked by the Office of Security during periodic polygraph examinations about unauthorized discussions of classified material should explicitly exempt SSCI and HPSCI personnel.

18. *Finally, the best assurance of quality intelligence analysis is a consumer community that asks pointed questions and reacts candidly to both good and poor intelligence products.* Specific questions and requests to include methodological information can help keep analysis objective. Pointed rejoinders or requests for clarification would also help. Useless "intelligence" should be noted as such, not ignored. Senior policymakers can ask for briefings or, better yet, discussions with analysts, and not just the usual briefs by managers better skilled in smooth deliveries and glad-handing than the subjects they are talking about.

Presidents need to keep special watch on CIA analysis. The DI is the final filter through which much of CIA's technical and human collection passes, meaning that a healthy DI is essential to the success of the Agency as a whole. A president's reactions to intelligence products get CIA managers' attention. He alone has the power to order immediate drastic actions. His actions, reactions, and inaction are extremely important. He is ultimately responsible for the quality and usefulness of CIA analysis.

Notes to Chapter 7

1 The Senior Review Panel was transferred from the DI to the NIC in 1982 and was not subordinate to the DDI from 1982 through the early 1990s, at least, as erroneously reported in John Ranelagh, The Agency, The Rise and Decline of the CIA *(New York: Simon & Schuster, 1987) pp. 684 and 742.*

2 "Agonizing" was a favorite expression of a EURA branch chief in the early- and mid-1980s who was known in EURA as "Norman Bates"—after the protagonist of the movie "Psycho."

3 Indeed, mandated accounting of analysts' time divided by category of activity would demonstrate conclusively the enormous resources consumed by the review process. The requests for accounting that do occur query about time spent working on projects, not the elapsed time of a project or speed of review.

CHAPTER EIGHT

PART II

PENETRATING THE FOG

The unflattering picture of the Directorate of Intelligence in Part I contrasts with much of the public literature on CIA intelligence analysis. This is partially attributable to the difficulty of penetrating fog surrounding an institution that works hard to maintain its privacy and has some legitimate secrets to protect. However, it also reflects a lack of independent inquiry into areas which are accessible to the public in full compliance with United States law and CIA regulations.

Much of the subject matter of academic discussions, moreover, concerns issues that simply do not concern analysis as the DI practices it. Some papers are thoroughly historical—like discussions of the assumptions of British intelligence about German behavior during World War II, for example—while some address theoretical issues with little day-to-day relevance to the draft/review process. Other critiques are obvious and innocuous. Still other attacks challenge specific judgments or cite "failures" that, because they often offer no systemic criticism, can be dismissed by individuals as others' mistakes or legitimate differences of opinion. The best evidence of the ineffectiveness of academic critiques is that, internally, the DI largely ignores them.

The Agency is partly responsible for this fog through its selective, and generally sophisticated, discussion by senior officers like Robert Gates. Undoubtedly intending in part to deflect serious criticism, such officials graciously admit some minor problems, including some of those of management, while keeping the attacks at the margin.[1] At the same time, the Agency under the guise of security controls prohibits employees generally from discussing intelligence matters, either substantively or institutionally, without permission. It is a bureaucratically foolish employee indeed who criticizes the Agency in any significant way in a public forum.

There are, however, many ways for Congress, the president, and the public to better examine intelligence analysis. Academics have fertile ground for investigation in the large number of former analysts, whose restrictions on talking freely are far smaller than those of current employees. The reason for this is simple. The secrecy oaths that all employees carry to their graves cover only classified or classifiable material—specifc judgments, names of CIA employees, and issues involving sources and methods, for example— while the key issues of the performance of the DI concern organizational, institutional, and ethical matters. Discussion of these—while protecting specific data like names, budgets, specific analytic judgments, and so on—at worse damage only reputations. There thus is little danger, when discussing the conduct of analysis, of running afoul of measures to protect legitimate secrets like those of the Directorate of Operations.

In the next three chapters, I offer suggestions for improving outsiders' assessments of CIA analysis. Chapter nine addresses some of the misunderstandings about analysis that have appeared in reputable publications in recent years. Chapter ten contains an attempt to describe in detail the characteristics and power of the culture of politicization— one that is very difficult to convey to people who have not experienced it; chapter ten also looks for lessons about review and politicization in one of Robert Gates' own memorandums. Finally, chapter 11 contains thoughts about a framework for analysis of intelligence analysis generally, using the DI's traits as examples.

Note to Chapter 8

1 See, for example, Gates' discussion comments in Godson, ed., Intelligence Requirements for the 1990s, *pp. 111-119.*

CHAPTER NINE

EXPLANATIONS, CORRECTIONS, AND COMMENTS

The relatively small body of literature on intelligence analysis is filled with judgments and assertions at variance with DI reality. Some articles contain factual errors. Some reflect understandable ignorance. Others reflect judgments which should be reexamined. In still other cases, important aspects of analysis have received little attention.

The Failure of Attacks on "Failures"

The recurrent attacks on "intelligence failures" caused by deficiencies of analysis involve judgments about individual issues and usually do little to address any institutional roots of misjudgments. They thus are fairly easily ignorable by the "mistaken" organization. In retrospect, these misjudgments may be embarrassing. They may cost tens of billions of dollars or exacerbate a cold war, but even the most serious criticisms of failure—like those surrounding estimates of Soviet strategic capabilities in the 1970s and 1980s, for example—usually boil down to differences of fact, method, opinion, or judgment that are understandable as human frailties. Bright, honest, knowledgeable people who work hard often differ over complex questions.

The implicit demand of critics that intelligence analysis never have "failures" is self-defeating. "Errors" in forecasts occur because intelligence organizations have the institutional courage to tackle difficult issues when facts are few, intentions obscure and developing, fog thick, and noise levels high. Intelligence organizations that want to avoid specific forecasting or estimative failures can do so easily by avoiding complex issues that could affect US interests in the future. When cornered by consumers to make a call, they can weasel to the point that their conclusions are consistent with most of the probable outcomes.

Chronic behavior of this sort is a systemic failure of intelligence—a far more serious failure that is consistent with the development of an intelligence bureaucracy overly fond of kudos and lacking institutional backbone.[1] Critics should be vigilant for institutional problems like repeated analytic failures by the organization as a whole when sound judgments at the analyst and junior manager level are squelched or edited beyond recognition by the review process. These, like the proliferation incident noted in chapter 4, happen. Intelligence bureaucrats may respond to attacks of this sort by arguing that: indeed they did note the development and reported it (albeit much too late to be of policy use); or, the development falls within the generic category of events discussed in some obscure document, which the policy community ignored.

Incongruous though it may seem at first glance, I believe the nation should welcome some intelligence "failures." These should not be too numerous, too severe, or involve military warning, of course; serious failures of collection should also be minimized if possible. However, some analytic failures are unavoidable if the intelligence community is to stretch aggressively, to "lean forward" in Bob Gates' parlance, to identify trends of importance to the United States—both threats and opportunities to exploit—as early as possible.

Social scientists might search for an "optimal" service/failure relationship, but I am skeptical that any general formula can be calculated or could be implemented in practice. The economists' concept of "satisficing" probably is a more useful. Under this concept, individuals (or nations' policymakers and intelligence services) recognize a series of important goals that are sometimes mutually exclusive (like long-lead time warnings, complete accuracy of forecasts, thoroughly policy-relevant analysis, and cost effectiveness) and try to patch together less than ideal outcomes for individual goals in hope of reaching the best total result.

In practice, the best strategy may encompass three elements that take time to develop: institutional courage to reach and sometimes "err" on forecasts of distant, perhaps low probability but high impact, events; management encouragement of initiative, imagination, and sometimes even apparently "off-the-wall" ideas by analysts; and, consumer and public recognition of the difficulty of providing warning, willingness to accept occasional "failures" as a price of initiative, and the development of their confidence that their intelligence community is doing the best it can. None exists now.

Differences Between DI Analysis and National Estimates

The literature on intelligence analysis contains assessments that often are vague on just what "CIA analysis" constitutes, and sometimes blend it with discussions of the analyses contained in NIEs and the other publications of the intelligence community overseen by the NIC.[2] In fact, CIA analysis is very distinct even though DI personnel often serve in community roles as NIOs, the NIC's offices for many years were physically located in CIA headquarters, and the CIA printing plant prepares the NIC's documents.

DI personnel write and review DI products independent of the rest of the community. Review normally stops at the level of the DDI, meaning that the DCI usually does not see DI products until they arrive in final form on his desk. In practice, the office directors control analysis, and determine significantly the shape of CIA positions in community discussions.

Community products, on the other hand, may be drafted by analysts from any intelligence community agency. The "principal drafter" of an estimate normally is an experienced analyst expert in the subject of the estimate. An NIO, who may likewise come from any agency of the community, and who has responsibility for the subject of the estimate, supervises the drafting of the paper. After review by the NIO, the chairman of the NIC or his representative (and often members of the Senior Review Panel as well) reviews the draft. After such coordination within the NIC, the draft goes to the rest of the intelligence community with responsibilities in the area of the estimate. After sometimes considerable alteration in language to reflect diverging views, and the taking of "footnotes" to indicate differences of opinion that cannot be reconciled, the draft is "coordinated."[3] Then, the DCI wearing his community hat, along with the heads of other members of the community, convene a National Foreign Intelligence Board (NFIB) session that approves the NIE (or SNIE). The chairman of the NIC alone approves lower level community products—Intergency Intelligence Memorandums (IIMs) and Special IIMs (SIIMs). The DI thus has an especially major role in the shaping of community judgments if one of its own is selected as drafter, but it must still contend with the views of the rest of the intelligence community.

Even the bureaucratic DI regards the community's coordination process as cumbersome and its products often improvable. While some estimates are very good, the intelligence community is prone to publishing NIEs either reduced to pabulum by compromise, or containing disjointed jumbles of opinions by agencies' insistence on inclusion of their opinions in footnotes. The NIC has even gone one step further than the DI in its "service" to consumers pressed for time. At the beginning of NIEs produced in the late 1980s, it mandated addition of a summary of key judgments, themselves a summary of the already homogenized views of the community. For a time, by dictum of the vice chairman of the NIC, these amounted to no more than four points, contained in a single sentence each. Recognizing the silliness and severe limitations of this directive, NIOs immediately began to make extensive use of semicolons.

Because the process often is slow, and NIOs usually pick good analysts as drafters, DI office directors interested in boosting their production numbers may be unenthusiastic about contributing drafters for community products. In addition, the selection of a good DI analyst to address a subject in a community product may preclude the DI from tackling the identical subject in a DI publication, and inhibit the office director from very strongly controlling the shape of the assessment. Because drafting a community paper usually does not count much toward satisfaction of DI production expectations, most analysts want to be a drafter only once—for the experience of understanding first-hand the fine points and frustrations of dealing with the community as a whole.

Moreover, much of the DI is suspicious of NIOs, as well as the other community agencies, for bureaucratic reasons. Always alert for infringements on their turf, DI managers want to know what NIOs are up to, and often require analysts to immediately report to them any communication with NIOs, including innocuous phone calls seeking data.

Myth of the Analyst as Key to Analysis

Non-Agency observers usually grossly overestimate the importance of the "analyst" as the key actor in CIA intelligence analysis because they do not understand the power of management to control ideas. The intelligence literature typically attributes virtually all of the perceived problems of analysis—lack of training, cultural biases, mirror imaging, and methodological problems—to analysts themselves. At the same time, the literature generally underestimates the importance of the review and coordination processes in shaping final, written judgments, and contains little discussion of them.[4]

While there are poor analysts, and the weaknesses in them that outside observers commonly lament do occur, DI analysts have become soldiers who obey orders. Managements in some major units of the DI have deployed their troops as research assistants and drafters in the service of their analytic visions.

The analyst weaknesses commonly cited by critics pale in comparison to the potential for intelligence failures—and simply poor day-to-day estimative analysis—caused by the ignorance, prejudices, personal interests, and capricious characteristics of a relatively small number of senior managers—primarily the office directors.

The continuing critical focus on analysts is akin to blaming riflemen, but not officers, for a defeat in battle. Continuing the military analogy, the existence of an adequate number of soldiers who can shoot straight is a necessary but not sufficient condition for battlefield success. It is a natural but irresponsible tendency of current and former CIA managers to blame their subordinates for their own inadequacies in assuring sound intelligence analysis. By focusing on analysts, students of intelligence analysis aim their critical arrows at the wrong targets, allowing in the worst cases DI managerial culprits to continue to avoid both their responsibilities and the punishments those actions and inactions warrant.

More generally, academic observers have largely ignored the role and importance of managers in the shaping of intelligence analysis at CIA in virtually all its aspects. These managers in many cases do not retain the analytical expertise that may have put them into management in the first place and often do not deserve the title "analyst" even broadly defined. Their knowledge sometimes has grown stale, and their usually considerable innate talents are devoted to bureaucratic battles. They may have supervisory responsibilities over analytical areas they never knew well; this trend is particularly pronounced as managers assume more senior positions and rotate laterally throughout the Agency. Key aspects of the control of managers include: criteria for organization and reorganizations; project selection criteria and the development of research programs; the review process generally; employee selection processes; training courses and priorities; and, the DI personnel system including rating and promotion criteria. The lack of public inquiry into the roles, impact, and competence of DI management is a significant deficiency that is subject to redress through survey work with former DI employees, at minimum.

The growth in the authority of DI management over intellectual judgments occurred in the 1980s and is a legacy of the Casey/Gates regime. It contrasts sharply with previous practice as described by former DDI Ray Cline:

> "... we have human beings. We try to get good ones and honest ones, and try to put them in the right slots at the right time for their talents and expertise, and have management only for the purpose of getting that expertise fully voiced for the benefit of policymakers."[5]

For DI analysts in the 1980s and early 1990s, this is a wonderful attitude that they rarely experienced.

Mirror Imaging Both an Asset and a Liability

Students of intelligence analysis long have noted that analysts' assumptions that foreign peoples act as they would in the same circumstance—the propensity to "mirror image"—can inhibit understanding and lead to surprises and sometimes significant intelligence failures. This is true. However, a propensity to mirror image, or at least respond to the desires of reviewers and consumers to receive judgments packaged in standard American cultural terms, is a major bureaucratic asset and, indeed, is often essential for bureaucratic success.

The mythical "reader" defined by each reviewer usually is an individual with limited time, modest intellect, and a desire for information or judgments that help resolve an immediate problem of the *United States* government. Most reviewers thus implicitly assume, and sometimes explicitly state to analysts, that policymakers want intelligence readily usable in their cultural context and do not want the sophisticated analyses acceptable in academe or even in the press.

A financial example illustrates the level of ethnocentrism and ignorance the DI attributes to policymakers, and shows a small measure of the mischief this condescension can cause. In the mid-1980s, the then-German Democratic Republic received two large loans from West German banks, denominated in West German Deutsche Marks (DM), that were guaranteed by the West German government. These guarantees were unprecedented and evoked considerable attention in the world political and financial media.

The DI also reported these loans. CPAS editors, presuming that readers of the *National Intelligence Daily* were ignorant of the nature and worth of the DM despite its importance as a major world currency, insisted that the loans be described as US dollar-denominated credits. Over a period of months, because the dollar/DM exchange rate was fluctuating considerably, the NID used the then-current exchange rate to print a series of different dollar values for the same two loans. The result—all in the name of making intelligence understandable to an American policymaker—was a series of references that erroneously reported the terms of the credits, confusingly misrepresented their values over time, and indicated that there were more loans than actually were made. The decision presumably also suggested to knowledgeable officials at the Departments of State, Treasury, Commerce, and elsewhere that CIA analysts were thoroughly incompetent, further contributing to the Agency's credibility problem.

This relatively innocuous example illustrates but part of the problem of including sophisticated analysis in DI products. The difficulty grows markedly when the goal of analysis is a forecast about the long-term political objectives of Middle Eastern leaders, for example. It is a rare analyst indeed who understands "esoteric political cultures," to use Paul Seabury's term, and who can regularly negotiate through rigid stylistic and review requirements to put sophisticated analysis that captures foreign cultures in American/intelligence jargon, briefly stated, on the desk of a policymaker who thinks it good enough to use.[6]

Most sound analysts are well aware of the differences between foreign cultures and their own, and of how important it is to include such understanding in their analyses. Critics thus tell good analysts little by stressing the importance of such knowledge. Tendencies toward mirror-imaging are much more likely to be the result of the review process or ignorance of facts, due to rotation to new accounts or inadequate training, than of ignorance of the concept of mirror-imaging. I believe that observers such as Eliot Cohen overestimate its importance as an intellectual impediment to sound analysis.[7]

Bureaucratization Hinders Ability to Recruit Diversity

Observers of intelligence analysis properly have noted that familiarity with foreign societies reduces the risk of mirror imaging and generally helps improve analysis. Yet, the increasing regimentation of DI analytic style—written and mental—appears to be having serious negative implications for the DI's ability to recruit and retain able individuals with initiative and imagination who are familiar with other cultures as well.

The DI's personnel practices clearly reward conformity and docility in thought and style, and some office managements actively discourage debate or discussion by branding it a form of anti-social behavior. Success is measured by one's ability to meet DI (or office) standards for slant and style of analysis. All new analysts, regardless of credentials, must prove themselves within this system. This requirement discourages application by experienced people and/or those of different cultural heritages, limits those of all backgrounds who want to expand their horizons, and discourages creativity.

The DI's standards thus seem most appealing to the very class of analyst least likely to appreciate foreign cultures—young people with mainstream backgrounds interested in adapting to, and doing well in, a new job. The DI hires a lot of recent university graduates—who are relatively easily molded—and comparatively few academics, retired military officers, or other capable, experienced people in mid-life who are more difficult to bring to conformity.

The Office of Security makes it still harder to hire people with foreign experience. The espionage cases of the 1980s involving CIA personnel and others with access to intelligence information have made the Office of Security still more wary of people with foreign contacts—further encouraging the hiring of young stay-at-homers. Security processing is slow, discouraging some applicants, and the rejection rate for applicants put into security processing (which occurs only after an office decides it wants an individual) is very high. One can only speculate about how many good candidates are disqualified by benign nervousness at the polygraph test and the paranoia of security officers. The tests are widely despised by cleared personnel undergoing normal reinvestigations; they regularly hear of unnecessarily unpleasant experiences during reexaminations, even as they know of the severe limitations of the polygraph and the problems they have caused the DO, in particular.[8]

Moreover, the DI poorly uses the diversity it has. Many new analysts have received initial duties that differ from their background and training. The personnel management system that encourages "troop rotations"—a reference to the Soviet Army's large semi-annual conscription and troop reassignment cycle—often cares little for exploitation of the expertise it has. The DI in the late 1980s and early 1990s maintained only a single computerized data base of analyst expertise which incomprehensibly equated skills with current duty assignments. Furthermore, the rigidities of the career service system, and the unhappiness that motivates many analyst requests for reassignment to other offices, virtually preclude effective use of the DI's quite large stock of expertise.

More Training May Not Make Analysis Better

Critics of CIA analysis for years have assumed that more training for analysts is better than less, and have proposed a series of areas for training and education as well as education-related hiring criteria. The Agency has introduced a few courses that serve at minimum to allow senior Agency officials to state truthfully that they have responded to such critiques. However, these in-house courses appear to be of limited use and may, in some cases, be counter-productive.

The only analytical courses the DI really stresses involve new employees and relate to judgments about the capabilities (and ignorance), writing styles, and methodological precepts these people bring to the job. The standard new analysts' courses presume that analysts are poorly trained by universities for intelligence work and need to be "deprogrammed," in the words of a DI manager, then rebuilt into real intelligence analysts.[9] In this way, new analysts' courses somewhat resemble Marine Corps basic training. Similarly, some analysts and managers pride themselves as being better than effete academics who do not deal with real world issues. This disdain also helps explain the reluctance of management to accept transfusions of academic blood into management or analyst ranks; in this view, there is little contribution that academe can make.

From the DI's perspective, universities fail to satisfy the needs of intelligence analysis in several key respects. Probably most important, in the view of many DI managers, universities do not value or teach "tight" writing.[10] Because the DI has adopted highly rigid styles and formats—literally including strict limits on numbers of words, sentences, and lines of print for some current intelligence publications—the ability to "package" is critical. The DI stresses the importance of the ability of an analyst to tell a "story" succinctly. Without packaging tools, an analyst's career will go nowhere—regardless of his knowledge or inherent analytic ability.

The DI breaks with academe in the relative importance it gives to understanding phenomena versus communicating beliefs. Because story telling skills are so important to maintaining DI "standards," the new analyst must learn to grasp for a simple message and support it with facts just sufficient to support the story line chosen.[11] DI managers generally judge it desirable to present a full discussion if possible; if a choice has to be made, however, many insist that a clear but incomplete or superficial story be presented rather than a lengthy, complicated one. This view stems directly from their concept of the limited capabilities and interests of the consumer community, and the orders of their superiors in the review chain which made full discussions difficult in any format.

Academic emphasis on methodologically sound work that can be replicated, which new employees bring from the universities, is a problem to be trained away. The academic's intellectual value system gives secondary importance to literary style, leads to longer but fewer articles that by definition mean less "production," implicitly imposes greater demands on competence of the review chain, assumes a different "reader," and puts an unwanted premium on intellectual integrity into the analysis/review process.

In other respects, DI concerns about the training of new employees make some sense. The DI's mission of forecasting, versus analysis of historical events, is a real change for many new employees; some individuals are much more comfortable poring over facts than they are in making judgments without the benefit of complete information. The Agency's role as a component of the US government places restrictions on the freedom of individuals to investigate at will; medieval furniture design clearly falls beyond the scope of fiscally responsible CIA inquiry. Still other new employees, like much of the population, can use help in crafting a paragraph.

Once at his desk, a new analyst's additional training in areas related to analytic ability is likely to be modest, and have little impact on his ability to do his job. Much of his training will concern technical topics like instructions on new computer systems, for example. For managers, analyst training usually is a secondary priority and may be a nuisance. Training can be a reward that gets an employee out of the normal office routine. It can be an unwelcome levy to fill quotas for unpopular courses that reduces analysts' time at their desks and thus cuts production. Training also is granted to employees who want it as the press of work permits.

In practice, despite a number of DI training and educational opportunities, I believe DI management little appreciates or encourages continuing education. As described in chapter 3, management (and thus analysts) regards expertise as less, not more important, than it once did. As analysts regularly rotate from office to office, training becomes an expensive luxury. If job description defines expertise, as is the case in some offices, the analyst needs little education beyond on-the-job training; analysts know this and may resist extensive training that would cut the growth of production files and thus promotion prospects. More training for these regular job changers, while perhaps of value to a neophyte analyst on a new account, will do little to improve the intellectual capital stock of the whole institution that is actually at work.

If the DI can decide that it really serves the United States government and not "the seventh floor," much of the Directorate would benefit from a course on how the US government works. Many Agency personnel understand foreign governments far better than their own. This is a direct result of prohibitions on CIA activities concerning the United States and helps account for some of the on-going wrangles about who the "reader" of DI products is. Better understanding of fellow public servants would assist analysts in preparing distribution lists for their papers. It also would better link the needs of consumers with intelligence activities by facilitating communications and increasing the chances for successful opportunity-oriented analysis. However, DI practice in recent years has been in the opposite direction—limiting contacts of all but management to consumer executive branch organizations and the Congress.

While there is periodic discussion of the need for both generalists and specialists (or experts), there is no distinction in the DI personnel system and no dual training programs to develop the best in either complementary approach to analysis. Decisions to take one or the other course are largely personal or may be made implicitly due to happiness with a current assignment, or such misery that the analyst just wants to go anywhere to get away from the present work environment. The decisions seemingly occur independently of the control and needs of the Directorate as a whole. OTE has no separate training curricula for the two career strategies.

The Intelligence "Eight"

Instruction in intelligence methods normally contains a diagram that is usually described as the "intelligence cycle" or "intelligence process." This cycle appears visually as a rough circle as shown in figure 5. In dynamic situations, the process is continuous. It is a fair representation of intelligence in aggregate.

In daily practice for many DI analysts, this cycle is modified considerably into what might be called an intelligence "eight" or even a "nine" (see figure 6). The following outlines procedures for product forms such as typescript memoranda or assessments—items often requested rather than generated at office initiative. The first step in the process is a request for a product—shown at the upper left of the figure. After (and sometimes before) project approval, analysts and management formulate initial hypotheses and stipulate format specifications including length. The analyst then checks or rechecks his personal files and Agency data resources for relevant information. If data are insufficient and time is plentiful, he may initiate formal written requirements for additional information through the DI's collection requirements staff. He may also make a quick phone call to a collector with whom he has developed a good working relationship—if the collection agency has not bureaucratically atrophied to the point that only formal written requests will be honored.[12] If he is lucky, the collection community will be able to respond directly to his request and he will be able to improve his analysis, or at least have another source to reference in the document that he eventually provides to consumers. The flow of requests and reports thus resembles the number eight.

More likely, time constraints or analyst pessimism about the speed and responsiveness of the requirements process will lead him to decide not to levy requirements; in this case, he will rely solely on data currently on hand or in the information pipeline. The collection organizations' normal operations may put some current reports at least peripherally relevant on his desk as he drafts because the community probably will already have

Figure 5

The Intelligence Cycle

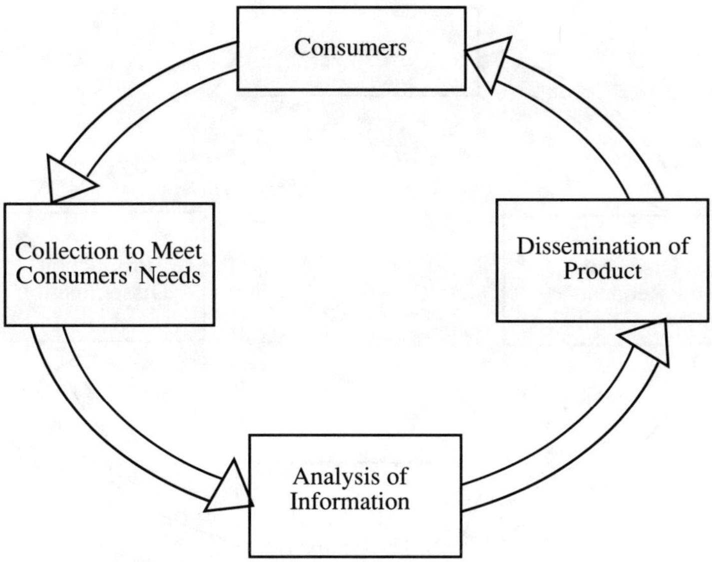

identified the topic as interesting. If there has not been an expression of interest via standing requirements, there may be no requirements levied prior to project conclusion. Without the left half of its lower lobe, the model of requests and reports resembles the number nine.

Diminished Methodological Considerations

Intelligence watchers over the years have variously criticized analysis for adhering too tightly to some analytical approaches or philosophies, or are in need of better use of others. Some proponents of "opportunity-oriented" analysis, for example, criticize the traditional approach for its allegedly excessive emphasis on empiricism—the preferred method of Sherman Kent. They also argue for use of "self-conscious

Figure 6

The Intelligence "Eight"

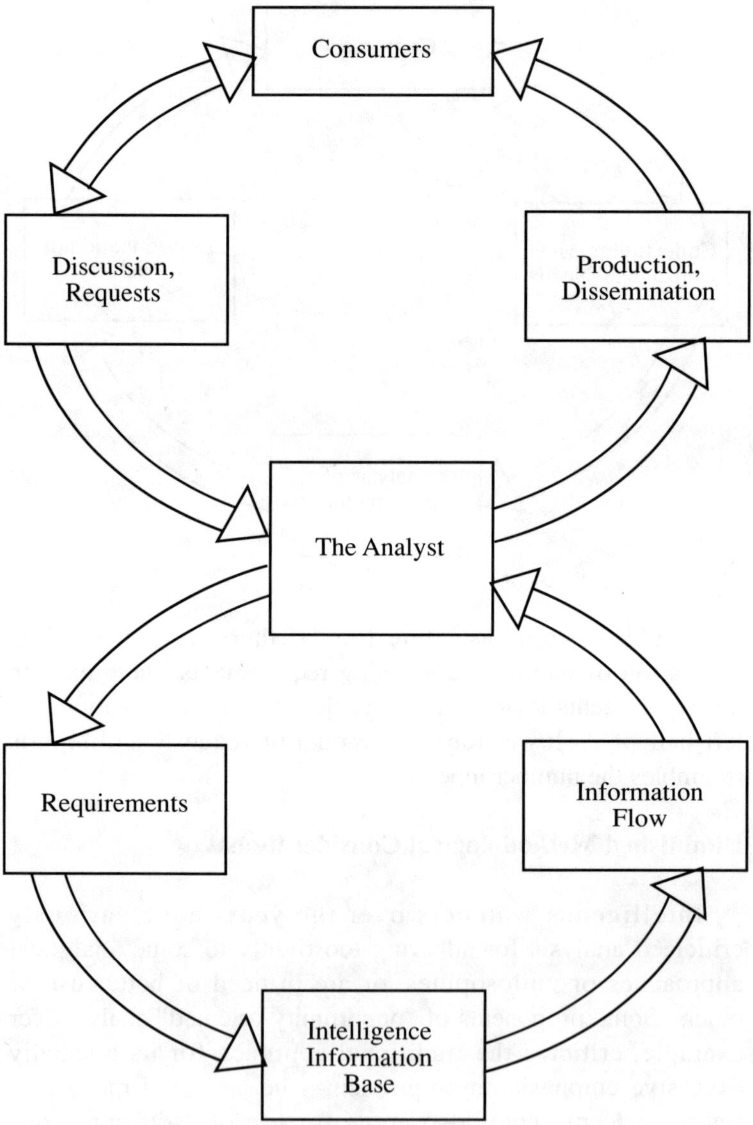

epistemology"—making clear what analysts know, do not know, and the theories or paradigms they use to reach conclusions.[13]

While some DI analysts and managers are very concerned with methods and a few are interested in methodology, the trend is away from use of such intellectual rigor. It is inconsistent with personal preference-driven review and offers analysts unwelcome opportunities to attack reviewers' changes on logical, factual, or methodological grounds. Rigor also gets in the way of packaging. Stylistic directives tend to discourage use of scientific methods that interfere with DI-style presentations, while imposing some requirements that ostensibly are quality control measures. It is a simple fact of daily life in the DI that issues like empiricism and epistemology are not topics of significant concern by analysts or reviewers.

Stylistic and presentational considerations normally dominate methodological issues, both in analysis and final document preparation. DI preference for the journalists' "inverted pyramid" method of presentation—dominant conclusion stated first with less important detail following—goes far beyond the admonition to formulate good topic sentences. It often precludes publication of background information, statements of assumptions, or definition of theoretical constructs used; these, it is argued, get in the way of provision of succinct judgments to busy policymakers unconcerned with trivia like how CIA reached its conclusions.

While empiricism is inconvenient for some reviewers, empirical facts, defined as the contents of raw intelligence reports, are often very important. In a mutant legacy of Gates' reasonable directive that judgments be supported by evidence, some office directors require the attachment of a reference of some sort to very elementary facts and basic analytical reasoning processes. Thus, in an extreme example, an analyst might be required to append a source (such as the *Farmer's Almanac)* to an obvious statement such as, "days in June in the United States are longer than nights." References—from intelligence sources or published articles, for example—might be required for even simple analytical judgments like, in another extreme case, "the sun probably will rise tomorrow morning in the east." Analyst failure to provide a regular stream of source attributions, through such phrases as "according to a generally reliable source ..." is grounds for criticism by managers. Such guidance encourages the use of "research" as a story support mechanism—rather than the beginning of study or analysis—and makes the presentation of complex reasoning more complicated. Creativity thus is too often discouraged because it usually goes well beyond simple assembly of others' views.

A Third School of Analysis?

Students of intelligence analysis have for years debated its proper role in the United States and, in the view of Roy Godson, fall generally into two categories. A traditional "school" descended from the views of Sherman Kent holds that analysts (should) objectively—independent of policymakers' concerns—describe and evaluate trends abroad, leaving policymakers to decide their importance and take action.[14] This was the dominant intellectual paradigm at CIA throughout the 1970s.

A second school, long a minority view, believes that intelligence analysis should be more activist, identifying policy opportunities through use of "opportunity-oriented analysis" and responding more effectively to a policy community that believes CIA to have become too isolated. Godson credits DCI William Casey and DDI/DDCI Robert Gates with developing new analytic products that have blurred the distinction between the types of analysis envisioned by each school.[15]

The mutation of the efforts of Gates and Casey—however originally well-intended—as described in chapters 3 and 4 differs markedly from Godson's assessment of their accomplishments. The record suggests the development of another de facto school of analysis that might be called "bureaucratic opportunism-oriented" analysis. One former analyst calls it the "apparatchik" school. In key respects, the reality of several offices of the DI in 1980s and the early 1990s, particularly some regional offices and RTT, fits neither of the two visions of analysis Godson discusses and deserves a separate name.

This third way involves fundamental policies of some senior managers, explicit or de facto, about the mission of the Directorate, its priorities, and its ethical standards. Figure 7 offers a rough tabulation of key characteristics of the schools for discussion purposes; there is no firm agreement on the first two, let alone the third.

Most important, Gates' changes evolved in the DI bureaucracy to the point that many in the DI believe that "policy relevance" is generated by providing products that satisfy consumers. This portion of the DI does not evaluate developments in the world, present them to the policy community, and let that community search for ways to use the intelligence. Instead, it discovers what consumers want, and provides formats, topics, and sometimes judgments that they desire. The difference between opportunity-oriented analysis and the third way is the latter's emphasis on message format and content that pleases rather than the selection of topics that show policymakers where, when, and how they have opportunities to advance US interests. The difference is basic.

The third way implicitly (and sometimes explicitly) assumes a markedly different type of intelligence consumer than the other two schools. It is a product of the Reagan years and presumes a substantively shallow consumer who is interested in entertaining intelligence stories. Both other schools assume higher levels of consumer competence. The traditional school presumes policymakers can glean useful judgments from analyses and incorporate them wisely into policy, while the opportunity-oriented school believes sound policymakers want intelligence help to aggressively conduct foreign policy.

A logical product of the belief that satisfaction of wants constitutes service is the implicit equating of the intelligence needs of policymakers with their wants in support of a policy position or a world view. This clearly opposes the traditionalists' aversion to purposefully serving intelligence as ammunition in policy debates. It also tends to generate fuzzy

Figure 7

The Three "Schools:" A Rough Comparison

	School		
Characteristic	Traditional	Opportunity-Oriented	Opportunism-Oriented
Analytically Objective	Yes	Yes	If Convenient
Pointedly Policy-relevant	No	Yes	Yes
Oriented Toward Wants or Needs	Needs	Both	Wants
Will Offer Unwelcome Assessments	Yes	Yes. Unlikely If Good Communication	Reluctantly
Assessment of Consumer	Capable	Capable	Not So Able
Research-heavy Analysis	Yes	Depends on Situation	No
Time Horizon	Long	Long	Shorter

analysis that weakly helps a decisionmaker who needs hard-headed intelligence support when launching a risky foreign policy initiative.

Because the mission is satisfying consumers, success is measurable by the receipt of kudos rather than the use, quality, prescience, or durability of analyses. Hence, evaluations of the accuracy of forecasts are unnecessary, reducing vulnerability to the embarrassment of examining one's own accuracy at the same time. This measure is dependent on the responses of consumers and the liaison officers who pass intelligence documents to policymakers, and their reactions back to CIA headquarters in return. With but partial feedback, however, the DI cannot accurately know how it is meeting its bureaucratic objectives.[16] Again, this implicit success criterion is different than that of both other schools.

This alteration of perspective allows considerable flexibility in the packaging of products, ostensibly in response to consumer and academic criticism, but actually in the service of the prime objective of preserving the bureaucratic interests of the Agency. The fact that the Agency wants to serve itself is hardly surprising. However, portions of the DI seemingly rate those interests above the mission of service and intellectual objectivity that were hallmarks of the Agency in its early years.

Notes to Chapter 9

1 For a good discussion of how diverse the opportunities for slips 'tween intelligence cup and consumer lip in the strategic arena, see Bruce D. Berkowitz and Allan E. Goodman, Strategic Intelligence for American National Security *(Princeton: Princeton University Press, 1989) pp. 30-32.*

2 In the late 1980s, the four main publications of the intelligence community were: the NIEs, often regular scheduled documents on subjects of continuing interest; special NIEs that tackle new or transitory concerns of major interest; Interagency Intelligence Memoranda (IIMs), which generally address more technical issues; and Special IIMs, which concern issues similar to those of the IIMs, published on more ad hoc bases. The criteria for titling estimates are not completely clear, but the listing above generally ranks them in descending order of perceived importance. In the late 1980s, the NIC introduced its own memoranda, which do not carry the authority of the entire community.

3 Disagreements on important issues appear literally as footnotes in the text or key judgments of an NIE. The footnotes state that the head of the dissenting organization believes something else.

4 For a very good checklist of what can go wrong, see Berkowitz and Goodman, Strategic Intelligence, *pp. 185-192.*

5 See Cline's comments in Godson, ed., Intelligence Requirements for the 1980's: Analysis and Estimates *(Washington: National Strategy Information Center, Inc., 1980) p. 79.*

6 See unnamed essay by Paul Seabury, in Godson, ed., Intelligence Requirements for the 1990s, *p. 103.*

7 See Godson, ed., Intelligence Requirements for the 1990s, *pp. 76-81.*

8 In one particularly unpleasant case, rumor had it in the late 1980s that polygraph operators quizzed a young mother who recently had lost a baby to Sudden Infant Death Syndrome about whether she had killed the child.

9 See page 2 of "Managing/Teaching New Analysts," a sanitized version of an classified article written by "One DI Manager for Other DI Managers" that appeared in the Fall 1986 edition of Studies in Intelligence. *In fact, this article was quite popular for a while in some DI offices, leading at least one office to require that the outline portion of IA and RP project definition papers consist entirely of questions to be answered. See also Eliot Cohen, "The 'No Fault' View of Intelligence, in Godson, ed.,* Intelligence Requirements for the 1990s, *pp. 71-76 and 90-92.*

10 See Robert Gates' comments in Godson, Intelligence Requirements for the 1990s, *p. 113.*

11 So strong is the drive to create good stories that a few analysts and managers stretch data or use relatively unreliable reports without the motive of politicization. I once had a reviewer who repeatedly changed numbers—hard facts—in the interest of improving the "story."

12 Some collection agencies require adherence by potential customers to extremely rigid, written request formats to get them to act. The National Security Agency is among the worst—leading many DI analysts simply to ignore tasking NSA.

The entire requirements mechanism is a source of frustration for most analysts. Periodic updates of general requirements called the National Intelligence Topics, or NITs, often are extremely vague, leading to periodic snide comments that "nit wits" make the NITs.

13 Godson, ed., Intelligence Requirements for the 1990s, *p. 8.*

14 Ibid., pp. 4-11.

15 Ibid., p. 6.

16 Liaison officers vary markedly in their provision of feedback from consumers. This undoubtedly reflects varying responses among consumers, but relates in some cases to sharply differing assessments of the value of feedback. Some former analysts, remembering the frustrations of working without knowing if their efforts were read by anyone outside CIA, are especially likely to give feedback. They also prefer to send positive rather than negative reactions of consumers. Thus, the kudo index of performance is inherently biased.

CHAPTER TEN

A PRIMER ON REVIEW AND POLITICIZATION

The principal way for a reviewer to both improve analysis and convey a political agenda is through provision of written comments on a draft paper. These often are marching instructions rather than debating points, although reviewers maintain varying degrees of willingness to discuss issues. Reviewers couch their comments across a spectrum of statements, questions, and directives. Analysts and managers study these comments carefully to determine what reviewers "really want," to use a fairly common DI expression.

A declassified review of an NIE draft by Robert Gates illustrates some of the phrases and orders that catch drafters' eyes. The February 14, 1982 memo, entitled "NIE on Soviets and the Third World," provides a wealth of specific guidance and pointed reaction (see Appendix B, page 298). While this memo provides some lessons, readers should remember that CIA declassified the previously secret document on the occasion of the 1991 Gates confirmation hearings as part of the effort to buttress his defense against charges that he politicized analysis. The name of the addressee of the memo has been deleted, but he was in fact the drafter of the NIE—Melvin A. Goodman. The memo is Gates' guide for remedial work, and an explanation of what he found objectionable.

The drafter and intermediate reviewers undoubtedly regarded the comments as severely negative. The first three lines give the judgment that a major rewrite, at minimum, is necessary: "… I have read the attached draft and, unhappily, find it rather dry and lacking any sense of Soviet involvement in the Third World and why involvement in the Third World is important to the Soviets." The specifics of Gates' problems and his solutions follow in the eight indented "ticks"—as they are called in the DI—that follow. (The first contains three paragraphs.) Generally, any such comments warrant careful study by a reviewee and should be regarded as the shape the reviewer wants to see in the next draft. They are orders, not suggestions.

The first tick provides both a reorganization scheme and a general analytical line; it begins the process of mandating the paper's conclusions. Organizationally, the tick orders a "historical introduction" pointing out the Soviets' "ideological motives" for an "activist role" in the Third World. Motives rarely can be ascertained with certainty, ensuring that Gates' personal judgment would shape the draft's entire discussion in its introduction. Gates then wants a "brief review" that spans thirty years—the early 1950s to 1982—that includes activities such as: types of assistance, kinds of setbacks, and changes in approaches and tactics. It specifies that the "brief" section should mention Egypt, Cuba, Chile, the United States, Ethiopia, Angola, Nicaragua, and Vietnam—in the context of foreign aid, political conclusions, military capabilities, and internal security. This is a great deal to cram into "three or four pages." DI papers, and thus DI-generated NIE drafts, are always double-spaced to allow for lengthy marginal comments.

In practice, Gates has defined the first part of the paper. The drafter will have noticed that Gates explicitly wants a description of the "conclusions *we believe [the Soviets] must have drawn* … (emphasis added)." If he did not know already, a drafter receiving such guidance would probably research what the "royal we" Bob Gates has said on the subject in internal CIA contexts or publicly. He presumably would keep his findings in mind for the duration.

The third paragraph of tick one states that the drafter missed the "whole historical significance" of Soviet activity in the Third World. It implicitly says that the drafter and intermediate reviewers were stupid not to understand the "significance" that Gates clearly believes he understands. Once again, such a determination is not a factual matter or an issue of the scope of discussion; Gates is saying that he wants his judgments reflected in the draft. He provides guidance on that judgment: "... the political and ideological imperative" must be considered; and, the Soviets believe "revolution is still alive." Gates does not ask for an assessment. He provides conclusions.

Tick two mandates inclusion of a conclusion that Soviet activities in the Third World had an objective of damaging US interests and resolve. It is consistent with the "evil empire" view of the Soviet Union then current. It clearly does not ask a question or suggest than an issue should be addressed; it directs the drafter to accommodate Gates' views. Note that this approach also is consistent with Gates' 1986 "War By Another Name" speech and article.

Tick three turns to economic matters and similarly reflects conclusions about Soviet tactics, strategy in its competition with the United States, and judgments about Soviet advice to its friends in Nicaragua. Again, he directs inclusion of judgments, not facts, and does not suggest that the drafter further explore some other aspect of the issue.

In tick four, beginning "on page 10 ...," Gates indicates that he wants other language about Soviet perceptions of the United States. He notes that differing assessments of Soviet perceptions constitute "a terribly important distinction in terms of the political message it conveys." Conveys to whom? The answer can only be intelligence consumers. The drafter is likely to have believed this tick amounts to a recognition by Gates himself that he considers consumers' "political" reactions to CIA reports as he reviews. In the world of nuance and subtlety that CIA analysts live in, this is clear commentary. In the world of Ronald Reagan in 1982, it meant that the president's reaction should be considered when drafting. This amounts, in my judgment, to a "smoking gun" admission of politicization by Robert Gates.

An analyst receiving this kind of commentary remembers it during drafting of his next paper, recalling that judgments, and therefore papers, are going to be reviewed in this "political" context. For many analysts, this admonition to be cognizant of consumers' political concerns amounts to politicization. In any case, simple discussion of the point flies in the face of the tradition of Sherman Kent that the political ramifications of CIA analyses "downtown" should not be part of the analysis process. Gates here stepped over the line between relevant intelligence that serves policymakers' needs and satisfying consumers' wants.

In the next tick, Gates scolds the drafter for pointing to Soviet difficulties in the Third World rather than agreeing with his assessment that new tactics boost successes. And at "no investment whatsoever" to boot! This reflects a fundamental difference in judgment, with Gates' view clearly factually wrong in hindsight. Granada came a cropper. He worries about a Libyan "client" that was weak and mercurial at best. Gates' view that the Soviets bore no burden but let the Cubans "carry the major burden" was demonstrably wrong even in 1982; the USSR long had given Cuba billions of dollars worth of aid annually. Gates' comment that the draft contained a "fundamental flaw" in this area instead shows a fundamental flaw in his own analysis. This is but one of many such errors over the years stated with such self-confident conviction; these had enduring consequences as standards for future "analysis."

The short sixth and seventh ticks concern the scope of the draft. They ask that other subjects be considered. This type of commentary is standard and completely legitimate.

The "In sum ..." tick, however, gets to the crux of the Gates' problem with the draft. He rejects the notion that the Soviets have troubles in the Third World, and argues instead that the Soviets are "creating new opportunities through different approaches, and that they are much better than we in exploiting problem areas that offer benefit more for the trouble they give to the West than for the advantages they provide to the East." He argues, in essence, that the Third World is but a theater in the global war against the West generally, and the United States in particular. "I see a lot more trouble for us in the Third World in the years ahead because it's easier to make trouble than it is to solve it." Once again, this judgment was not one of Gates' most prescient.

Note that a reader of the memo put three question marks on page two. In the DI, these normally mean one of two things: either the language is confusing, or the message makes little sense. In this case, both may have been at work. Gates has crammed major judgments into a few lines, and has not fully explained himself. Generally, this may mean that the drafter is left to try to interpret cryptic comments; his success at doing so may not be apparent until the next review.

This review is important for another reason. It is evidence for the debate over whether Gates was/is a tough task master who flustered intellectually flabby analysts—as he and his supporters claim—or whether he was/is intellectually arrogant, sometimes wrong, prone to politicize, and disrespectful of people with whom he disagrees.

The NIE was killed. Clearly concerns about its direction were too great for editing "fixes." While Gates as DDI in 1982 could not have killed the estimate on his own, his views presumably carried some considerable weight with then-chairman of the NIC Harry Rowan and/or DCI Casey, both of whom had such life-and-death power. The issue did not die, however, and was resurrected periodically in later years. Finally, an NIE on the subject was published in 1985.

* * *

More generally, senior intelligence officers employ a variety of methods to move analysis in a direction of their liking. Their objectives may be to improve good or bad analysis, change a focus, raise additional questions—all legitimate goals of review—or demand changes in conclusions to support an objective other than sound analysis. I believe that a functional definition of politicization in an intelligence context is:

> The alteration of an otherwise objective, methodologically sound course of the conception, production, and review of

an intelligence product to serve a personal, bureaucratic, ideological, policy, or political purpose.

The portions of the definition most often discussed are the ideological and political, but I believe that politicization normally has a significant bureaucratic or personal element as well. Individuals at mid- and lower-levels politicize by pandering to perceived political or ideological wants of mentors because they seek to gain personal or organizational favor. Senior intelligence officers seek to curry favor with Congress, the president, or cabinet officers for personal promotional, budgetary, or bureaucratic turf reasons, for example. The clear lesson of the Gates years of the 1980s is that such parochial motives are acceptable within the DI. I believe this recognition through much of the organization warrants Mel Goodman's use of the term "systematic"—a word that drew much fire from Gates partisans and Gates himself at his 1991 confirmation hearings. Goodman's definition of politicization was "the systematic slanting of analysis to serve policy interests."[1] In his March 16, 1992 speech to employees admitting continued concern among CIA personnel about politicization, Gates defined it as "deliberately distorting analysis or judgments to favor a preferred line of thinking irrespective of evidence."[2] The Agency task force DCI Gates asked to look into concerns about politicization defined it, according to Bush Administration officials, as "changing, delaying or killing an analytical assessment to avoid offending a policy maker."[3]

The practical methods employable to achieve politicization range from the explicit to very indirect techniques. Some are so vague that, while clear to the communicator and the communicatee at any time, they defy easy "proof" that such discussions occurred or that interpretations actually were correct. This inherent difficulty, combined with Office of the Inspector General's exceptional demands for proof, render OIG extremely ineffective at policing politicization. The increasing concern about the issue, evidenced by Gates' 1991 confirmation process, is likely to make managers inclined to such behavior even more careful not to leave incriminating evidence. Alternatively, they can act to back such politicized judgments with paper trails indicating defensible methods of review—given a selected part of the available evidence. They also can minimize their own vulnerability through careful selection of additional reviewers who they expect will come to similar conclusions.

How then does politicization occur? The most obvious way is a simple command that an article is to be written containing a specific message and, perhaps, to a specific format. This type of directive rules out an order to determine whether a reportable issue really exists—a legitimate management directive. It also eliminates the possibility of a dispute because of legitimate disagreements about substantive issues. It simply is procedurally out of order. For these reasons this type of politicization is relatively unusual. I experienced it only a few times. Some fortunate analysts never have such experiences.

More common is guidance to analysts to keep a particular set of senior managers' comments or writings in mind while drafting a paper. While this guidance can refer to stylistic issues, it often contains significant substantive elements. It is for this reason that speeches and articles of senior Agency officers like Robert Gates can have significant, long-lasting influence internally. These words provide statements of "slant" or "party line." Middle managers reinforce the importance of following such leads by referring to the degree an article follows a stated preference during sessions reviewing papers.

Similarly, managers provide oral and sometimes written guidance on issues, types of data, or judgments to avoid. This is the category of Gates' comments in his "NIE on Soviets and the Third World" memo. These often quickly become known and are communicated within offices rapidly; they form a pattern that gradually (or quickly) establishes an orthodoxy in the more politicized offices like SOVA. Prior to the Gates years, such preferences generally were restricted to personal quirks about language. Thus, for example, wags in the late 1970s kept a "dictionary" that contained both word and phrase preferences of

Bruce Clarke—then head of the National Foreign Assessment Center, the DI's predecessor organization—as well as pet peeves on words and sentence construction he did not like to see in drafts. In RTT, where bureaucratic expediency in the late 1980s and early 1990s was more important than ideology, preferred "story lines" often changed with little apparent rhyme or reason. Other, better managed offices, normally have no such established orthodoxy.

Once a paper has been drafted and handed to managers for review, a new series of opportunities for politicization occur. Sometimes, reviewers simply craft new language and direct that it be included in the final text; they insert new words into the draft as they review. This re-crafting sometimes is extensive and is couched as improvements or "fixes." In other cases, sections are excised, and marginal comments demand inclusion of data, issues, or judgments with specific language left to the ostensible author and lower level reviewers. It is a rare analyst or junior manager who tells a senior reviewer that he is wrong and demands a return to original language. Such a position generally is considered indicative of an "uncooperative attitude." As a result, virtually any review comment forces at least some language modification in the direction of the reviewers' wishes; these demonstrate "responsiveness" to reviewers' wants.

Manager/reviewers tip their hands by repeated pushes to get a specific message into a draft. For example, during review of a paper I wrote in 1987 about training of Third World personnel in an East European country, my reviewer repeated directed that I find examples of graduates of such programs who had reached senior positions in their governments and were clearly anti-American. He was unmoved by my statements about the positions, and thus potential influence, attained by these graduates. His fairly clear, but then unstated, intent was to demonstrate the effectiveness of these regimes as Soviet clients engaged in political warfare against US interests. Why would he do this? Gates and Casey had made clear the danger for the United States and the West posed by Soviet activities in the Third World and this individual wanted to provide some support. (This individual earlier told me that he intended to prosper bureaucratically and that people were either with him or against him in this quest; he presumably was motivated primarily by the belief that these ambitions would be furthered if he could satisfy Gates, as well as the director of EURA—a man closely allied with Gates who long has had a reputation for politicizing analysis.) The distinguishing feature in this type of case is preference for a specific message or specific language—as opposed to a concern about style, or scope, or methodological soundness of analysis, or any of the host of other concerns that must be addressed in preparation of a major paper.

The conduct of politicization requires a purposeful effort to convey specific messages and thus requires a motive which rarely is stated explicitly. How can one identify such a motive and distinguish it from an honest difference of opinion between analyst and reviewer, simple ignorance, or incompetence? Usually analysts tell because they have come to understand the views and personalities of their bosses through observation, including oral comments, written review comments, briefing remarks, general attitudes as expressed in formal and informal settings, and even body language. Another tip-off is the degree of conviction of reviewers and the extent to which they will discuss issues, rather than mandate positions, during the review process.

Former SOVA analyst Jennifer Glaudemans told the SSCI of a personal experience:

> Thus, in August 1989, I was asked to write a paper on the implications for Soviet foreign policy should Gorbachev be gone. Initially, I was not told what the answer was supposed to be, but that became apparent in the "review" process. My (and my branch chief's) analytical approach to this hypothetical scenario was to examine how factors, such as when and how Gorbachev might be gone from the scene, would determine the outcome. The original outline suggested that should Gorbachev die unexpectedly from a heart attack or even

> an assassin, it was quite likely that the reformists could hold the center of power at least over the short term. If such event occurred after a sufficient period of time for glasnost and democratization to become more institutionalized and rooted, the longer term prospects for reform were fairly good. Should he be ousted, the outcome would depend on who in fact ousted him. Quickly, we were not even allowed to consider a political threat from the left, representing those who were dissatisfied with the slow pace of reform. At that time at least, the Yeltsin alternative could not be considered in the hypothetical. [Director of SOVA] Mr. Kolt flat out rejected it. The only ouster scenario we could consider was one from the hard right; from those who wanted a return to Neo-Stalinism."[4]

The practical manifestations of politicization motivated by bureaucratic concerns—an issue that received little discussion during the Gates confirmation hearings but for which he also is heavily responsible—are usually somewhat different. In these cases, managers care little for specific judgments but worry a great deal about the reaction their superiors will have to the work of their units. If they perceive that a superior wants (or wants to avoid) a particular slant, they insist on papers that provide such a message for the purpose of pleasing the senior reviewer and enhancing their careers. Because the Gates/Casey line was so clear, they had little difficulty during the Casey years in divining acceptable slants and making clear their own similar wishes to their subordinates. This bureaucratic motive heavily drives politicization by omission.

Gates' inability or unwillingness to recognize this phenomenon among his appointees reflects a fundamental managerial failing. Dick Kerr, especially expert at bureaucratic self-preservation, continued to accept and I believe encourage the practice as DDI and DDCI. It is now institutionalized. The "Cowey Report" on the Agency's work on the attempted assassination of Pope John Paul II recognized it in 1985;

discussing the role of senior Agency management in the series of reports on the subject, Cowey and his colleagues concluded:

> "… there was a perception of upper-level direction, which became more pronounced after new evidence of Soviet complicity was acquired. In the event, however, our interviews suggested that *it was not so much DCI or DDI direction as it was an effort on the part of some DI managers at the next one or two layers down to be receptive to perceived DCI and DDI desires* (emphasis added).[5]

I believe it not coincidental that these managers added to the immediate beginning of the above quotation, "So, despite the DDI's best efforts …" despite the lack of discussion about any direct actions by any senior managers in the entire section entitled "External Influence and the Role of Senior Management."[6] This is a transparent effort to absolve DDI Gates, the requester of the memo, of responsibility for the widespread perception the team found that senior management had politicized the IA. Thus, bureaucrats Ross Cowey, John McLaughlin, and Christine Williams were themselves being receptive to perceived DDI desires.

The difficulty of describing the magnitude and power of this tendency is shown by the views Senators John Chafee and John Warner expressed to their colleagues after the 1991 Gates hearings ended. After listening to the testimony of Jennifer Glaudemans and others, Republicans Chafee and Warner—who also had obvious partisan political reasons for their comments—cavalierly dismissed the effect, its ubiquity, and its importance. After citing the Cowey report passage above and noting the "DDI's best efforts" as a reason to support Gates, they erroneously concluded:

> "In short, some people wanted to please their boss. This is a natural instinct and a problem inherent in the work place. But the strong ethic of honesty in the

> Intelligence Community, as well as the careful vetting process that estimates go through within CIA or within the Intelligence Community, help insure that 'skewing intelligence to please the boss' is minimized."[7]

The "vetting" process cannot work, however, when the "vettors" are the bosses who want to be pleased.

Personnel moves can indicate a tendency toward politicization derived from many motivations. Analysts who show an inclination toward an unfavored judgment or approach are replaced by individuals more politically orthodox or respectful of the Agency's bureaucratic imperatives. I believe this happens relatively rarely because senior managers normally select junior managers and drafters who they feel confident will approach the task properly; expectations are well known and "mistakes" thus occur relatively infrequently. Politically motivated managers have been able to find "hired-pens," as they have been known in SOVA and elsewhere. Former SOVA manager Mel Goodman gave an example of such a tack in his testimony to the SSCI:

> "Casey and Gates wanted an intelligence product that linked drug dealers and international terrorists. The task was given to a senior analyst who concluded that no such link existed and who then refused Gates' pressure to reach a different conclusion. The analyst was replaced by another intelligence officer, who complied with the request."[8]

Still another coincident indicator of a tendency toward politicization is an office director's strong direction of a paper during its formative stages through micro-management of what is known as a "concept paper," which usually is accompanied by an outline. The greater the degree of specific direction about format, length, and issues to be covered, the stronger the likelihood of a predetermined position. Such inflexibility limits analysts' freedom to alter analysis as research warrants, and hints at a motive to serve a political or bureaucratic constituent;

I have had papers' contents specified to the number of paragraphs prior to the commencement of drafting and before research was complete. (Depending on the office director, this attitude can also reflect simple poor judgment that is not a symptom of politicization.)

Sometimes there are genuine gray areas. Reasonable and responsible people can and do differ over complex issues. Moreover, reviewers overconfident of their abilities may make poor judgments when good sense and sound management principles would have dictated that they leave judgments to their analysts and subordinate managers; these unfortunate decisions can be interpreted as politicization. While undoubtedly some analysts mistake differences of judgment for politicization, this type of disagreement also provides reviewers cover by allowing them to equate analyst unhappiness over real politicization with "poor analysis"—analysis that warrants either modifications or outright rejection. This approach implicitly holds that seniority confers expertise and better judgment, regardless of the actual currency of reviewers' knowledge and expertise, and that analysts should listen to their betters. It is consistent with the attitude of Gates and some of the office directors that they are good senior analysts whose judgments are superior to their analysts' views. It also is a time honored, major method of ensuring that analysts indeed accept politically correct positions; Robert Gates used such an argument to defend himself against charges of politicization on September 16, 1991. Admiral Bobby Inman, a vocal Gates supporter, despite his first-hand ignorance of Gates' performance after he left CIA in 1982, added:

> "That ... is the analyst's first complaint when someone challenges their analytical judgments. Bound to be political. Can't be because they are wrong. I may even have been guilty of that a time or two myself as a young analyst."[9]

Jennifer Glaudemans rejected the notion that charges of politicization occur because analysts are "too finicky, too egocentric, too whiney, or too academic."[10] She found the arguments of Gates, and by extension Inman, "the most smug, condescending, and callous answer to such a sensitive question I could possibly imagine."[11]

After the publication of papers, managers reinforce incentives to slant analysis in certain ways by selectively reporting consumers' reactions to papers. They also push future papers in certain directions by selectively rewarding producers of acceptable papers. These can take the form of favorable comment, which analysts generally assumed to indicate a degree of favor that will pay dividends at promotion board time. Reviewers may grant modest cash awards or indicate favor through a variety of informal and personal ways.

At the same time, senior reviewers can make life difficult for those analysts who stick to their principles and resist politicization. These techniques include: critical comments; no promotions and poor comparative rankings; denied travel opportunities; shunning and slow review of papers which translates into missed deadlines and low quantities of production—evidence of "poor performance;" lack of career-enhancing opportunities for good assignments; and so on. These punishments become known and become part of the incentive structure built into the personnel management system.

It is difficult to understate the importance of these institutionalized incentives as motivators for DI employees. These similarly are hard to convey to people who have not experienced them. Even the SSCI staff—ostensibly familiar with CIA—clearly failed to appreciate them adequately prior to the 1991 Gates confirmation hearings.

Even for the most politically minded senior official, real politicization of analysis occurs only infrequently for several reasons. First, a sound project's conclusions may support pre-determined value judgments. One OGI manager once confided to a SOVA manager that he felt the same pressure to produce intelligence documenting extensive Soviet activity in the Third World, but was more fortunate than the SOVA person; he caught no flak from Gates because his office could deliver what Gates wanted without compromise of its intellectual integrity. Second, the potential politicizer may not be interested in the subject. Third, overt alteration might be too time consuming or too obvious to make it worthwhile—and worth the risk. Fourth, the power of suggestion and the revealed preferences as demonstrated by other reviews, articles, speeches, staff meeting commentary, for example, over time communicate the senior officer's real desires and make direct action unnecessary.

Thus, the astute long-time senior officer like Gates will always be able to provide, especially with the help of a legion of research assistants, selected documents that show no obvious politicization. If that same officer has been careful to sprinkle his articles and speeches with admonitions for better, more timely analysis, and strict adherence to the highest ethical standards, he provides himself and his supporters with a strong defense against charges that his actions differed from his written words. It is a simple tactic that can work quite well.

Politicization sometimes is provable after the fact, via paper trails and the consistent testimony of witnesses to a specific directive, but much more often it is subtle, hard to demonstrate, and difficult to explain. While malcontents exist and sometimes verbal communications fail badly, it is clear that human communication often occurs without much written or formal spoken language. The discrimination against black men in the old South years ago was real. So is the fear of whites who wander accidently into Harlem in the 1990s. The courts recognize the subtle discrimination of chauvinist men against women as grounds for awarding monetary damages, and the Senate in 1991 recognized sexual harassment as a potential reason for rejecting Supreme Court nominees. Jennifer Glaudemans put it another way:

> "... politicization is like fog. Though you cannot hold it in your hands, or nail it to a wall, it does exist, it is real, and it does affect people's behavior."[12]

Why do some DI personnel perceive politicization that

others never notice? There is no simple, single answer. I believe, however, that there are several general categories of reasons. The first, and best, is that there may be none to notice. This surely occurs in some offices, and in some divisions in moderately poorly run offices due to the force of character of division chiefs. Politicization also is much less likely to occur in areas where political motives and controversies are weak and topics are not "hot"—like some scientific areas, for example. It is for this reason that the confirmation hearings testimony of Lawrence K. Gershwin, National Intelligence Officer for Strategic Programs, should be regarded as largely irrelevant to the debate about whether Gates politicized analysis.[13] Larry Gershwin never worked in the DI and never worked in CIA proper.[14] (Nor, for that matter, did Gates supporter Graham Fuller ever work in the DI.) He never had to contend directly with the DI review process on his main product—the annual NIE 11-series document on Soviet strategic programs.

Others presume that colleagues and superiors have only the best of intentions and are willing to give the benefit of doubt. Graham Fuller addressed the difficulty of identifying politicization in senior intelligence officers involved in the process of producing and reviewing National Intelligence Estimates:

> "In principal good people are supposed to be at the top, where they can exercise their own judgments about the true import of events. They may appreciate the analyst telling them about what happened, but they will not relinquish the right to interpret events for themselves if they wish. The same goes for the President in reading CIA reports. Is this wrong? Sometimes the policy-maker's analytic instincts might be better than the analyst's. There is no right or wrong here, only a permanent dilemma. The process must accommodate both, for the quality of judgment may be found anywhere. The very principle of NFIB is that senior experienced people in intelligence work have the right to

> pass judgment even on the NIO's work and change the judgments as they see fit. Politicization? Or seasoned judgment? You tell me."[15]

Fuller's argument that senior people alone have the "right" to make intelligence judgments, with the research support of "experts," while probably fairly reflecting Gates' tendencies, is new. Gates himself noted in 1987 that it is important to distinguish "formal assessments from personal views expressed by individuals at all levels of the agency, from analysts to senior operations officers to the director."[16] Gates continued:

> "It is worth remembering that in 1962 Director John McCone disagreed with the entire intelligence community over whether the Soviets might install missiles in Cuba. He told President Kennedy they would, and he alone in the executive branch was right. As long as all points of view are fairly represented and reported, the director of central intelligence (sic)—the president's chief intelligence adviser—is entitled (even obliged) to have put forward his own views."[17]

Gates' distinction is a good one. Many CIA people clearly believe that he has not followed his own good counsel. They believe he has been and will be unwilling to let "all points of view" be "fairly represented and reported," and mention examples like the NIE review comments cited above.

Those who weakly hold the tenets of Sherman Kent believe that the decisions of superiors determine sound judgments, and accept that standard. Many of these people believe that CIA is a quasi-military organization where the determination of virtue and right is easily made upon observation of a uniform collar—or knowledge of a pay grade. These people, without exception in my experience, do not know how the military actually works. This is a strong variant of Fuller's argument that seniority confers analytic prowess.

Others view the production of acceptable papers as the

primary goal. Reviewers define what is acceptable. These people are not bothered by larger questions; they are not worth the effort.

Still others are active, willing participants in at least the bureaucratic aspects of politicization. These are opportunists. Sometimes they admit so candidly. They see nothing wrong with the practice of sycophancy; it pays tangible dividends. Virtually by definition, these people see no politicization. Such people constitute a minority of DI personnel, I believe, but they are essential to the operation of the DI as Gates and Kerr modified it. These people lack critical moral qualities and the intelligence principles of Sherman Kent, but they prospered bureaucratically under DDIs Gates, Kerr, and Helgerson. They occupy many mid-level and senior positions, and are a major part of the DI's problems. Gates and Kerr could not have done the damage to the DI that they have inflicted without the willing collaboration of such people.

And, a large number of analysts came to CIA with well established value systems and a desire to serve. These individuals note and resist politicization when it occurs. The degree of opposition, and the overt manifestations of unhappiness, vary considerably by individual and situation.

On the other hand, some undoubtedly are too quick to see politicization. For these relative few, some of Gates' defense rings true. A few take personal criticism too hard. A few fail to recognize fully the need to compromise in the production of CIA "corporate" products. Some indeed are whiners or malcontents. Some are poor analysts. These relatively few people normally discover quickly that they are in the wrong business, however, and usually leave the DI or the Agency.

However, Gates' argument that he has been the victim of complaints of malcontents, or misfits who failed to adjust to a tough boss or a reorganization, is specious. Gates long has maintained the silly argument that the reorganization of 1981 was a leading cause of attrition as late as the mid-1980s, yet raised it again a as defense in 1991. The argument of Douglas J. MacEachen is perhaps worse. MacEachen, speaking about individuals concerned about politicization, insisted: "... it only takes a few to poison the atmosphere. It is particularly so when many of these are experienced veterans who become role models for young, new, impressionable officers."[18] Such respected veterans seem unlikely pathological malcontents. However, there undoubtedly are many who agree with MacEachen's self-assessment:

> " ... since I was responsible for the SOVA product during part of Mr. Gates (sic) tenure as DDI, any charge of skewing SOVA products to suit alleged consumer biases gets absorbed into my consciousness as charges—not in a legal sense perhaps; as a non-lawyer I would leave that to experts—but in a moral sense—that I was an accessory if not a co-conspirator."[19]

I wrote or co-authored over 230 papers of various sorts during my years at CIA. I experienced excellent review and editing, miserable review and editing, and politicization. After a while, I found it easy to spot the extremes in each category.

Notes to Chapter 10

1 Melvin A. Goodman, "Testimony of Melvin A. Goodman to the Senate Select Committee on Intelligence," p. 2.

2 Elaine Sciolino, "C.I.A. Chief Upset Over 'Politicization' Seen within Agency," New York Times, *March 28, 1992, p. A7.*

3 Ibid.

4 Glaudemans, "Written Statement," p. 11.

5 Cowey, et al., "Review of Production on the Attempted Assassination of Pope John Paul II," p. 19.

6 This four-paragraph section consumes a page and a half on pages 18 and 19.

7 Senate, Exec. Rept. 102-19, "Additional Views of Senators John H. Chafee and John W. Warner," p. 222.

8 Goodman, "Testimony," p. 5.

9 Senate, Exec. Rept. 102-19, p. 104.

10 Ibid.

11 Ibid.

12 United States Senate, Transcript of Proceedings Before the Select Committee on Intelligence, Evening Session, September, 25, 1991, p. 96.

13 Written Statement of Lawrence K. Gershwin, National Intelligence Officer for Strategic Programs, before the Senate Select Committee on Intelligence, 1 October 1991.

14 National Intelligence Officers report through the Chairman of the National Intelligence Council to the DCI wearing his intelligence community hat. Thus, despite the fact that NIOs work at CIA headquarters and have CIA security credentials, they are not regular CIA employees.

15 Graham E. Fuller, "Statement of Graham E. Fuller, Former Vice-Chairman, National Intelligence Council, CIA (sic)," for the Senate Select Committee on Intelligence, 1 October 1991, p. 11.

16 Gates, "The CIA and Foreign Policy," p. 227.

17 Ibid, pp. 227-228.

18 Statement of Douglas J. MacEachen, Special Assistant to the DCI for Arms Control, before the Senate Select Committee on Intelligence, 25 September 1991, p. 12.

19 Ibid., p. 10.

CHAPTER ELEVEN

TOWARD A CRITICS' PARADIGM

Students of the analytical portion of US intelligence need a systematic framework for the evaluation of intelligence analysis. If done well, this work could put specific critiques in broader contexts, allow more coherent assessments of the performance of the CIA's Directorate of Intelligence and its evolution over time, and provide criteria for comparison of intelligence services. It might help potential consumers better understand the capabilities and limitations of intelligence analysis, assisting them to better formulate requests for support. Built well, this framework might help refine or reform the operations of CIA and other intelligence agencies. It also could help identify flawed assumptions or judgments about missions, the causes of disagreements within intelligence organizations or between producers and consumers about their mutual relationships, and simple failures to properly implement.

Criticism of intelligence analysis over the years has covered a broad spectrum of individual issues, ranging from the philosophical to narrow, practical attacks on specific forecasts. Recommendations for reform or improvement similarly have been fairly specific. While in many cases valid, these individual observations have not been sufficiently significant in scope, or integrated, to offer a general assessment or to generate pressure for real, much needed reform.

Construction of a general framework can proceed from

evaluation of a series of factors related to intelligence organizations' avowed mission and their operations in practice. Just as analysts make implicit assumptions and use theory in evaluation of their information and formulating their analysis, so intelligence agencies make conscious or implicit decisions about the meaning and role of their work. Key among them are the purpose for which the organization does analysis, the consumer to be served, and the time horizons that analysis and the consumer community deem appropriate. From these spring decisions about the types of products to produce, including questions to address and the formats of presentations. These also help determine standards of performance.

The Purpose of Analysis

Purpose is a critical question that cuts to the heart of the debate between the two traditional schools of analysis and will probably be a topic of increasing importance as US political/economic relations with much of the world become more complex in the post-Cold War period. There are other possibilities already exploited by other nations' intelligence services that will undoubtedly receive continuing attention as the United States refines the roles of its intelligence agencies.

First, the traditional school of Sherman Kent regards analysis as an activity that generates judgments for the use of government policymakers at their convenience. It is to be objective, independent, and methodologically sound. It is organizationally independent of its consumers because it wants to avoid taint from politicians who want intelligence backing for their positions, or who could engineer organizational or other changes that could have politically significant results.

Second, the proponents of opportunity-oriented analysis argue that it should be methodologically sound but should be targeted to serve specific legitimate needs of government. Direct support for the rest of government is not politicization, it is effective intelligence—a view Sherman Kent's work supports as well. In the Kentian context, it is improvement of the intelligence response to policy community guidance.

Third, the more vapid bureaucrats at CIA see "analysis" as a process that generates enough papers to satisfy Congress that the current year research program is sufficiently close to completion to warrant another appropriation. It is production process. Numbers mean bureaucratic success for the organization and its individuals; they mean continued prosperity.

Fourth, the purpose of analysis can be expanded in scope to include broad national interests of varying sorts. Giving service to non-governmental users of information in the economic sphere is a prime candidate. Industrial espionage has become a world-wide industry that supports corporate decisionmakers' needs for data on competitors' abilities and their intentions. Foreign intelligence services target American and other firms. Analysis, with collection assets, arguably can foster national interests by improving the ability of nations to compete by providing details in areas like technological developments, marketing plans, cost structures, foreign government/firm cooperation, defenses against foreign industrial espionage, and others. The payoffs are growth of exports, bigger profits, more jobs, larger market shares, and greater national economic power. A major debate about the desirability of such economic intelligence—offensive and defensive in the form of counter-intelligence—was underway within the US intelligence community, Congress, and American business itself in the late 1980s and early 1990s.[1] Adoption of such roles would expand the responsibilities of intelligence well beyond all of the first three roles and would not reflect merely an alteration of the environment in which the other roles operate.

The net purpose of DI analysis in the early 1990s probably is best described as a combination of the first and third goals. The proponents of opportunity-oriented analysis should be disappointed because Agency bureaucrats have transformed Gates' apparently well-intended reforms—which seem at least partially supportive of opportunity-oriented analytical objectives—into very heavily self-serving activities of the third type. The fourth would require a change in national policy as well as numerous, significant decisions about implementing details. Many other nations plainly have already decided to use their intelligence services in support of economic objectives like acquisition of controlled technology, for example.[2]

Organization, Size, and Focus of Analysis

Intelligence organizations can vary considerably in organization and size. These characteristics can follow decisions about the appropriate scope of activities (a region of the world or concentration on military threats, for example) or be consequences of budget or other decisions. The DI has evolved considerably in size and organization in its history. It is much different than other US intelligence analytical organizations like DIA and INR, and is very different from some foreign intelligence services. Some students of intelligence like Angelo Codevilla argue that organization can be important.[3] I believe that key characteristics of the DI—such as the conduct of review and thus the quality of analysis—are heavily determined by the organization of the production offices.

Characteristics of The Consumer

Any analytical organization must make at least implicit assumptions about the identity of its consumers—and the interests, wants, needs, and abilities of those people. Individual analysts and reviewer/managers in the DI have such disparate definitions of the "reader" as to indicate that there is no clear definition, or even a useful series of identifying characteristics, to suggest who consumers are or should be. Distribution lists for papers usually are lifted from other papers, and the regular turnover of personnel in consumer agencies means that even CPAS can not keep track of the names of people in positions in those agencies it has identified as having need for intelligence information.

Identity

The key decision about how to focus intelligence products concerns the bureaucratic level of intended readers. A decision to focus on very senior officials could, in the extreme, generate brief snippets for an unengaged president disinterested in foreign affairs. On the other hand, emphasis on low-level governmental "worker bees" might produce much more detailed intelligence the junior officials could use in preparation of the reports and recommendations they make to their superiors. While the president and junior civil servants receive intelligence, the DI's most common "reader" probably is an imaginary assistant secretary who does not have time to replicate analysis or question its methods. He presumably trusts the competence of CIA and will not ordinarily question the judgments he reads. National Security Council staffers also are acceptable consumers with roughly similar presumed reading habits and interests.

The DI disdains provision of intelligence support to the civilian bureaucracy as a whole. While providing data (through series like the unclassified *Handbook of Economic Statistics*), occasional short papers, and some of its serial publications, the DI does not normally plan projects to provide assessments for individuals who are not "policymakers."[4] The staffs of these people are largely ignored. There are at least two relevant bureaucratic reasons: "worker-bees" do not give valuable kudos, and their use of CIA material in their own work diminishes the acknowledged value of a DI contribution. The DI seems not to recognize that policymakers are served when their staffs are served. A DI analyst who transferred to the Foreign Service, and was at one time a desk officer, recounted her own experience to me in 1991. She said that during her time as an analyst she was told (and thought) she was writing for some single policymaker. She later came to realize that there are many policymakers, including herself as a relatively lowly desk officer feeding data and judgments to an office director and a bureau assistant secretary who more prominently make State Department policy.

Much of the DI also disdains provision of intelligence support to the Department of Defense and the uniformed military services. Apart from SOVA's active participation in the debates about the Soviet military over the years, DI offices often have little to do with Defense. In part, this reflects anti-military prejudice. In also reflects distance, the regular rotations of military personnel which hinder the development of good personal working relationships, cumbersome telephone connections, and suspicions about the security-consciousness and competence of military personnel in the intelligence arena.

DIA and NSA, in contrast, have much closer relationships with the uniformed military services; they explicitly are parts of the Department of Defense. Bureaucratic procedures worked out with DIA which inhibit the flow of CIA information to the military account for some of the distance, but not all. Many DI officers are content to work primarily with civilians and "target" departments other than Defense. My Army Reserve tours with several major military commands indicate that the military does use DI products in preparation of daily briefings, but that military intelligence officers normally call DIA or NSA analysts with questions.

In wartime, as the Persian Gulf war experience demonstrated, the value of DI analyses to the military can be expected to drop further. No document prepared in Washington can replace a trusted intelligence officer at the right hand of a field commander. Moreover, the agonizing DI review process is simply too cumbersome, and its style too "policy-relevant," to offer much useful tactical- or even operational-level intelligence support to a commander in battle. The National Photographic Interpretation Center (NPIC), a part of the Directorate of Science and Technology that has analytical functions, is potentially far more helpful, despite the fact that it was a major target of General Schwarzkopf's critique of CIA support during the Persian Gulf war.[5]

The president is not a usual "target" for much of DI analysis. He is too "high." The PDB staff's production is a clear exception to this generalization; it lifts material from other DI products and modifies that output as it sees fit, sometimes without the etiquette of compromise that accompanies normal coordination. This staff also tasks DI components for papers at the request of the president, the vice president, some cabinet officers, or White House staffers.[6]

The DI is deeply ambivalent about its relationship with Congress. On the one hand, CIA is an executive branch organization that works for the president, and its production plans target executive branch needs. On the other, Congress controls budgets and therefore must be satisfied to at least some extent. Growing Congressional influence on CIA is a part of the much publicized general struggle between the presidents and Congress for power generally and over foreign affairs in particular. The DI's emphasis on slickly published research programs and reports about quantities of papers published is at least partially attributable to an assessment that these help get money from the Hill. Briefings or papers for Congress, however, are always potentially risky because they threaten to embroil the Agency in a fight between a president and Congress. Analysts talking to Congress thus are on even shorter leashes than they are when dealing with executive branch agencies.

Presumed Capabilities

Analysis is shaped by the perceived intellectual capabilities, discipline, competence, objectivity, background, and experience of the target audience. Comparative studies of the intelligence services of several countries show sharply different types of intelligence reflecting these variables.[7] Intelligence analysis in the United States arguably is best when consumers are competent and demand the best intelligence support in the service of sound policy.

DI perceptions in the early 1990s of the consumer community reflect dealings with the Carter and Reagan/Bush Administrations. The Gates/Casey initiatives of the early 1980s were responses in part to the troubled producer/consumer relations of the late 1970s as well as the desires of Reagan and his appointees. For most practical CIA purposes, the Bush Administration (including Bush's choices for DCI and DDCI—William Webster, Robert Gates, and Richard Kerr) is a continuation of the Reagan Administration.

Perceptions of, and assessments about, the consumer community vary considerably within CIA. Rightly or inaccurately, however, many DI officers regard consumers as amateurs weak in foreign policy substance but often with strong opinions. They cite the regular turnover of senior officials during the Reagan years and the insularity of a small number of insiders at the State Department of James Baker, as an example. They see the clear and simple, even simple-minded, world views of officials including Reagan. They note the appreciation in kudos communications for pretty graphics and simplicity of verbiage. It all translates into a perception of a less than fully competent "reader." Other DI personnel retain a more traditional, complimentary view of consumers.

If much of the DI of the 1990s underestimates its readers, the DI of the 1970s, while adhering to the views of Sherman Kent, probably overestimated its consumers. The early DI implicitly assumed that consumers were competent and could screen gems of useful intelligence from its studies. It placed confidence in consumers' interest in intelligence and their desires and ability to wade through analyses. The numerous complaints from policymakers about analysis over the years indicate flawed DI analysis about them, as well as periodic misjudgments about foreign developments. I cannot shake the nagging suspicion that Kent's 1940s assessment was on the mark, but that his prescriptions became less applicable as the calibre of senior government officials deteriorated in later years.

Wants and Needs

Intelligence serves consumers who need intelligence information to do their jobs and have wants for data and judgments. In many cases, these are identical. Both the traditional and the opportunity-oriented schools implicitly assume such unity. The DI of the early 1990s, however, operates much more in support of the fairly well-understood wants of its senior officials and the perceived wants of consumers. In extreme cases, the dichotomy justifies provision of shoddy and even dishonest work for the purpose of making consumers happy. The DI's de facto view of the wants of the consumer community reflect directly its perceptions of the abilities and objectives of that community.

Time Horizons

An intelligence organization's operations are highly dependent on the time periods of the forecasts it wants to make, or its consumers ask it to make. Prognostications about next week require far less preparation and insight than a time horizon extending several years into the future. Forecasts about more distant events may also encourage greater use of historical analysis to better gauge long-term trends. The acceptance of distant horizons is ambitious; it requires a greater degree of institutional self-confidence and a willingness to be "wrong"—as unforeseen events unfold or successful warnings generate policy changes that alter the course of developments and make valid warnings appear inaccurate. More distant horizons also are far more valuable for proponents of opportunity-oriented analysis; they give policymakers more time to act.

Because it is so reactive to the wants of consumers, the time horizon of much of the DI is quite short. While some parts of the DI make prognostications out 10 years or more, much analysis (and a large share of analysts' time) is focused on situations that require immediate government attention: the likely outcome of a party congress later in the week; strategy at the next round of trade talks; the next battlefield moves of antagonists. Such topics reflect reactions to policymakers' already piqued interests. In chronological time, the horizons may be weeks, days, or even hours—varying by individual issue—as opposed to months and years.

Short time horizons usually mandate shorter papers that are short on "research" and long on gisting the most recent "traffic," or in-coming reports. Real expertise thus is less important, explaining the DI's less than robust interest in analyst expertise. Similarly, the conduct of this type of analysis renders the establishment of a significant base of detailed assessments less valuable.

The growing tendency to write papers to short deadlines to satisfy immediate concerns—catering to consumers' short time horizons—makes excellent standing requirements more important. These generate much of the information that analysts take "off-the-shelf" from the Agency's stock of information. Yet, there is much less incentive in the analytical community as a whole to ponder potential future informational needs—known as "requirements"—if exploitation of the information on hand usually is adequate to satisfy consumers. With the process of revising requirements cumbersome as well, analysts usually are unenthusiastic about revising them.

The time horizons of the DI in the late 1980s and early 1990s, heavily focused on providing current policy support, arguably have been shorter than those implicit in both the traditional school and opportunity-oriented analysis. The search for opportunities to exploit requires evaluation of foreign trends, strengths, weaknesses, and vulnerabilities that are not obvious or subjects of current international discussion. The quest for opportunities to exploit also places a premium on the development of wisdom—an attribute the DI does not much value.

The DI has consciously decided to largely dispense with evaluations of the lessons of history. It rationalizes that the past is the theater of academics and the collection of data the job of librarians. This reflects a significant departure from the practice of the DI in its early years—when a major product was the series of *National Intelligence Survey* (NIS) documents. The NIS was a standard format product that addressed a broad range of political, economic, military, geographical, sociological, and other factors. They were major intelligence reference documents that covered such non-perishable data as harbor features, for example, that they still are valuable and still are used.[8]

Because the DI's focus heavily is toward forecasts of immediate policy interest, much of its intelligence product is very perishable. That is, it is irrelevant after a while. For example, there is little continuing need for a paper assessing prospects for a close election after the election is held and results are publicized. Thus, the papers of recent years rarely have the enduring value of a NIS document.

As part of its decision and evolution over the years, the DI has forced out analysts who chose not to adapt to the "investigative journalism" approach to analysis, and literally threw away huge amounts of data deemed dated, and thus irrelevant. DI managers also forced disposal of information they deemed more specialized than the nebulous "reader" wants, sometimes over the objections of analysts. Incredibly, another reason for discarding books and files is managers' desire to make work spaces visually attractive to rare VIP visitors.[9]

The DI's strong focus on the short term represents an abdication of a part of its responsibilities to provide warnings to the nation. Threats develop over time. Capabilities to threaten take longer to develop than decisions to use those capabilities. Someone must make an analytical decision that an issue is important and warrants monitoring before the collection requirements systems can be refined. The short term focus of analysis thus limits the intelligence community's usefulness by hindering the development of collection assets. This myopia perhaps reflects a complacency about the absence of genuine threats to the United States; in the strategic military world of MAD—Mutual Assured Destruction—most analysts long have regarded nuclear war with the Soviet Union as a low probability, albeit high impact, event.

Types of Analyses

Analytical product types can be of several types that reflect objectives, time horizons, and consumers' characteristics. These types are the result of decisions about what is important. Major analytic types are: historical, warning, and evaluative or estimative. DI products overwhelmingly are of the third type.

The DI virtually proscribes historical analyses. While there are a few on specialized issues, the DI generally deems historical studies to be academic activities outside the realm of intelligence analysis. Within DI products, historical examples or lessons generally must buttress judgments or forecasts and have little independent value.

Evaluative analyses serve policymakers by assessing forthcoming events or current trends from the perspective of perceived US interests. The primary purpose is to forecast events in pithy prose. These analyses are to be policy relevant in the sense that they support current policy community concerns. Yet, much of the government is regularly concerned with "putting out fires" and has little time for more reflective policymaking. DI analysis tracks the fairly short time horizons of these consumers.

Because it wants to serve policymakers' current needs, the DI places little emphasis on warning of threats (or opportunities). It risks criticism that it is free lancing. Warning messages by definition occur before events are obvious, risking "error" and subsequent ridicule. Warning may offer unwelcome and thus unappreciated news. Moreover, warning analysis is difficult.

Events that warrant warnings can occur at unpredictable intervals; they thus are anomalies not susceptible to research program planning. The conduct of warning analysis thus plays virtually no role in the priorities of the DI, is seldom mentioned in the Directorate, and is not an employee evaluation criterion. Few DI analysts take OTE's warning course. Warning simply is not an important part of DI analysis—a sharp contrast to the priorities of intelligence services of nations at war or with powerful potential enemies.

Role in Generating Requirements

Analytic offices potentially can have sharply varying roles in the formulation of collection requirements. The traditional intelligence cycle model puts collection before analysis, for example, largely leaving analysts out of the requirements process. However, as the intelligence "eight" model shows, DI analysts have sometimes significant roles in addressing collection needs for individual projects.

The participation of analytic offices in the determination of requirements can make a difference in the overall quality of intelligence and the ability of intelligence to best develop future capabilities. Ideally, analysts should be very aware of the current state of knowledge, consumers' wants and needs, information gaps, and collection assets and capabilities generally (even given rules of compartmentation). They thus should be able to communicate with, and understand, the organizations that make the entire intelligence cycle.

Other participants in the cycle may have less clear understanding of the whole. For example, consumer agencies may be preoccupied with current needs, be unaware of the state of intelligence knowledge and levy redundant requirements, or waste collection assets by asking for information virtually impossible to acquire. Collectors might be tempted to concentrate excessively in areas where their assets are strongest and neglect harder targets of great interest to consumers; collectors too are rated on quantity of production. Designers of collection equipment might be more interested in engineering sophistication than the ability of those systems to satisfy the needs of consumers they rarely meet.

Standards of Performance

Finally, any organization must have standards against which to measure its performance and provide institutional incentives. These can come from principles, doctrine, or degrees of adherence to trivial standard operating procedures. Production numbers or quality of analysis can be weighed more heavily. Standards can reflect and reward successful aggressiveness or encourage avoidance of controversy. They can demand the highest standards of integrity of employees or condone expediency and deceit. These values also can encourage service to the nation or bureaucratic self-interest.

Notes to Chapter 11

1 "Should the CIA Start Spying for Corporate America," Business Week, *October 14, 1991, pp. 96-100.*

2 Such examples are numerous. The Soviet Union and its allies for years have used intelligence assets to procure militarily important technology. Third world countries like Iraq have done the same. The United States and its allies have responded by establishment of technology transfer control regimes that have themselves caused frictions between regime partners over the proper degree of trade restriction.

3 Angelo Codevilla, "Comparative Historical Experience of Doctrine and Organization," in Godson, ed., Intelligence Requirements for the 1980's, *pp. 11-36.*

4 Some of these series are released to the general public, while others are classified.

5 NPIC is an unusual hybrid organization that, while a CIA entity, also has many military employees.

6 Vice President Dan Quayle has been an avid reader of DI products and has asked repeatedly for more. DI personnel have appreciated his interest.

7 See Adda Bozeman, "Political Intelligence in Non-Western Societies," in Roy Godson, ed., Comparing Foreign Intelligence *(Washington: Pergamon-Brassey, 1988) pp. 115-155.*

8 I used one myself during an Army Reserve tour in October 1989 at the Intelligence Center, Pacific—the major intelligence organization of the US Pacific Command located at Camp Smith, Hawaii.

9 The Director of EURA in the mid-1980s communicated as much to subordinate managers, who in some cases energetically discarded material to please her on later inspection tours.

APPENDIX A

CIA's Credo

The following CIA credo hangs on a wall in CIA headquarters near the credit union and car pool information. Many analysts pass it twice daily on their way to and from the cafeteria. Most ignore it. The credo and its values play essentially no role in their working lives. It nevertheless provides a standard against which DI performance can be judged. Its irrelevance to most employees reflects both the gap between promise and reality, and employees' lack of confidence that the gap will be closed.

Director Casey mandated creation of a credo after reading the best selling book *In Search of Excellence*, by Thomas J. Peters and Robert H. Waterman. Jr., which recommends such a measure. The Agency bought large numbers of the book and many employees purchased their own. For a time, copies prominently adorned desks throughout the Agency. When the fad appeal of the book faded, they disappeared too.

Casey directed that components of the Agency hold employee meetings to come up with suggestions for the credo. The final version, of course, reflected the views of senior Agency management.

Central Intelligence Agency
CREDO

We are the Central Intelligence Agency.

We provide timely and high quality intelligence for the President and Government of the United States.

We produce objective and unbiased evaluations and are always open to new perceptions and ready to challenge conventional wisdoms.

We perform special intelligence tasks at the request of the President.

We conduct our activities and ourselves with the highest standards of integrity, morality, and honor and according to the spirit and letter of the law.

We measure our success by our contribution to the protection and enhancement of American values, security and national interest.

We believe our people are the Agency's most important resources. We seek the best and work to make them better. We subordinate our desire for public recognition to the need for confidentiality. We strive for continuing professional improvement. We give unfailing loyalty to each other and our common purpose.

We look to our leaders to stimulate initiative, a commitment to excellence, and a propensity for action; to reward and protect us in a manner which reflects the special nature of our responsibility, our contribution, and our sacrifices; and to promote among us a sense of mutual trust and shared responsibility.

We derive our inspiration and commitment to excellence from the inscription in our foyer: "And ye shall know the truth and the truth shall make you free."

Appendix B

Intelligence Documents

The six documents of Appendix B provide a glimpse of the feelings of DI personnel and show some of the ways they communicate with each other. The first is my letter of resignation from the Agency. This document struck a chord with numerous personnel and was widely reproduced and distributed. I received, directly and indirectly, numerous comments to the effect that it was accurate, and thanks that I had put other peoples' concerns on paper. The sole negative critiques of which I am aware hold that my criticisms were somewhat too strong. I suspect that this reaction comes mainly from people lucky enough to have been in the better managed DI offices and those co-opted by the system. In any case, I have few regrets about the letter now. The second document is DDI John Helgerson's report to the troops in response to my letter. It was declassified in mid-1991.

The third document is Thomas Barksdale's memorandum to then-DDI Robert Gates over the handling of the intelligence supporting what became the Iran-contra affair. It was declassified and released to the public in late 1991.

The fourth and fifth documents are depositions to the SSCI by two experienced DI hands—Carolyn Ekedahl and John Hibbits—against Gates in 1991.

The last document is Robert Gates' memo to Melvin A. Goodman in reaction to Goodman's NIE draft. The Agency declassified and released it in late 1991 on the occasion of Gates' confirmation hearings.

16 November 1990

MEMORANDUM FOR: Deputy Director for Intelligence

FROM: John A. Gentry

SUBJECT: Resignation

I hereby resign from the Central Intelligence Agency, effective 30 November 1990. After years of often challenging, enjoyable work, the increasingly oppressive intellectual climate, bureaucratic morass, and institutionalized lack of integrity in this Directorate have overwhelmed the positive aspects of analysis that lead me to this Agency in the first place.

I can no longer work in an organization in which satisfaction of bureaucratic superiors is more important than superior analysis; in which the key analytic question often is "what does the boss really want?" rather than "what is really of significance to US foreign policy and national security?"; in which subservience of intellectual integrity to the wants of superiors is essential to bureaucratic success; in which analysts' fear of "managers" has created an analytical corps of "scared rabbits," as one fairly senior Ph.D. economist in RTT recently characterized it--including him/herself; in which analysts too often are relegated to the role of research assistant or propagandist in the service of de facto senior analysts up the review chain who inject personal political opinions and desires into Directorate products, regardless of fact or analysts' judgment.

It has been genuinely distasteful to have worked for:

o A division chief who ordered a politically pointed current intelligence article based on a press clipping despite numerous hard facts to the contrary, my judgment to the contrary, and the opposition of other DI components. In discussions about the issue, my branch chief questioned my loyalty to the Office of European Analysis, but not to honesty, the Agency, or the Nation. These men repeatedly made clear that they intended to serve a political constituency and to choose their data selectively--often picking information scraps specifically refuted by numerous, more reliable reports. Both have since assumed more senior positions in an office whose director recently stated that politization had occurred during his predecessor's tenure, but preposterously claimed he had stamped it out.

- These same and other supervisors who "cook the books" by omission by avoiding issues or judgments they know/knew would offend the political or bureaucratic sensitivities of readers--in CIA headquarters and in policy organizations like the Department of the Treasury, for example.

- An office director who received numerous complaints from many analysts about division- and branch-level managerial dishonesty and incompetence but simply dismissed them out-of-hand.

- A deputy office director, now an office director, who made it clear that having a concern about management was itself--alone--evidence of unsatisfactory performance.

- A deputy office director who ordered a branch chief in my division to write critical performance appraisals on two analysts in his branch. When he responded that the analysts were doing good jobs, the deputy office director said that he should write negative PARS or expect to receive one himself. The spineless branch chief capitulated. The victims left the DI.

- A division chief who, in his office, threatened to kill an analyst.

- Numerous supervisors who could/can not be counted upon to tell the truth consistently.

- A supervisor who admitted to having neuroses, acted like it in my view, and permitted regular lies by a staff member about US intelligence capabilities to visiting foreign intelligence officers, NSC staff personnel, and Defense Department officials, at least.

- A branch chief who repeatedly, purposefully, altered the facts contained in articles--creating factual errors--in the alleged interest of making sentences and paragraphs more "readable."

- A branch chief who stole my personal property from my desk.

- Another branch chief who rummaged through analysts' desks to discover, according to him when confronted, "what kind of analysts" he had in his branch.

- Division- and branch-level managers who recruited

UNCLASSIFIED

secretaries to inform on analysts' comments and actions, rewarding those who accepted with Agency awards and babysitting fees. Secretaries who declined these requests were not so favored.

- An office director who, in reviewing a research paper, said he didn't like what he saw, didn't care what the revised terms of reference/concept paper he agreed to contained, recognized that his oral and written comments were not very clear, but said he would know what he wanted when he saw it.

- Numerous supervisors for whom the concept of leadership was foreign and loyalty was/is single directional--up only.

These anecdotes concern only individuals in my direct supervisory chain (including deputy office directors) and do not include numerous others about actions that have afflicted and now afflict offices in your directorate.

I have reached the conclusion that the lack of personal and intellectual integrity is not only no impediment to "success" in the DI, it is an advantage. Dishonesty is rampant and is a management tool. Dishonest men and women demonstrably "succeed." This is not surprising to me when the week-long OTE course that I took in early 1989 on managing in CIA contained not one word about an ethical standard for the Agency. I believe that the lack of a statement of organizational principles and standards of acceptable conduct sends a clear implicit message that ethics are not important. At the same time, the principles of leadership--duties and responsibilities as well as perquisites--that I am accustomed to as a US Army Reserve officer received no attention in the OTE course and get much too little in the DI on a daily basis. Many analysts share this view: one well-respected senior analyst has decided that he will not accept a branch chief's job because he believes the unethical behavior expected of branch chiefs by senior managers conflicts with his Christian values.

The recruiter's promise that CIA analysts provide timely, relevant intelligence to senior US policymakers rings hallow indeed when managers insist, pointedly or implicitly, that we write for a "reader" who is stupid, lazy, ignorant, interested only in entertainment, or all of the above. Much of management clearly is interested in providing stories that please, not analysis that serves these presumed incompetents. This arrogance too regularly produces "intelligence" that is an embarrassment to this Agency when it goes to sound, knowledgeable policymakers who are looking to CIA to provide genuine intelligence support. The director of OTE made the point succinctly when he said to an OTE class in March 1990 that analysts are in the

UNCLASSIFIED

UNCLASSIFIED

"investigative journalism" business. This regular, intended shallowness of "analysis" often has led me to muse that CIA analysis is to analysis what classic comic books are to classics.

Perhaps you recall that last year an economist resigned from the Agency lamenting what he called the Office of Soviet Analysis' preference for "economic journalism" over research. I believe his point, reinforced by the OTE director's comment, is that pretty words are valued more greatly than expertise or sound judgment in SOVA and other offices. The DI has a fundamental problem when expertise is conferred by position description or desk occupied, not knowledge or experience, and the main criterion of analytical success is publication, not accuracy of forecast or soundness of judgment. I have never, in all my time in this Agency, heard of a single post-mortem review of the accuracy of DI publications except to find a reference somewhere, however obscure, to refute charges of an intelligence failure. I long will remember the branch chief cited in the first bullet above laughingly say to a new analyst, legitimately concerned about his qualifications to write in a current intelligence publication, something close to, "who cares if it's right, you're getting a publication, aren't you?" Sound analysis is possible only through work and the development of expertise. You poorly serve the nation by fostering the managerial attitude that research is an effete academic pursuit that real intelligence analysts eschew and management cannot tolerate because it cuts "production."

You likewise will continue to have trouble keeping economists and others when they are hamstrung in pursuit of methodologically sound analysis by the demand that analysis be reduced to the blacks and whites allegedly expected by the mythological "reader" whose changing identity is known only to each reviewer. Technical economic expertise suffers when, despite one's best efforts, reviewers virtually automatically demand further "clarification" which usually deteriorates into simplicity and too often simple-mindedness. In early 1990, for example, a division chief in RTT proclaimed that all paragraphs should contain only one thought and that, in essence, all mitigating or extenuating facts are "extraneous." This attitude is foolish at best.

The review process generally could hardly be more destructive of creativity and timeliness if it were intended to denigrate the work of the Directorate. The determination of nearly every reviewer to modify papers in his/her own image to accommodate the perceived wants of more senior reviewers--not genuinely review for substance or edit--means that ever more amateur, less expert, more politically motivated analysis is injected into products, even as the coordination process tends to produce blandness. These

UNCLASSIFIED

UNCLASSIFIED

papers, moreover, are too often late due to managerial dithering, insecurity, and simple incompetence; but one example is that 27 of the 30 papers requested of the Office of Soviet Analysis by the White House in advance of the Bush/Gorbachev summit in Malta late last year failed to reach the President because SOVA division and group chiefs sat on the papers until after he left the country. It is no wonder that policymakers often say that they prefer INR products to CIA papers, one Congressional intelligence committee staffer says he usually opts for the Washington Times over CIA publications, and DI analysts often experience greater senses of relief than accomplishment when their hard-cover papers are published.

The Directorate cannot have high-quality analysis while having a management system that insists that analysts accept all changes made in the review process, or risk having challenges even to the injection of factual error regarded by management as unacceptably combative behavior. Management too often abdicates its basic responsibilities to mediate differences by punishing analyst challenges to shoddy review. By so doing, the Directorate is encouraging "team players" over sound analysts. The extent that this trend has developed is shown in management's finding, I am told, that "getting along with others" is the premier success characteristic for analysts. This is odd indeed when almost all analyst assignments are individual and management personnel often resist the formation of teams because, as I have heard repeatedly, they cannot adequately judge individual performances on team projects. The term "getting along..." has become a euphemism for being a pleasant, docile subordinate, particularly in the review/rewrite process. Heaven help him/her whose sense of intellectual integrity gets in the way of bureaucratic expediency and managerial laziness.

These new generation team players, increasingly in senior positions by dint of their obsequiousness, do not like to take risks and so tend not to provide useful intelligence warnings to the nation. They obfuscate, waffle, or wait until events are clearly taking shape. The trend in Directorate personnel policy is fostering future intelligence failures--particularly failures to alert the policy community of opportunities to exploit. These failures are bureaucratically safe; they almost never generate the recriminations of Pearl Harbor because only unseen opportunities remain unknown.

A sharp operations officer last year said to me, "'Agency management' is an oxymoron," and I am convinced that her comment applies to much of DI "management." Real managers know how to delegate. Real managers are consistent in their standards and fair in their appraisals and treatment of employees. They are concerned about efficiency

UNCLASSIFIED

and don't waste massive amounts of analysts' and managers' time--and taxpayers' money--by marginal dithering and simply inexcusable delay; I well remember a Director of European Analysis taking exactly 105 days to return a research paper with but minor comments. Real managers know how to develop initiative and responsibility in subordinates, rather than tell them what to do, foster subservience, and like one current office director chasten them by asking regularly what outside source can corroborate even their straightforward judgments. Good managers also are leaders; it has long seemed to me incongruous that the Directorate has an Office of Leadership Analysis but so few leaders.

Stupid managers blame analysts for their unhappiness and concentrate more on recruiting than retaining expensively recruited personnel; I well remember one division chief who weekly lambasted his branch chiefs over failure to recruit even as his division hemorrhaged personnel--precisely because of them. Self-delusive managers pretend that people leave because of personal problems, like failure to adjust to office reorganizations, or to accept 6-digit salaries; all is well because some other government agencies have higher turnover rates, according to the silly argument of a senior official of the Office of the Inspector General this year. There is a lesson in Agency statistics on attrition by Directorate and DI attrition by office that complacent DI managers will continue to ignore. Such comfortable self-assurance remains in the presence of clear ignorance; the Director of Personnel told me last year that he was unhappy that the Office of Personnel's exit interviews are so perfunctory that he did not really know why people leave the Agency. Would you like the name of a political analyst who took a 5-digit annual pay cut to get out of the Office of European Analysis?

It is clear that significant portions of Agency and Directorate management are unwilling to recognize that problems exist, let alone do anything to resolve them. With the very idea of a problem anathema, the bureaucratic/ideological orthodoxy of many managers reminds me of the post-1968 Czechoslovak Communist Party, in which stolid apparatchiks exiled competence and outlawed even the use of the word "reform." Large numbers of analysts regularly rotate offices in your directorate in search of decent working conditions. The number of good places to go is declining. I once asked a long-time China analyst why he had transferred into a notoriously poorly managed division of the Office of European Analysis, commenting half-jokingly that I thought he was smarter than that; he responded that he knew he was entering a "hell-hole," but he wanted to work in a different "hell-hole." This analyst later resigned from the Agency.

UNCLASSIFIED

While you inherited these problems, you also show no signs of making meaningful changes. Your initiatives have been at the margin, and you recognize no serious problems. I am disappointed, but no longer surprised, that you declined to respond in any way to my note of May 25 offering specific proposals for corrective measures.

The Office of the Inspector General is useless at best as an agent of positive change; at worst it is a detriment to better DI management and a bureaucratic danger to concerned analysts with the courage to try to effect change. I am reminded of the story of an analyst who complained about his office management in July 1989 and received word in February 1990 that the OIG had refused to query any of the individuals referenced in his complaint or to address any of the points of the complaint because it, the Office of the Inspector General, already knew what was going on in the referenced office. Amazed, the analyst complained that he had not even been able to verbally explain his concerns to the assigned "investigation" team. The OIG response was that dropping the documents at the OIG and casual conversations with an OIG officer satisfied his written request for consultations. The analyst met the "investigators" for the first time shortly before they handed him a written rejection of his complaints, citing at the same time comments of individuals the analyst had complained about. This travesty defies all but bureaucrats' logic. I wonder if it reflects accurately the Judge's sense of judicial fair play, or only not-so-benign neglect.

Dick Kerr once said to me something close to, "the solution for anyone who has problems with the Agency is for him to leave the Agency." At the time, it was a conversation stopper. Now, I am convinced that his comment accurately reflects de facto DI policy. Clearly, many bright, creative people have chafed under the intellectual orthodoxy imposed on much of the Directorate--however strenuously DI management also claims an interest in encouraging cultural diversity--and have taken that advise. I now happily join them.

The systemic problems of the Directorate lead me to question its basic integrity as an organization ostensibly dedicated to serving the US Government and the American people. I question the institution even as I salute the many fine people in it who strive and often succeed in producing good intelligence despite, not because of, the system you head.

John A. Gentry

UNCLASSIFIED

UNCLASSIFIED

cc:

DI Analysts
DI MAG
Chairman, SSCI
Vice Chairman, SSCI
Chairman, HPSCI
Ranking Minority Member, HPSCI
OCA
Inspector General
Director of Personnel
Chairman, NIC
General Counsel
Publication Review Board
MPSS
DDCI
DCI

UNCLASSIFIED

DDI Message to the Directorate on the Subject of Politicization

14 June 1991

Last year, an analyst who resigned from the Agency charged that DI analysis was politicized. A thorough inquiry by the Inspector General did not substantiate the analyst's allegations. It did, however, surface some general concerns about this issue among analysts.

I believe that our sensitivity to this issue is healthy. New employees know that in my remarks to the New Analyst and CT courses—as in written messages to the Directorate—I have underscored the importance of providing consumers our findings objectively and dispassionately. At the same time, we attempt to make the length and level of generality of our material responsive to the consumer's needs. In remarks at the Persian Gulf awards ceremony last month I noted my pride in our analysts' "relentless determination to find the facts and objectively present them to policymakers."

I remind you of our continuing attention to this matter to underscore the point—which I repeat in this message—that we in the DI do not sanction and will not tolerate deliberate distortion of our intelligence products to match anyone's preconceived views. Clearly, this would be anathema to our mission and our role as a trusted source of timely, objective intelligence for policymakers.

We all know that the credibility of DI intelligence products rests on the integrity of the analytic process, in which objectivity is both our guide and our goal. Anything that weakens that integrity undermines the Directorate's ability to meet its responsibilities. We must be careful, of course, not to misconstrue strongly held views or appropriate editing and substantive review as evidence of bias. Our intelligence publications are, in the end, not the product of an individual but the product of the Agency. Nevertheless, it is only by paying attention to the possibility of bias and ensuring that alternative outcomes and minority views are reflected that we can safeguard the credibility of our product.

I have recommended that the general issue of analytical integrity be addressed in all appropriate training courses, and I urge you to reflect on and discuss among yourselves in your branch or division our professional responsibilities in this area. Indeed, you have the obligation to make sure that our products do not reflect bias. Anyone with concerns about politicization is welcome, in confidence, to contact me, the Associate Deputy Director, or the Inspector General.

My years of experience in this Directorate have given me the utmost faith in the integrity of the employees of the Directorate and their commitment to producing objective finished intelligence. Working together and sharing our concerns, we will remain true to this mission.

John L. Helgerson
Deputy Director for Intelligence

UNCLASSIFIED

2 December 1986

MEMORANDUM FOR: Deputy Director for Intelligence

FROM: Thomas M. Barksdale, NESA/PG/I

SUBJECT: The Iranian Imbroglio: Implications for the Intelligence Process

1. I want to express to you my concern over the circumvention and misuse of the intelligence process in connection with the contacts between US and Iranian officials and the transfer of US arms to Iran. It is my perception that normal intelligence procedures have been ignored throughout this affair. Iranian analysts in the DDI were never consulted or asked to provide an intelligence input to the covert actions and secret contacts that have occurred. In my judgment, this exclusion of expert opinion contributed significantly to the current foreign policy disaster. [redacted]

2. My concern is not only the exclusion of DDI analysts from playing an intelligence role in the recent events. I do not believe this is an isolated case that is already past history. I believe the Iranian affair has revealed serious problems about the intelligence process and this Agency's role in it. I am concerned over the manner in which the entire process becomes skewered when a small coterie of people claiming access to exclusive raw intelligence and acting without coordination with relevant offices are allowed to provide intelligence and advice to US policy makers. In my view, this development in connection with the Iranian arms affair has embarrassed this Agency and the Intelligence Community in the eyes of those officials we are supposed to be serving. But much more importantly, it has squandered the resources of this Agency and prevented it from performing its central mission: the provision of timely and informed assessments to policy makers to guide them in making their decisions. [redacted]

3. The immediate problem. I have become aware since the Iranian arms deal became public that there has existed within the Central Intelligence Agency a unique channel for providing intelligence to the NSC on Iran. This channel apparently includes a person under contract to the DDO and the NIO/CT. We have had only sporadic glimpses of the activities of this channel. I have on about two occasions over the past year been allowed to read "exclusive dissemed" TDs dealing with US-Iranian relations. [redacted]

4. Subsequent to the public revelations of US contacts with Iran, a draft NID/PDB brief on growing popular unrest in Iran was held over

UNCLASSIFIED

[redacted]

UNCLASSIFIED

for 24 hours because DDO was sending an exclusive report to the White House on Iranian political developments. Neither I nor, so far as I know, any other DDI analyst was allowed then or has been allowed since to have access to this report. On my return on 24 November from a TDY, a fellow political analyst informed me that during my absence a jointly drafted PDB item on Iranian political factions written prior to my departure had been published. He was subsequently told that an exclusive DDO report had been delivered along with the PDB. At least one reader had noted that our assessment and the DDO report were contradictory. My colleague was then allowed to read the TD on which the DDO exclusive assessment was based. My colleague was asked to incorporate his assessment of this report into a package of briefing material prepared for the DCI. I do not know whether this assessment received any further dissemination. [redacted]

5. On 26 November 1986 I became aware of yet two more instances in which intelligence on Iranian domestic politics was provided to senior levels of the US Government without coordination with NESA/PG/I. I received a copy of a Memorandum for the DCI drafted by CTC entitled "Iranian Support for International Terrorism." This memorandum contains a section on Iranian political factions. The factions are defined in ways that none of the three political analysts in NESA nor, so far as I know, anywhere in the Intelligence Community have ever used before. Some of the information is factually wrong. Flat assertions are made about the attitude of a so-called "middle-of-the-road" faction toward relations with the United States that are at odds with the judgments of NESA and, I am confident, with the judgments of other components of the Intelligence Community. These assertions are also at odds with the overwhelming bulk of intelligence reporting both from US sources and foreign intelligence services. [redacted]

6. Also on 26 November, I became aware that the NIO/CT had briefed officials of the NSC and National Strategy Planning Group on, among other issues, Iranian leaders' attitudes toward the United States. He also discussed the leaders' contacts with US officials. NESA Iranian analysts were not informed that this briefing was to take place, nor were they asked to provide an assesment of the attitudes purportedly held by Iranian leaders. I believe the issue of Iran's relations with the US is much more complex and nuanced than that presented by the NIO/CT. [redacted]

7. All of this, of course, takes place against the background of press reports that for a considerable period of time US officials have

[redacted]

UNCLASSIFIED

UNCLASSIFIED

been involved in secret contacts with Iranian leaders involving arms deals and our hostages in Lebanon--contacts that took place without anyone involved drawing on the professional expertise available in the DDI to provide an understanding of the broader issues and pitfalls involved in such dealings. [redacted]

8. The above incidents represent to me a perversion of the intelligence process staggering in its proportions. It violates the professional standards of conduct that have governed me and most of my colleagues throughout the Intelligence Community during my 18 years as an intelligence officer. Apparently it is now possible for a small number of people claiming access to an exclusive and almost personal data base to run their own intelligence operation with disdain bordering on contempt for their colleagues who have every right to be consulted and included in the process. I believe that the system as it has worked in regard to Iran over about the past 18 months has resulted in distorted, uninformed, and in some instances inaccurate information being presented to officials of this government who presumably believed they were receiving the collective judgment of this Agency. I am appalled that in the midst of a grave foreign policy crisis this helter-skelter, ad hoc, uncoordinated way of doing business has continued. I worry that we risk repeating or perpetuating the mistakes that contributed to the onset of the crisis. [redacted]

8. Over the past five years, this Agency and the DDI have enjoyed a recovery of public prestige and and infusion of resources. We have hired new analysts in sizeable numbers; on instructions from our managers, we have expanded our contacts with the academic world and other experts through personal meetings, attendance at professional conferences, and the sponsorship of seminars; new collection systems have been brought on line; tasking functions have been given new priority; funds have been made available to allow analysts to travel extensively in their areas of responsibility; new slots have been created for overseas assignments; a research program has been implemented to focus us more on mid- and long-term problems and away from fighting fires; and funds provided to hire outside contractors to expand our knowledge and data even more. [redacted]

set back for us too!

9. In the end, all of this activity and commitment of resources did not amount to a pitcher of warm spit as far as providing the US Government with judgments about one of the most significant foreign policy initiatives ever undertaken. As an intelligence officer concerned about the reputation of this Agency and the integrity of what I call an intelligence process; and as an American citizen with some regard for the use of the taxpayers' money, I am hard pressed to justify resources committed against gains achieved. [redacted]

[redacted]

UNCLASSIFIED

UNCLASSIFIED

10. As for specific grievances: Any of my superiors in this Agency or this Government are privileged to disregard my analytical judgments at any time. I claim no inherent right to have them exalted above any others. What I do claim--and what I was denied in this instance--is the right to have my judgments heard and taken into account when this Government makes policy on the country on which I am the senior political analyst. If such a right does not exist, or if it can be arbitrarily suspended by any of my superiors at any time, then this Agency is operating in a condition of anarchy bereft of the standards of conduct that I had assumed motivated all of its employees. Any organization in which regard for proper procedures--particularly those that go to the heart of its existence--has become a trivial concern is living on borrowed time as far as its ability to perform its functions effectively or to continue to attract the caliber of employee it would like. [redacted]

11. I must also protest the way in which advocacy of a certain line of analysis by people claiming access to closely held information inevitably pushes the intelligence process toward divisions into cliques pleading their particular cases. When, for example, certain components assert exclusive raw intelligence data indicates Iranian leaders are abandoning terrorism, analysts who are not privy to this information and analysing more ambiguous information tend to lean harder on the conclusion that Iran is a strong supporter of terrorism. It is a natural human tendency. This undermines the process in which everyone with knowledge of the same data is required to defend their conclusions under rigorous intellectual debate--a process that never works perfectly under any circumstances but at least provides some hope of producing the best finished intelligence possible for policy makers. Instead, we have a process in which the debate becomes personalized as those relying on one set of data cling more forcefully to their principal line of analysis, lest they be accused of themselves adjusting their conclusions to conform to those based on the exclusive data. [redacted]

12. I am concerned over the potential for abuse when components are allowed to advocate a line of analysis based on exclusive information. It seems to me to undermine the ability of the CIA to provide objective analysis when the same limited number of people apparently have the authority to cultivate sources, determine the reliability of those sources, provide advice to policy makers based on the information derived from those sources, and determine the relative credibility to be given those sources when weighed against other, and even contradictory, information. I am concerned that there does not seem to be a self-correcting mechanism to subject those sources and the information they provide to rigorous cross-examination, even when the conclusions have, according to available empirical evidence, proved to be faulty. [redacted]

[redacted]

UNCLASSIFIED

UNCLASSIFIED

13. I do have one particular grievance.

During the course of [redacted] briefings, the question of Israeli arms transfers--and in one instance, even the question of a US role in such transfers--inevitably came up. I gave what I believed to be the objective facts: Israeli arms transfers were a small and relatively insignificant part of the Iranian inventory, and the US opposed Israeli arms deals with Iran. As we now know, this assessment was wrong. I told a lie to my [redacted] hosts who had every right to believe they were getting an impartial briefing. This, to me, constitutes a violation of the trust that I have a right to demand from this organization. There are no circumstances that justify having an intelligence analyst deliver a briefing in ignorance of contravening facts available to other components of the CIA. The potential for abuse if DDI analysts become shills for covert action is, I hope, all too apparent. Once the lies are revealed, it certainly will do nothing for our relations with foreign governments [redacted]

14. I am being denied access to the reports stemming from contacts between US and Iranian officials. It will be difficult if not impossible for me to analyze Iran's internal politics and its attitudes toward the US and terrorism until I know what Iranians were approached, what they said, and what deals were made. [redacted]

15. The more general problem. As a DDI analyst, I increasingly find I am being denied timely access to the full range of data I need to do my job as I think it should be done. I become aware data I have not seen is in exclusive or restricted channels. I may not see it at all, or see it after it has been disseminated to policy makers, and then I may be allowed only a cursory FYI glance. I am not supposed to analyze this information or incorporate it into a data base. The reports I am referring to are mainly "exclusive dissemed" DDO TDs; some of it is SI. [redacted]

16. With the expansion of the Agency's manpower and creation of new components, there seems to have been an increase in the number of people who are guaranteed a hearing at high levels of the Agency or the government without the necessity of coordinating their opinions with other components. [redacted]

17. I obviously have not conducted a poll of my colleagues, but I believe a sampling of opinion would reveal widespread malaise on the part of most employees connected with Iran, the hostages, and Iranian terrorism over the manner in which the issue of contacts with Iran

[redacted]

UNCLASSIFIED

UNCLASSIFIED

has been handled by the Agency. Morale has been dealt a serious blow with the realization that much of their work has been only a sideshow, a spinning of wheels isolated from the main show. This is one other factor to be weighed against the justifications that will undoubtedly be offered for limiting knowledge of the Iranian contacts. [redacted]

18. It is dificult to make recommendations about correcting these perceived shortcomings. The problems I have cited involve basic questions of how this Agency does its business. I cannot tic off a few easily implemented solutions. In general, what I am asking is:

--A review of all the intelligence production provided the NSC over the past 18 months related to Iranian internal politics and Iranian relations with the US that was passed without coordination with NESA. The right to make known to the recipients of this production any NESA differences with the judgments provided.

--If this is not feasible, an explanation of the circumstances under which finished intelligence on Iran can be provided to policy- making levels of the US Government without coordination with NESA.

--An explanation in writing of the relative responsibilities and relationships between NESA/PG/I on the one hand and CTC and NIO/CT on the other, particularly regarding their respective obligations to coordinate with each other in the production of intelligence. An explanation of why the memorandum entitled "Iranian Support for International Terrorism" dated 22 November 1986 was sent forward without NESA coordination.

--The right to be consulted when any CIA component is writing an assessment or making recommendations to policy makers or senior Agency officials regarding my areas of expertise.

--An end to any practice of sending raw intelligence to policy makers without its being reviewed by relevant DDI offices. A mechanism for resolving the issue if DDI and DDO disagree on whether the information should be sent.

--A review of the practice of keeping some information in exclusive or restrictive channels, to determine whether this is necessary, and, if so, to improve the procedures whereby DDI analysts can be given timely access to such information.

--Assurances that never again will I or any DDI analyst be allowed to present information to any recipient that any other component of the CIA or US Government knows to be inaccurate. [redacted]

[redacted]

UNCLASSIFIED

UNCLASSIFIED

19. I have so far given you what I believe are legitimate concerns about our activities. What follows is more presumptuous. I appeal here to the fact that I have spent my entire adult life in the employment of this Government, either here or in the US Army, including a tour of duty in the infantry in Vietnam. I have worked here under five Presidents, all of whom have done things that I disapproved of, but nothing so grievous as to cause me to have doubts about continuing as a part of this Government. Even before this Iranian business broke, this perception had begun to change. To simplify for the sake of discussion, there appear to be two strains of thought underlying the conduct of US foreign policy. One views the world as a complex place, requiring US leaders to have a sophisticated knowledge of foreign countries. According to this view, the US can perform its role only if it has an informed awareness of the forces that motivate other countries and deals with these forces with a thoughtful blend of its moral, military, and economic resources. [redacted]

20. The other strain has a more simple view. It believes what the US wants sets the standard by which other countries are to be judged. They are right or wrong, according to the degree to which they support or oppose US policies. From this standpoint, it follows that any country can be dealt with by any method the US believes proper. US leaders are not required to conduct foreign policy openly and with the support of the American public. They can place much reliance on force. They can turn to a small clique of individuals unaccountable to any institution and only tenuously if at all acountable to the rule of law. These individuals in turn feel free to choose methods more suited to the Mafia than to a government presuming some moral superiority. Hence the US ends up conducting its foreign policy by arming various brigands, mining international waters (putting us in the same boat with Qadhafi), attempting to reestablish relations with a previously hostile country through furtive contacts with men of questionable motives, and engaging in under-the-counter arms deals contrary to our own stated policies. [redacted]

21. I have within the past four years had a front row seat on two occasions to witness the disasters that result when this latter strain is allowed to govern foreign policy. I was the Palestinian analyst and served on the Lebanese task force when Israel invaded Lebanon. There, too, great diplomatic vistas were to open up if Israel invaded Lebanon and ended the "Palestinian problem" through military might; if US Marines were used not just temporarily to separate warring factions but to provide the US with a basis to intervene in Lebanese internal politics; if the battleship New Jersey blasted hostile Lebanese factions; if carrier bombers made a show of force against the Syrians. All of these uses of military force were to cut through the complexity

[redacted] [redacted]

UNCLASSIFIED

UNCLASSIFIED

of the Middle East peace process, Lebanon's factional politics, and Syria's role in regional affairs and and allow the US to impose its own solutions. They not only failed to do that; they left the region more destabilized and peace further away than ever, and they left in their wake immense human suffering that continues to grow. [redacted]

22. These policies in Lebanon failed because they were inherently flawed. What's more, there were people in this organization saying at each step of the way that they were flawed, would not work, and would probably be counterproductive to any objective this country wanted to achieve. The killing of our and State Department employees; the deaths of over 200 Marines; the radicalization of Lebanese Shias; the transformation of an already conflict-ridden Lebanon into a charnel house; these events did not just happen, much less did they happen because evil terrorists persist in their terrorism. They happened in large measure because those in charge of US policy remained ignorant of the forces at work as they single-mindedly pursued militarily imposed solutions. [redacted]

23. How incredible that four years later the same ignorance in even more virulent form has produced yet another disaster for the United States and its prestige. How incredible that 25 years after the Bay of Pigs, action-oriented adventurers are let loose to do their thing without any necessity to seek the advice, much less the consent, of experts who might have warned them they were on a fool's errand. How incredible that three weeks after the judgments about Iran put foward by certain CIA components are revealed to be seriously flawed, those same components are free to continue pushing the same line unfettered by any neeed to consult with other components with different viewpoints. [redacted]

24. Adventurers who achieve results by cutting through the details can justifiably find tiresome those who constantly insist that the details of a complex world should be given due regard before the US seeks new worlds to conquer. The adventurers become intolerable when all they can point to is a string of failures that have left US prestige further tarnished and more innocent human bodies lying in their wake. [redacted]

25. I would hope that events of the past few weeks have laid to rest the notion that US foreign policy can be conducted on the basis of a small handful of people engaging in covert action, clandestine contacts, and other too-cute-by-far tactics uninformed by consultations with the chief foreign policy instruments of this government. I would hope DDI analysts through proper channels will always have a central role in providing the assessments on which policy makers base their decisions. [redacted]

[redacted]

UNCLASSIFIED

26. As for me personally, I can only express to you my profound disquiet about being part of a government that conducts its foreign relations without regard for the norms and proper procedures of a democratic system based on the rule of law. If any other employee of this Agency finds these concerns trivial, I would welcome consulting with them in a forum of their choosing. I would like to hear their opinions of how the same person at the age of 25 could fight a war in which he did not believe out of concern that at that particular time his obligations to society outweighed his personal feelings, but now deserves only condescending dismissal if he asserts that his own morality seems to be at odds with his professional duties. I hope I do not hear that if a person's role in great affairs is minor, that individual is excluded from the necessity to reach moral judgments about what is happening. If that is the rejoinder, I would like to hear a discussion of the differences between the obligations of a government employee in the United States today and one in Germany in, say, 1942. [redacted]

[redacted]

UNCLASSIFIED

UNCLASSIFIED

APPENDIX

I would like for the record to repeat what I said to you about the substance of US policy in our meeting on 25 November. DDI Iranian political analysts have consistently pointed out the factionalism within Iran's leadership. We have said that anti-US attitudes stem from deeply held perceptions that will not be easily abandoned, especially while Khoemini is alive; we do not believe that Iranian leaders yet have a sincere desire to improve relations with the US and would at best engage in probing to see what practical benefits Iran might derive in return for open ended promises to seek improved relations; any Iranian leader claiming to want better ties probably would represent only a faction or clique and would be unlikely to have the authority to commit Iran to a rapprochement; he would in fact, be seeking ways to further his own political fortunes. The power struggle, we said, would have to work itself out more before the US could deal confidently with Iran. [redacted]

We also pointed out that while our policy makers must decide whether to deal with Iran while officials who held our diplomats hostage in Tehran and were linked to the murder of US Marines in Lebanon and the bombing of our Embassy there continued to hold high-level positions in the Iranian hierarchy, it seemed to us that a test of Iran's willingness to seek a rapprochement would be whether these officials had their wings clipped. We further assessed that it might send exactly the wrong signal to Iranian leaders if the US were perceived as the supplicant, begging for better relations while Iran remained uncompromising and unapologetic about its past transgressions. In sum, had our assessments been heeded, the US would not be in the mess it is in today. [redacted]

[redacted]

UNCLASSIFIED

STATEMENT TO SENATE SELECT COMMITTEE ON INTELLIGENCE

SUBJECT: CIA POLITICIZATION

FROM: Carolyn McGiffert Ekedahl[1]

DATE: September 30, 1991

The bias built into CIA reporting during the Casey/Gates era continues to undermine the agency's ability to produce quality intelligence. While the issue of politicization is difficult to confront, the problems created by flawed intelligence are significant enough to require serious and concentrated attention. I believe that, given Mr. Gates' past performance, his confirmation as Director of Central Intelligence would send a strong and demoralizing message to intelligence analysts--and would be a disservice to the very real need of U.S. policymakers for objective intelligence analysis.

TOPIC 1: Soviet-Third World Relations

The committee has requested a copy of a paper on the Soviet position in the Third World, written by a colleague and me in 1985. There is no copy of the paper; it was killed and never published. I believe the paper was killed for political reasons; it did not support the views of the 7th Floor.

When I was first asked to write the paper, by my deputy division chief (Robert Korn) in late 1984 or early 1985, Korn told me that Douglas MacEachin, Director of the Office of Soviet Analysis (SOVA) had requested an assessment that would provide a "balance sheet" of Soviet activities in the Third World. I requested that he go back to MacEachin and make sure he wanted such a paper, because my experience was that nothing we could write on that particular subject of an analytical nature would be

[1] I currently am CIA's Officer-in-Residence at Georgetown University. I have been an intelligence officer with CIA for 29 years and have worked on Soviet foreign policy for most of that time. In September 1985, I left the Office of Soviet Analysis because of issues involving politicization that I will discuss in this memorandum. I have subsequently worked on the National Intelligence Council's Analytic Group (1985-1986) and the Office of Near East and South Asian Analysis (1986 to date). I have continued during this period to work on Soviet foreign policy and have written a book, several book chapters, and a number of journal articles.

acceptable to the seventh floor.[2] Korn told me several days later that he had raised the subject with MacEachin, who had said to go ahead.[3] My division chief, Melvin Goodman, subsequently also agreed that we should write the paper.

After collecting a considerable amount of data, Raymond Duncan, a visiting scholar, and I began to draft an assessment; by March 1985, we had a rough draft prepared. Material compiled by OGI and ~~Soviet~~ SOVA revealed that most indicators of Soviet Third World activity were either leveling off or declining by the mid-1980s--after increasing rather rapidly in the 1970s. Given the fact that the Soviets were continuing to put large amounts of material assistance into various beleaguered client states (Afghanistan, Ethiopia, Angola, Cambodia, Cuba, Vietnam), the data suggested that Soviet expansionism in the Third World had peaked and that the costs of an expanding empire could not be sustained.

Following the purge of SOVA (a major reorganization involving the replacement of various managers) that occurred in March 1985, Ray Duncan and I were asked to submit our preliminary draft to the new management team and were then summoned to a meeting with those officers. We were told that the paper was off the mark, that it had no particular relevance or utility, and that it should be published on the outside--not inside the CIA where it had nothing new to offer.[4] I asked why MacEachin had asked for the paper if it was irrelevant and was told that MacEachin had never heard of the paper and didn't even know it was on the research program. The paper was killed. Shortly thereafter, I left SOVA.

TOPIC 2: Soviet Involvement in International Terrorism

I was the drafter of the original estimate on Soviet involvement in international terrorism in February 1981. Robert

---

[2] By that time, we were exercizing a considerable amount of self censorship. There seemed little point in spending a lot of time on a project that had no chance of moving through the system.

[3] I'm emphasizing these exchanges because MacEachin subsequently denied that he had ever asked for such a paper--or, indeed, even heard of it.

[4] Subsequently, over a three-year period and in our spare time, Ray and I took the theme of the draft and wrote a book. It was published by Westview Press in 1990 and is titled, Moscow and the Third World Under Gorbachev.

Gates has claimed that the drafters wanted to "stick their finger in the policy maker's eye." This is totally false.

State Department requested a special estimate on the subject after Secretary Haig made a speech in late January 1981, charging that the Soviets were behind much of the terrorist activity in Europe. I was informed by a State Department official present at the meeting that the Director of State Department's Bureau for Intelligence and Research, Ron Spiers, had told Haig that there was little evidence to support his charges and had then requested an interagency effort to address the issue. The CIA's National Intelligence Council (NIC) was tasked to prepare a special estimate, and I was asked to be the drafter.

Because of the importance of the request and the volatility of the issue, exceedingly high priority was giving to collecting and evaluating <u>all</u> available information dealing with Soviet involvement, direct and indirect, to <u>any</u> group dealing in terrorist activities. I worked extremely closely with the Directorate of Operations (DO) to make sure it provided every piece of information it had, as well as with the State Department and the Defense Intelligence Agency (DIA); we discarded <u>no</u> piece of evidence and, when I wrote the draft, I included an annex with all the evidence, good and bad, carefully described and [redacted] explained.

As I drafted the estimate, I maintained close contact with my colleagues, and when I finished the first draft in late February, I informally coordinated it with them. We agreed that the Soviets consistently stated, publicly and privately, that they considered international terrorist activities counterproductive and advised groups they supported not to use such tactics (we had hard evidence to support this conclusion). We emphasized, however, that the Soviets had little moral compunction about the use of terrorism, made little if any effort to prevent its use, and furnished assistance to various groups, such as the PLO, the ANC, and ZAPU, which used terrorism as one of their tactics. We reported that we had found no persuasive evidence of Soviet support for those European terrorist groups (the IRA, the Red Brigades, and the Red Army Faction) about which Secretary Haig had specifically asked. There was <u>no</u> effort to "stick our finger in the policy maker's eye." On the contrary, we had expanded the scope of the paper to include groups in which Haig had expressed no interest so that we could point out that the Soviets <u>did</u> support militant groups and <u>did</u> pursue destabilizing policies.

I sent the draft to the Acting NIO (Jeremy Azreal) on February 25, 1981. It drew a strong reaction. The Key Judgments were rewritten by Azrael and Gates (at that time the assistant to William Casey) to suggest greater Soviet support for terrorism, and the text was altered by pulling up from the annex reports that ~~exaggerated the extent of~~ overstated Soviet involvement. The rewriting was done in one day and the draft was prepared to be sent out for interagency coordination. My Branch Chief (Richard Rogers) and I protested the changes to the draft. At this point, the DO also intervened; on behalf of his officers, John McMahon protested that DO information was being misused in the new text. On February 28, a meeting of DO, NIC, and NFAC (now DI) officers was held and the draft was returned to me. After further coordination and discussion, a draft was sent out for interagency coordination on March 6.

From March 9 through 11, coordination meetings on the draft were held; they proved very difficult. All the DIA analysts who had been involved originally had been replaced by people new to the subject who insisted on language emphasizing Soviet control of international terrorist activities. When the estimate, now ~~in stripped-down form and~~ lacking much analytic input, was finished on March 20, DIA submited alternate judgments.

Director Casey read the estimate on March 24 and rejected it; he asked DIA to prepare a new draft. The second draft, completed on April 8, asserted that the Soviet Union was directly supporting and controlling most international terrorist activity. Casey liked the draft, but was convinced by the Director of NFAC (Bruce Clark) and the Director of the NIC (Richard Lehman) that, if issued, the draft would undermine the credibility of the intelligence community.

A completely new team was then selected to try a third draft. It was chaired by Ambassador Lincoln Gordon, newly arrived at CIA as a member of the Senior Review Panel. The new drafter, Richard Mansbach, was a visiting scholar from Rutgers University who had arrived at the agency in January. A new NFAC representative was chosen and NFAC was informed that it would not be allowed to note its dissent from the text.[5] Instructions were given to start again, but Mr. Lehman emphasized that the paper was being written "under constraints."

I was the only one of the original group of analysts (all with experience in Soviet policy) who attended the coordination meetings on the third draft. I was told that I could not speak unless I were asked a direct question; Ambassador Gordon was gracious, however, and I did speak when what I considered to be serious misuse of operational material occurred.

A new draft was completed by mid-May. Its basic approach

---

[5] Intelligence estimates usually represent the concensus of the community. When an agency differs from the agreed text and no compromise language can be found, a "footnote" may be taken. In a footnote, the dissenting agency is identified and makes its case.

was to widen the scope of the paper and to avoid definitions of terrorism and terrorist tactics. Rather, the draft subsumed terrorism into a broader category of revolutionary violence and emphasized that the Soviet Union, by providing support for revolutionary violence, supported international terrorism. I considered the approach misleading.

My division chief, Mel Goodman, and I wrote a memo to Director Casey, protesting the convoluted nature of the estimate and its implicit support for conclusions that could not be supported by evidence. We argued that such an estimate did a disservice to our policymakers by giving them a misleading picture of Soviet activities. We argued that this could distract attention from threatening (and real) aspects of Soviet policy and that it would undermine our credibility on other issues. We got no response.

TOPIC 3: <u>Manipulation of Intelligence Process</u>

I believe that the experience with the estimate on Soviet involvement in international terrorism convinced Casey that he needed better control over the estimative process. With its emphasis on coordination, institutional independence, and analytic objectivity, the process was not sufficiently responsive to Casey's interests. With the help of Bob Gates, Casey took a number of institutional steps designed to insure better control. The first was to stipulate that terms of reference and estimate drafts be cleared by the DCI's office before coordination. The second was the appointment of Gates as DI, giving him the ability to clamp down on intelligence production. During the period of Gates' tenure, the DI was effectively prevented from dissenting when its analysts disagreed with estimates of interest to Casey/Gates.[6] The third, and most effective, action was to

[6] The most damaging instance of this occurred in the May 1985 estimate on Iran. The SOVA analyst participating in that exercise, Brian McCauley, ~~had written the Soviet~~ defended SOVA contribution to the estimate. The NIO for the Near East, Graham Fuller, wrote his own version. According to Brian, Fuller announced at the coordination meeting that Gates had chosen his version. Although the Fuller version was not acceptable to Brian, he felt that there was little point in pursuing a dissent because the DI (Robert Gates) had already pronounced judgment. At a subsequent meeting of the DI's Management Advisory Group with Assistant Director of Intelligence Richard Kerr, I raised the subject of Brian's dilemma on this estimate in the context of a discussion of intimidation in SOVA. Kerr responded that, even if the analyst had been told that Gates, then the DI <u>and</u> Chairman of the NIC, had rejected his language, Brian should have pursued the issue. I considered such a response totally inadequate, ~~to~~ he failed to appreciate the lone and difficult position the analyst was in.

appoint Gates as Chairman of the National Intelligence Council. He thus had control of the two most important producers of intelligence analysis and was able to exert pressure on both.

Casey and Gates used various management tactics to get the line of intelligence they desired and to suppress unwanted intelligence. The latter is relatively simple because a given report or estimate can be dismissed on a variety of grounds (insufficient evidence, irrelevance, poor analysis, etc.) not clearly traceable to politicization. Direct pressure to produce supportive analysis, on the other hand, is risky because it requires open flaunting of the basic professional ethic of intelligence--that is the pursuit of objective reporting and analysis.

Personnel management is the most effective way to ensure consistent production of the desired line. Replacing experts with people willing to cooperate became a central element in the Casey-Gates approach to intelligence management, and the effects of this policy continue to hinder the production of quality intelligence.

TOPIC 4: <u>William Webster's Efforts to Deal With Politicization</u>

When Judge William Webster became DCI in 1987, he brought with him several aides. One, Mark Matthews, was interested in the issue of politicization and, on Judge Webster's behalf, conducted an internal investigation. I have no idea how many people he talked to, but I talked to him for several hours, trying to explain the culture and the corruption of process which had occurred under Casey and Gates. On my way in and out of his office, we were both careful to prevent my being seen by Bob Gates, who was then Deputy Director. This reflects the atmosphere of paranoia that pervaded the place by that time.

In subsequent telephone conversations, Mark told me that the Judge was very aware of the problem of politicization, that the Inspector General had included a paragraph on that subject in its report on SOVA, and that the IG personally had met with Judge Webster alone (specifically without Bob Gates) and had informed him that the inspection had yielded results even stronger than those found in the written report. I never saw the report nor did I have first-hand knowledge of such a conversation between Judge Webster and the IG, but I have no reason to think Mark Matthews was not telling the truth.

~~addressing the serious problems of the directorate and the agency.~~

Personal Conclusions

The culture in the intelligence directorate changed radically during the Casey/Gates years, and that culture continues to define the process. Whereas the pre-Gates ethic emphasized analytic independence and objectivity, the new culture is that of the "hired pen," loyal to the current leadership and its views. Whereas intelligence production should be based on informed and objective analysis of the available evidence, in the Gates' culture it is based on the anticipated reaction of senior managers and officials.

There is no question that reasonable people can differ--and, certainly, reasonable analysts can differ because evidence is always subject to interpretation. That is why the intelligence process was structured to ensure the airing of these differences and the necessity of dealing with them. That was the reason for competing offices, for coordination requirements, for the right to express dissent. That is also the foundation of the professional ethic of the intelligence analyst--the commitment to search for truth in the labyrinth of evidence, to pursue compromise where possible but to express dissent freely when compromise is not possible.

I swear the above statement is true to the best of my knowledge and belief.

Carolyn Ekedahl

Oct 2, 1991

Statement of John Hibbits before the Gates Hearings 2 October 1991

I am here to testify about my role in the production of the CIA paper linking the Soviets to the plot to kill the Pope. In May 1985 I wrote a critique of that paper. At that time I was Chief, Foreign Activities Branch in the Office of Soviet Analysis(SOVA). Currently, I am Deputy Chief, Russia/Union Division in SOVA.

I have spent some 30 years of my life in government service, over ten with the Navy and almost 20 with the CIA. I started out in the intelligence business in the 1960s with the Navy as a junior officer. After completing a year of Russian language training I served as an operational intelligence officer in Japan during the Pueblo Crisis and the shootdown of a naval patrol aircraft off the coast of Korea. In 1969 I left the Navy and came to Washington to work as a civilian analyst for the Director, Naval Intelligence at the Pentagon, and to earn a graduate degree in Soviet affairs from Georgetown University. I did my undergraduate work at Fordham University before joining the Navy In the Pentagon I observed the tough bureaucratic and political pressures involved in producing national and departmental intelligence.

I joined CIA in 1974. I was a naval analyst in the Office of Strategic Research under DCIs Colby, Bush and Turner., and later spent two years in the Directorate of Operations on the CI Staff. In 1981 I received the DCI Certificate of Merit for my service there.

In the early 1980s I returned to the DI as an analyst and later a branch chief working on Soviet issues in the DI and the National Intelligence Council. I worked closely for Doug MacEachin and Larry

Gershwin, both exceptional leaders in intelligence. I observed during those years, however, that relations between SOVA and both Gates and the NIC were adversarial rather than collegial; the DDI was highly critical of the SOVA product and papers regularly came back from the 7th floor with strong correctives of substance as well as style that seemed to go beyond what would be expected in a "tough review."

Over time managers and eventually analysts in SOVA understood what would and would not get through the front office and there developed within the office, divisions, branches, and minds of the analysts a self-censoring atmosphere. Some reaction was subtle and some more obvious. In planning our research program, for example, a paper on Soviet use of chemical agents in the Third World was rejected at the middle management level because it would have no payoff; it would not show clear Soviet use and therefore would likely only upset Gates. So I had to tell the analyst who had proposed the subject in hopes of clarifying the record that he should work on something else. At the same time, offices outside SOVA, knowing Casey was consumed by the Soviet problem, began writing about Soviet activities, often duplicating effort and wasting resources.

How well agency managers could craft intelligence that would keep criticism from the DDI to a minimum became a measure of one's value and there arose a danger of being out of the loop if you were not responsive. Many professionals adjusted without seriously compromising the essential integrity of the product in their own mind, but it became difficult to remain completely objective. As professionals, many began to anticipate criticism and write papers that Gates would like or at least find convincing. Even with these constraints, many of us were able to write and manage a number of what I believe were solid intelligence analysis, but the process was very difficult. Others simply sought jobs outside SOVA or the Agency.

It was this atmosphere that prevailed when I was Chief, Foreign Activities Branch in SOVA and Doug MacEachin came into my office in May 1985 with some special tasking. As I can best recall he told me that a compartmented paper had been drafted on the papal assassination attempt of 1981 and it was about to be disseminated. He asked that I do a quick assessment of the paper looking critically at the case being made for Soviet involvement. I was told it had to be done as soon as possible because Gates was anxious to get the paper out. My impression at the time was that MacEachin initiated the critique and was not enthusiastic about the thrust of the papal assassination paper. As I read it for the first time I saw it as an effort by Casey, using Gates, to push the case further than the evidence would take us. I feared that the most senior policymakers in Washington would quickly read the key judgements, as their busy schedules usually dictate, and come away with the view that CIA as an agency believed that the Soviets were behind the papal assassination plot.

I can remember having just a couple of days and nights to put my comments together, coming in the ofice early one morning to finish it and send it to MacEachin. I distinctly remember him coming down to my office with paper in hand, highly satisfied with the critique and recommending just a few changes. I also remember that I was reviewing what we call a dylux copy of the study which is the print-ready copy of the paper just before it goes to press. I was told that the paper was not yet disseminated. One of my criticisms of the paper was that it was speculative and did not make clear to the reader that this was so. It did not meet the usual standards for a SOVA paper: it did not contain alternative scenarios, analysis or views, and the key judgements were not fully representative of the body of the paper.

MacEachin immediately hosted a meeting in his office with all involved and a rebuttal by the authors was attached to my critique. I was told that Gates would decide on what to do next. I was not permitted to keep a copy of the paper and was not told of its dissemination. Several weeks later I was interviewed by the panel of three senior DI officers that wrote the post mortem in July 1985. That was the last I heard of the incident until now.

A sensitive NIE written in 1987 made it clear that we still had no conclusive evidence of any Soviet involvement in the assassination attempt. Whether or not the Soviets were involved can still be debated. We have had new evidence on both sides of the issue. We may never know the answer for certain even though access may be given to KGB files.

To me, the more important issue, however, is not who was right or wrong on the call, but how the game was played. Did the intelligence process in the CIA provide policymakers with a balanced and dispassionate analysis of the event with uncertainties and alternative analysis appropriately rendered. I thought this was not the case. Reading the Gates cover memo on the study sent to then Vice President Bush, my reservations about the assassination study and how it would be presented to top officials appear to have been warranted.

Senators, you are hearing two different views of how well Bob Gates managed intelligence production. I know Mr.Gates only from a distance professionally. During his tenure, however, I have seen severe problems develop in the Office of Soviet Analysis. Some changes probably were needed in the 1980s to put the DI on a steady analytic course and a new manager has the responsibility to implement hard choices. Analysts will grumble about change, but they usually adjust and come to accept new guidelines and standards if these are clearly stated, consistent, and unbiased. But I respectfully submit that the policies I experienced were of a different nature. I believe the people who worked there then --the vast majority of both analysts and managers--believe that Gates subverted the intelligence process. It is difficult to know the truth from listening to a few of us here during the confirmation process. But I hope that you become concerned enough to continue investigating these reports.

Major analytic differences on political intelligence often stem from differences in political philosophy. It is essential that we develop an analytic process where opposing views are encouraged and seriously weighed with the goal of producing a balanced and useful product. In many instances, fine intelligence analysis has and is being produced at the Agency. Some credit must go to Mr. Gates, but more, I believe, must go to the professional men and women working there who always have had high standards of academic excellence and integrity. Thank you for allowing me to speak before you.

I swear the above statement is true to the best of my knowledge and belief.

John A. Hibbits

2 October 91

UNCLASSIFIED

DDI 1200-83
14 February 1982

MEMORANDUM

FROM: Robert M. Gates
Deputy Director for Intelligence

SUBJECT: NIE on Soviets and the Third World

Per your request, I have read the attached draft and, unhappily, find it to be rather dry and lacking any sense of the dynamics of Soviet involvement in the Third World and why involvement in the Third World is important to the Soviet Union.

—The draft could do with an historical introduction pointing out that the Third World has had ideological and political importance for the Soviet Union since the Revolution and the subsequent Baku Conference. There is no need to belabor this point or turn it into an historical tract, but without such a section one has only a snapshot of Soviet involvement in the Third World that tends too much to reflect on present opportunities and power balances and less on the ideological and political motives that have impelled the Soviet Union to an activist role in the Third World now for more than 60 years. This should be followed then by a brief review of Soviet involvement beginning in the early 1950s, including the kinds of assistance provided during the 1950s and 1960s and the kinds of setbacks that the Soviets suffered culminating perhaps in their expulsion from Egypt in 1972.

This section would then draw the distinction between the policies that the Soviets pursued until the mid-1970s and then the different kind of involvement that the Soviets have sponsored since that time, including a modernization of the Cuban armed forces to encourage Cuba's greater role abroad. This description of the change in Soviet tactics and approach should very explicitly point out the conclusions we believe they must have drawn from the US explusion from Vietnam and the perceived carte blanche that it was likely to give them in the Third World for at least some time. The shift in tactics to which I refer draws both on the lessons of Egypt and Chile and pointed the Soviets in the direction of greater support for regimes supported directly by surrogate forces or foreign help and dependent upon those forces to remain in power. Angola, Ethiopia and to a lesser extent Nicaragua are outstanding examples of this change. Moreover, the improvement in the military capabilities of each, and especially the internal security forces, are important points to note.

UNCLASSIFIED

UNCLASSIFIED

SUBJECT: NIE on Soviets and the Third World

In sum, this estimate misses the whole historical significance of Soviet involvement in the Third World and the ways in which their tactics and approach have changed in the postwar period. The reader cannot understand Soviet activities in the Third World without some understanding of these changes. The importance of the changes is reflected by the fact that the Soviets have allowed their relationship with the United States to founder in many respects over the last eight years over the question of their involvement in the Third World. This cannot be explained only by striving for marginal advantage. It is the political and ideological imperative that must be considered as well. Involvement in the Third World is proof to the Soviets that their revolution is still alive. The change in tactics is a reflection of their determination to avoid wherever possible repetition of the failures of the 1960s and early 1970s. This whole section need be only three or four pages long. ?.

—As for one of the major Soviet motives, particularly in Central America, the draft fails to mention the benefits involved in diverting the US from larger issues such as Europe/INF, the strategic competition, and also the potential impact of further splitting US opinion over foreign policy thereby making it more difficult for the US to respond not only in the Third World but elsewhere as well. ?.

—On the question of economic support, I think the draft should point out that we are likely to see Soviet behavior very much in line with its approach to Nicaragua, that is, warning them not to throw away the benefits of trade aid and investment from the West. They simply will not provide the kind of economic assistance that is needed. Political and military assistance will be made available in all possible ways ? but the Soviets will counsel the country on how to best take advantage of divisions in Western Europe and the US in order to get the financial and trade advantages.

—On page 10 the estimate draft contends that Moscow believes that the US is is now more willing to counter Soviet activities in the Third World than during the immediate post-Vietnam years. I think it is not possible yet to draw that conclusion and I think the Soviets themselves have not drawn that conclusion. So far, except in El Salvador, the Soviets principally have seen American rhetoric since 1975 and very little action. We are still not a player in Angola. Other than diplomatically we are not involved elsewhere in southern Africa, and we are playing no role at all in the Iran-Iraq war. The only place they know we are involved to any degree at all is in Afghanistan. In short they may see a greater willingness to let CIA carry some burden for the United States abroad, but they do not yet see the willingness of the American people and Congress to support an overt American role in the Third World. This is a terribly important distinction in terms of the political message it conveys.

UNCLASSIFIED

UNCLASSIFIED

SUBJECT: NIE on Soviets and the Third World

—On page 24, the draft indicates that Soviets will have more difficulty in gaining new clients than after first becoming active in the Third World in the 1950s. Again, this does not reflect the change in Soviet tactics. It is much easier for the Soviets to let the Cubans or the Libyans or others develop such clients and to support them indirectly than it is to do so directly. Examples include Grenada and potentially Suriname. The Soviets make no investment whatsoever but the Cubans carry the major burden and then the Soviets can come in behind with support. This would be true in the event Libya is successful in Chad as well. In short, the estimate misses a major historical and political development in failing to point out the change in Soviet tactics in the last eight years in Soviet involvement in the Third World and just how surrogates are used in the Third World. This is a fundamental flaw in the draft in my judgment.

—The draft fails to take adequate account of recent information [redacted] we have acquired on the nature and extent of Soviet active measures in the Third World in Africa, the Islamic world, and elsewhere. These reports and political strategy they convey should be discussed in some detail in the estimate in my view.

—Finally, the draft does not document some mundane, but very important, advantages the Soviets bring to the Third World competition, including training of all kinds—from insurgent training to scholarships at Lumumba University. In this and other ways, they are simply better organized for the competition than we.

—In sum, the estimate is basically a snapshot with a great deal of detail and the problems and opportunities confronting the Soviets in the Third World. But what I find lacking is any sense of the change in the Soviet approach to the Third World over the last several years and that pulls together for the policymaker something more than the specifics we have been feeding them for the past three or four years—something that provides a synthesis of what it all means in terms of larger Soviet imperatives and motives in that part of the world. The estimate seems to conclude that fewer opportunities will present themselves to the Soviets in the 1980s than before for a variety of reasons and that the opportunities the Soviets have exploited will begin to present them with increased problems. I think this overlooks the creativity of the Soviet approach in the last seven or eight years, the fact that they are creating new opportunities through different approaches, and that they are much better than we in exploiting problem areas that offer benefit more for the

UNCLASSIFIED

UNCLASSIFIED

SUBJECT: NIE on Soviets and the Third World

trouble they give to the West than for the advantages they provide to the East. These points are not brought out at all. What the policymaker needs right now (and has needed for several years) is the synthesis of where the Soviets are coming from in the Third World historically, how their tactics have changed over time to give us the present situation, and future directions—the depth of their commitment to present policies in the Third World. In short, I see a lot more trouble for us in the Third World in the years ahead because it's easier to make trouble than it is to solve it. This estimate does not convey the dynamic opportunity this gives the Soviets given their own tactical creativity.

RG.

Robert M. Gates

UNCLASSIFIED

Glossary of Intelligence Acronyms

ALA — Office of African and Latin American Analysis.

CPAS — Office of Current Production and Support.

DCI — Director of Central Intelligence, head of CIA and the nation's chief intelligence officer with oversight responsibilities for the entire community.

DDCI — Deputy Director of Central Intelligence.

DDI — Deputy Director for Intelligence, head of the DI. In the early- and mid-1980s the term also referred to the Directorate of Intelligence—what is now called the DI.

DI — Directorate of Intelligence.

DIA — Defense Intelligence Agency.

DDO — Deputy Director for Operations.

DO — Directorate of Operations.

EURA — Office of European Analysis.

FBIS — Foreign Broadcast Information Service.

HUMINT — Human intelligence.

IA— Intelligence Assessment.

IG — Inspector General.

IIM — Interagency Intelligence Memorandum.

NESA — Office of Near East and South Asian Analysis.

NFAC — National Foreign Assessment Center, the name the Carter Administration gave the DI. NFAC became the DI again in early 1982.

NFIB — National Foreign Intelligence Board, composed of the heads of the agencies of the intelligence community.

NIC — National Intelligence Council, composed of National Intelligence Officers and headed by a chairman who advise the DCI and perform intelligence community coordination functions.

NID — National Intelligence Daily, CIA's main current intelligence publication and "publication of record."

NIE — National Intelligence Estimate.

NIO — National Intelligence Officer, member of the NIC who advises the DCI and chairman of the NIC. NIOs have substantive regional or functional responsibilities, supervise preparation of estimates, and perform liaison and coordination functions. Some NIOs have no significant intelligence backgrounds.

NPIC — National Photographic Interpretation Center.

NSA — National Security Agency.

OEA — Office of East Asian Analysis.

OIA — Office of Imagery Analysis.

OIG — Office of the Inspector General.

OIR — Office of Information Resources.

OGI — Office of Global Issues. In existence from 1981-90, it was replaced by RTT, which assumed somewhat different responsibilities.

OSE — Office of Slavic and Eurasian Analysis.

OSS — Office of Strategic Services. The OSS was an intelligence/special operations arm of the US government during World War II and was the immediate predecessor of the Central Intelligence Agency.

OSWR — Office of Scientific and Weapons Research.

PAR — Performance Appraisal Report.

PDB — President's Daily Brief.

PES — Product Evaluation Staff.

PFIAB — President's Foreign Intelligence Advisory Board.

RP — Research Paper.

RTT — Office of Resources, Trade, and Technology.

SIIM — Special Interagency Intelligence Memorandum.

SNIE — Special National Intelligence Estimate.

SOVA — Office of Soviet Analysis.

SRP — Senior Review Panel.

INDEX

About the Author

John A. Gentry spent nearly 12 years as an analyst at the Central Intelligence Agency until his resignation in November 1990. He worked initially on economic analyses of the Soviet military. For nearly seven years, his responsibilities centered on several East European countries. In 1987-89, Gentry was senior analyst on the staff of the National Intelligence Officer for Warning, where he tracked world-wide issues of potential warning interest to senior US intelligence officers and policymakers. His last duties involved analyses of trade relations between selected countries and the economics of counter-insurgency operations.

Gentry is a United States Army Reserve infantry officer. His active duty was with a Special Forces unit in east Asia. His reserve assignments have been in intelligence, special operations, field artillery, and air defense artillery areas. He currently is an instructor with an Army Reserve school.

Gentry is a graduate of the University of North Carolina at Chapel Hill, where he majored in history and was a member of Phi Beta Kappa. He studied economics in graduate school, also at the University of North Carolina. Gentry graduated from the Phillips Exeter Academy.

The author now works as an economist in the Washington, D.C. area. He is married and has a young daughter.